HOSPITALITY AND FOOD MANAGEMENT

M. C. METTI

ANMOL PUBLICATIONS PVT. LTD.
NEW DELHI - 110 002 (INDIA)

ANMOL PUBLICATIONS PVT. LTD.

H.O.: 4374/4B, Ansari Road, Darya Ganj,
New Delhi-110 002 (India)
Ph.: 23278000, 23261597

B.O.: No. 1015, Ist Main Road, BSK IIIrd Stage
IIIrd Phase, IIIrd Block
Bangalore - 560 085 (India)
Visit us at: www.anmolpublications.com

Hospitality and Food Management

ISBN 978-81-261-3243-0

PRINTED IN INDIA

Printed at Mehra Offset Press, Delhi.

Contents

	Preface	*vii*
1.	Introduction to Food Management	1
2.	Hospitality and Food Management	42
3.	Food Safety and Management	80
4.	Food Preservation	133
5.	Food and Drugs	162
6.	Food Waste Management	198
7.	Food Planning	227
	Index	271

Preface

In order to succeed in today's business world, hospitality managers must have a wealth of knowledge when it comes to food. *Hospitality and food management* provides this essential information. Covering the technique used in each segment of the hospitality industry - lodging, foodservice, and tourism. This book offers an in-depth look at how hospitality managers can most effectively use food management to benefit their business, and is a must-have resource for students and professionals seeking to learn more about this cutting-edge topic.

The food management in hospitality industry is very much. Business should be well planned for long term benefits. Besides providing all the demands of every client, the management department much gives depth concern regarding food.

Hospitality and food Management prepares readers to succeed as managers in the hotel industry, while developing a solid foundation for a long and successful career. This comprehensive resource combines detailed presentations of each department in a hotel or lodging establishment along with a close examination of organizational structure and the interdependent relationship among departments.

This book is a comprehensive tool to help readers develop the understanding, knowledge, and skills to be tomorrow's management leaders.

Author

Chapter 1

Introduction to Food Management

Food habits in India are traditional in nature and are varied across the country. Changing consumer mentalities, busier schedules, and a growing number of working women has collectively led to an increase in the demand for ready-to-eat traditional foods. These foods are based on a variety of raw materials such as cereals, milk, fruits and vegetables, and are prepared in large varieties in the country. As a segment of the food industry, traditional foods are the largest, both in terms of tonnage and value. However, production is done at different scales, mostly in the unrecognized sector, barring a few large-scale industries. Most of the operations are manual at best batch type even in relatively large-scale units. This causes variation in quality and shelf life. Hence, the need of the hour is automation of the traditional food industry, irrespective of the scale.

FOOD SERVICE

Food service managers are responsible for the daily operations of restaurants and other establishments that prepare and serve meals and beverages to customers. Besides coordinating activities among various departments, such as kitchen, dining room, and banquet operations, food service managers ensure that customers are satisfied with their dining experience. In addition, they oversee the inventory and ordering of food, equipment, and supplies and arrange for the routine maintenance and upkeep of the restaurant, its equipment, and facilities. Managers generally are responsible for all of the administrative and human-resource functions of running the business, including recruiting new employees and monitoring employee performance and training.

In most full-service restaurants and institutional food service facilities, the management team consists of a general manager, one or more assistant managers, and an executive chef. The executive chef is responsible for all food preparation activities, including running kitchen operations, planning menus, and maintaining quality standards for food service. In limited-service eating places, such as sandwich shops, coffee bars, or fast-food establishments, managers, not executive chefs, are responsible for supervising routine food preparation operations. Assistant managers in full-service facilities generally oversee service in the dining rooms and banquet areas. In larger restaurants and fast-food or other food service facilities that serve meals daily and maintain longer hours, individual assistant managers may supervise different shifts of workers. In smaller restaurants, formal titles may be less important, and one person may undertake the work of one or more food service positions. For example, the executive chef also may be the general manager or even sometimes an owner.

One of the most important tasks of food service managers is assisting executive chefs as they select successful menu items. This task varies by establishment depending on the seasonality of menu items, the frequency with which restaurants change their menus, and the introduction of daily or weekly specials. Many restaurants rarely change their menus while others make frequent alterations. Managers or executive chefs select menu items, taking into account the likely number of customers and the past popularity of dishes. Other issues considered when planning a menu include whether there was any unserved food left over from prior meals that should not be wasted, the need for variety, and the seasonal availability of foods. Managers or executive chefs analyze the recipes of the dishes to determine food, labour, and overhead costs and to assign prices to various dishes. Menus must be developed far enough in advance that supplies can be ordered and received in time.

Managers or executive chefs estimate food needs, place orders with distributors, and schedule the delivery of fresh food and supplies. They plan for routine services or deliveries, such as linen services or the heavy cleaning of dining rooms or kitchen equipment, to occur during slow times or when the dining room is closed. Managers also arrange for equipment maintenance and repairs, and coordinate a variety of services such as waste removal and pest control. Managers or executive chefs receive deliveries and check the contents against order records. They inspect the quality of fresh meats, poultry, fish, fruits, vegetables, and baked goods to ensure that expectations are met. They meet with representatives from restaurant supply companies and place orders to replenish stocks of tableware, linens, paper products, cleaning supplies, cooking utensils, and furniture and fixtures.

Managers must be good communicators. They need to speak well, often in several languages, with a diverse clientele and staff. They must motivate employees to work as a team, to ensure that food and service meet appropriate standards. Managers also must ensure that written supply orders are clear and unambiguous.

Managers interview, hire, train, and, when necessary, fire employees. Retaining good employees is a major challenge facing food service managers. Managers recruit employees at career fairs, contact schools that offer academic programmes in hospitality or culinary arts, and arrange for newspaper advertising to attract additional applicants. Managers oversee the training of new employees and explain the establishment's policies and practices. They schedule work hours, making sure that enough workers are present to cover each shift. If employees are unable to work, managers may have to call in alternates to cover for them or fill in themselves when needed. Some managers may help with cooking, clearing tables, or other tasks when the restaurant becomes extremely busy.

Food service managers ensure that diners are served properly and in a timely manner. They investigate and resolve customers' complaints about food quality or service. They monitor orders in the kitchen to determine where backups may occur, and they work with the chef to remedy any delays in service. Managers direct the cleaning of the dining areas and the washing of tableware, kitchen utensils, and equipment to comply with company and government sanitation standards. Managers also monitor the actions of their employees and patrons on a continual basis to ensure the personal safety of everyone. They make sure that health and safety standards and local liquor regulations are obeyed.

In addition to their regular duties, food service managers perform a variety of administrative assignments, such as keeping employee work records, preparing the payroll, and completing paperwork to comply with licensing laws and reporting requirements of tax, wage and hour, unemployment compensation, and Social Security laws. Some of this work may be delegated to an assistant manager or bookkeeper, or it may be contracted out, but most general managers retain responsibility for the accuracy of business records. Managers also maintain records of supply and equipment purchases and ensure that accounts with suppliers are paid.

Technology influences the jobs of food service managers in many ways, enhancing efficiency and productivity. Many restaurants use computers to track orders, inventory, and the seating of patrons. Point-of-service (POS) systems allow servers to key in a customer's order, either at the table, using a hand-held device, or from a computer terminal in the dining room, and send the order to the kitchen instantaneously so preparation can begin. The same system totals and prints checks, functions as a cash register, connect to credit card authorizers, and tracks sales. To minimize food costs and spoilage, many managers use inventory-tracking software to compare the record of sales from the POS with a record of the current inventory. Some establishments enter an inventory of standard ingredients and suppliers into their POS system. When supplies of particular ingredients run low, they can be ordered directly from the supplier using preprogrammed information. Computers also allow restaurant and food service managers to keep track of employee schedules and paychecks more efficiently.

Food service managers use the Internet to track industry news, find recipes, conduct market research, purchase supplies or equipment, recruit employees, and train staff. Internet access also makes service to customers more efficient. Many restaurants maintain Web sites that include menus and online promotions, provide information about the restaurant's location, and offer patrons the option to make a reservation.

Managers tally the cash and charge receipts received and balance them against the record of sales. They are responsible for depositing the day's receipts at the bank or securing them in a safe place. Finally, managers are responsible for locking up the establishment, checking that ovens, grills, and lights are off, and switching on alarm systems.

The hospitality industry is notorious for their staffs turn over which costs untold millions of dollars. Experienced employees are difficult to find, and even if hired, still require additional training to understand the inner workings of the procedures of each department in the property. Managers often fail to understand that they must know each facet in every operation and then manage detail. After all, the success of each hospitality business depends on detail. In order to achieve any level of perfection, each manager must first learn, and then get subordinates to perform the task. There is always something new to learn if you want to implement a procedure. The business environment changes constantly as do the expectations of guests. What have been acceptable a year ago my not be so today. The challenge to learn new things daily and implement him or her in the operation is the responsibility of each manager.

Technology changed needs and expectations. While only a few years ago running an operation was a relatively simple task, today's managers must, in addition to all other tasks, be able to understand and manipulate electronic systems. The flow of information and intelligence accelerated due to such devices, and response time decreased accordingly. A guest expects a certain level of comfort and service based on the category of establishment. In many instances, imagers and all employees must anticipate needs and deliver them before the guests asks, This requires not only experience but also an innate sense of service and study of human behaviour. Good management goes beyond technically achieving objectives by co-ordinating human resources with materials to produce profits. Leadership requires a thorough knowledge of the job, extreme commitment to duty, interpersonal skills, delegation of responsibilities, anticipating changes, and ability to deal with stress on individuals and its ill effects. Hospitality employees are particularly exposed to stress, as there is no formula or set workflow to serve a guest.

They are in constant, direct contact with guests whose needs; wants, moods and demands change from minute to minute. Successful operations have an informal mentoring system. Experienced managers take potential managerial "material" under their wings and guide them to techniques "reserved" for privileged managers. They spend time with their understudies and impart information on how to speak with important business partners, how to present themselves, how to behave in formal settings and the finer points of delivering an important proposal. They stress the importance of teamwork, the importance of structure, process, planning and human resources development.

Processes must be based on solid criteria in an attempt to be able to deliver services if an important (key) employee is absent, or leaves unexpectedly, or even must be relieved of his/her duties. Respected leaders know the importance of communication in daily management, planning and implementation of strategies. Leaders have visions, and it is ultimately a vision that drives an organization. A leader knows that a title looks on paper, and that a true leader makes the world believe in his/her beliefs and visions by making a guest feel at ease.

Future Development

The best strategies, conceived by experts are doomed if improperly implemented. This is the Achilles' heel of most large and medium-sized establishments. Only a few companies are able to implement strategy properly to yield expected results. The best strategies could be stymied in the absence of correct implementation and the right people. Experience shows that having the best team is no guarantee for success. Experienced and result-oriented managers give sufficient freedom to their workers to ensure continues evolutions and success. Experienced managers are all too aware that success comes through getting work accomplished by others. Those who insist on supervising every detail (micromanaging) will end up working unduly hard, and in the process frustrate co-workers.

Leaders know the value of giving subordinates freedom to think and accomplish work according to parameters. Organizations thrive or fall by people. Leaders must have their fingers on the pulse of the establishment all the time; this can be achieved through daily and frequent walks through the plant. Also, meetings with department managers must be held regularly to ensure a continuous flow of information up and down the chain of command. It must be understood by all that systems and procedures can aid performance, but only employees can drive it. All employees must commit their energy and creativity to ensure profitability of the operation. Leaders tend to have an uncanny ability to detect talent and are acutely aware of the importance of people's needs and aspirations.

They create a environment conducive to develop talent. Leaders commit effort and resources to determine the correct level of freedom for talented employees to achieve their potential. Industries dependent on production lines can count on checks and balances, systems and procedures, through which the product passes before eventually reaching the end user. In the hotel and restaurant industry the end user contact is direct and frequent. In fact, often goods and services are produced on demand. The product must be customized for every individual. The entire product depends on people, not on pre-ordained models. Employees must be trained to deliver seamless and consistent service. All must believe, regardless of their position, in the fact that they all involved in the production of all goods and services reaching the end user – the guest. The only practical; and feasible way to achieving this objective is by training employees in one-on-one interaction with guests.

All must be trained to handle out-of-ordinary requests and/or situations. It is important to empower front line employees to make instant decisions if and when a dish fails to meet the expectations of a guest, or a bottle of wine is oxidized, or front office fails to deliver an important message on time. The level of perfect service depends on the leadership of an establishment. Successful leaders believe that perfection is a moving target and can only be improved, never fully achieved.

FOOD PROCESSING

Food processing is the set of methods and techniques used to transform raw ingredients into food for consumption by humans. The food processing industry utilizes these processes. Food processing often takes clean, harvested or slaughtered and butchered components and uses these to produce attractive and marketable food products. Similar processes are used to produce animal feed. Food processing covers a spectrum of products from sub-sector comprising agriculture, horticulture, plantation, animal husbandry and fisheries. India is one of the major food producers in the world and has abundant availability of a wide variety of crops, fruits, vegetables, flowers, live-stock and seafood. Diverse climatic conditions and a long coastline have contributed to India's position as a leading food producer. Before the advent of food processing, fresh food spoiled, it was that simple. In medieval times, people attempted to cover up the smell and taste of tainted food by using fragrant herbs in the cooking and serving process. Even earlier, people used salt to preserve meats, and they used smoking and drying, especially for meats.

However, none of these processes was totally satisfactory, and there was still no way to preserve many fruits, vegetables, and baked goods. Therefore, Americans, and others around the world, relied on fresh food when it was available, usually during the warmer summer months, but in the winter, early spring, and late fall, most of the food available was meat or freshly baked goods, and some root vegetables that would keep through the colder months. The development of food processing technology changed all that, and allowed the world to eat a wider variety of foods all year round. It was a breakthrough in technology, but it was also a breakthrough in the eating habits of Americans, because they could enjoy more food, and more freshly processed food, creating variety in their diet, but giving them many more healthy food options, too. In addition, even people in rural areas, far from the produce and food centers of the country, could eat the same foods that others could eat, despite their isolation.

Modern food processing technology in the 19th and 20th century was largely developed to serve military needs. Nicolas Appert developed a vacuum bottling process to supply troops in the French army with food, which would eventually lead to tinning and then canning by Peter Durand in 1810. Although initially expensive and somewhat hazardous due to lead used in the cans, canned goods would later become a staple around the world. Pasteurization, discovered by Louis Pasteur in 1862 was a significant advance in ensuring micro-biological safety of food. Food processing dates back to the prehistoric ages when crude processing incorporated slaughtering, various types of cooking, such as over fires, smoking, steaming, oven baking), fermenting, sun drying and preserving with salt. Foods preserved this way were a common part of warriors and sailor's diets up until the introduction of canned food. These crude processing techniques remained essentially the same until the advent of the industrial revolution.

Benefits of food processing include toxin removal, preservation, improving flavour, easing marketing and distribution tasks, and increasing food consistency. In addition, it increases seasonal availability of many foods, enables transportation of delicate perishable foods across long distances, and makes many kinds of foods safe to eat by removing the microorganisms. Modern supermarkets would not be feasible without modern food processing techniques, long voyages would not be possible, and military campaigns would be significantly more difficult and costly to execute.

Modern food processing also improves the quality of life for allergics, diabetics, and other people who cannot consume some common food elements. Food processing can also add extra nutrients. As our ancestors learned to use fire, they learned simple cooking, such as broiling hunted game or baking meat on hot stones. By smoking raw meat, we can not only store meat longer, but also meat tastes better, with smoke elements added. It is said that smoking was the first food processing in the world. Fermentation and putrefaction of food are caused by the action of microorganisms. This scientific discovery by Pasteur is applied in the vinegar industry. And now also in the area of bread making and in the meat processing industry, they are developing their technology, based on an organic chemical research.

For instance, we can colour food more evenly and more beautifully with pigment extracted from a plant than with a crushed plant. Methods of producing high-grade effective elements have been developed in succession, by analyzing the effectiveness in food of natural elements contained in plants or animals and applying chemical synthesis in which some chemical reactions produce other elements. Recently the ratio of processed food against household food spending has been increasing. Today we have the administrative law systems that scientifically guarantee the safety and functions of food processing techniques, in addition to the wisdom of the ancients based on experience in the history of food culture.

While India has an abundant supply of food, the food processing industry is still nascent: only two per cent of fruit and vegetables; and 15 per cent of milk produced are processed.

- Despite these low volumes, the processed food industry ranks fifth in size in the country, representing 6.3 per cent of GDP. It accounts for 13 per cent of the country's exports and 6 per cent of total industrial investment.
- The industry size is estimated at US$ 70 billion, including US$ 22 billion of value added products.
- The sector has been attracting FDI across different categories.

Mechanism

Food processing is a highly complex multi-disciplinary activity involving the application of chemistry, biochemistry, biophysics, nutrition, microbiology and also different branches of engineering. Today, consumers have an increasing concern regarding food safety and sensory qualities, which make them, look for minimally processed foods with least distortions to the profile of the food during processing.

The efficiency of the existing equipment used at large for drying and dehydration is very low (say, 10-15 per cent only). Adaptation of conventional equipment used in the chemical industries for food processing is difficult mainly due to factors such as high moisture content, thermal labile nature with respect to notation as well as colour and most importantly, rate of drying which influences food characteristics significantly. Hence there is a need for design of efficient dehydration and similarly competent drying equipment.

Since the cost of energy is increasing all over the world, alternate sources of energy such as solar energy and fossil fuels such as LPG (liquid petroleum gas) will improve the economics and the present status of the industry. Application of LPG will even enhance the efficiencies due to the provision for recycling. Solar energy based equipment also has potential. For many years, thermal processing was the main technology for the preservation of food and extended shelf life, although in most cases loss of fresh flavours, vitamins, and some physio-chemical characteristics were the price of the safety and long-term stability. Increasing consumer demand for new products with very high organoleptic and nutritional qualities has led to extensive research for new alternatives to food processing.

FOOD PROCESSING TECHNIQUES

Virtually all foods undergo some form of processing before they are ready to eat. At its most simple, processing can be peeling a piece of fruit or boiling potatoes. The oldest, traditional methods of food processing include sun-drying, smoking, pickling and salting. These methods utilise the fact that water removal increases shelf life. Fermentation and freezing are also very traditional methods. Canning, pasteurisation and sterilisation are techniques that have been used for many decades but are still important techniques in the modern food processing industry. However, they are now being joined by many new processes, and a number of others are already waiting in the wings.

One of the key factors that has stimulated the availability of a diversity of products is consumer interest in health and related issues, such as 'naturalness' and 'added value'. This interest has led to the development of products that are lower in fat, sugar and salt and higher in fiber and products that have specific vitamins or minerals added to them. The addition of nutrients to foods and drinks is used around the world as a public health measure and as a cost effective means of ensuring the nutritional quality of the food supply. The addition of nutrients requires careful attention to food regulations, a suitable nutritional rationale and that the final product remains acceptable to consumers.

Food processing includes any action that changes or converts raw plant or animal materials into safe, edible, and more palatable foodstuffs. Food processing also provides us with the means to extend the shelf life of otherwise perishable foods. Without food processing it would not be possible to sustain the needs of modern urban populations, and the choice of food available would be very limited and largely seasonal. Changing lifestyles and family structures have resulted in a largely consumer led demand for an ever-growing selection of foods, particularly ready-prepared and partially prepared products.

A recent example of this approach, in the UK, is the voluntary addition of folic acid to bread and breakfast cereals as a means of increasing the folate status of women of childbearing age. This has been stimulated by recognition that low folate status is associated with an increased risk of neural tube defects. Vitamin and mineral fortification is common in Britain, and many foods are fortified to some extent. In some cases the addition of micronutrients is mandatory, e.g. fortification of margarine with vitamin A and vitamin D, whereas in the majority of cases it is voluntary, e.g. the addition of a range of vitamins and minerals to breakfast cereals.

Food processing can improve the nutritional value of certain foods. For example, severe heat treatment destroys trypsin inhibitors, which are anti-nutritional factors present in a range of foods. Prolonged boiling also destroys the harmful lectins present in legumes, such as red kidney beans. Food processing can also increase the bioavailability of nutrients in foods and the organoleptic qualities of foods. On the other hand, however, any form of food processing, even slicing, washing and cooking foods in the home, can result in a loss of heat sensitive, oxygen sensitive and light sensitive nutrients, especially certain vitamins.

Leaching of vitamins and some minerals into the cooking water can also occur with vegetables. The main commercial processes that cause nutrient loss are blanching, heat processing, and drying or dehydration. However, in some cases, processed foods actually retain more nutrients than the unprocessed form. The best examples are frozen vegetables, which are picked and frozen within hours of harvest, whereas 'fresh' vegetables may have been stored for several days before purchase or use. Even with unprocessed vegetables, however, modern storage and transportation techniques can help retain nutrients.

An example of a potential health concern arising from food processing involves trans fatty acids. Vegetable oils are often hydrogenated to improve their oxidative stability and functional properties, e.g. during the manufacture of margarine, and during this process trans fatty acids (a group of unsaturated fatty acids) can be produced. It is thought that trans fatty acids behave more like saturated fatty acids than unsaturated fatty acids after ingestion. However, the general consensus in the UK is that current intakes of trans fatty acids do not present a problem.

Many new processing techniques have been developed in response to changing nutritional concepts and consumer demand for less processed foods e.g. Ohmic heating and high intensity pulsed electric field processing. Such processes are sometimes called non-thermal processes or minimal processing techniques. The objective is to produce high quality, safe foods that are convenient, fresher and considered more natural. The nutritional implications of some of the techniques that are still in development have yet to be established and will almost inevitably determine whether or not these techniques achieve commercial success.

Functional foods are the latest refinement in a continuum of products developed to provide 'added value'. One commonly used definition of a functional food is: 'a dietary ingredient that affects its host in a targeted manner so as to exert positive effects that may, in due course, justify certain health claims'. Within this context, there is increasing interest in prebiotics, probiotics and synbiotics. Prebiotics are substances, e.g. oligosaccharides, that are not digested but which beneficially affect the host by selectively stimulating the growth of specific bacteria in the colon.

It is now recognised that the composition of the bacterial population of the large bowel is important for human health, and can potentially be manipulated by the type of food eaten. Another approach to influence the gut microflora involves the incorporation of live micro-organisms (probiotics) into foods, such as yogurts. A third approach, the use of synbiotics, is a combination of the above two approaches. The use of genetic modification in food production is a relatively new process and has many potential applications. For example, a plant can be modified to resist disease, microbial attack or insect infestation, or to produce fruit with a better flavour and improved keeping qualities. Plants can also be developed to resist certain herbicides that are applied to kill weeds. Other possibilities include drought resistance (very important in developing countries) and resistance to fruit damage.

The use of genetic modification offers substantial potential benefits to the food industry and consumers, but it is recognised that some consumers may have reservations about this new and unfamiliar technology. To help in the recognition of foods which contain genetically modified material, regulations have recently been published that require all foods containing ingredients produced from genetically modified soma or maize to be labelled, except when neither protein nor DNA resulting from the genetic modification is present in the food itself.

Coagulants

The terms flocculant and coagulant are sometimes used interchangeably, but it is more accurate to use the term coagulant for a chemical that contributes to molecular aggregation, rather than particular aggregation. Usually dissolved substances are aggregated into microscopic particles by a coagulant and then these particles may be flocculated into a macroscopic floc with a flocculant. In general, coagulants will have higher net charge and a lower molecular weight than flocculants.

Creaming

Creaming, in cooking, is the technique of blending dry ingredients – usually granulated sugar – together with a solid fat like shortening or butter. The technique is most often used in making cake batter or cookie dough. The dry ingredients are mixed or beaten with the fat until it becomes light and fluffy and increased in volume, due to the incorporation of tiny air bubbles. These air bubbles, locked into the semi-solid fat, remain in the final batter and expand as the item is baked, serving as a form of leavening agent.

Butter is the traditional fat for creaming, but vegetable shortening serves as a more effective leavener for a number of reasons. The low melting point of butter means it aerates best at temperatures cooler than most kitchens (18°C/65°F), while shorting works best at higher temperatures. Because of the coarser crystalline structure of its fat, butter allows larger air bubbles to form than shortening; large bubbles can rise in and escape from thin batters. Also, most shortening is made with preformed nitrogen bubbles and bubble-stabilizing emulsifiers, both of which enhance its leavening ability.

Creaming, in the labouratory sense, is the migration of a substance in an emulsion, under the influence of buoyancy, to the top of a sample while the particles of the substance remain separated, as compared to flocculation (where particles clump) or breaking (where particles coalesce).

Deflocculating

A deflocculant is a chemical that is added to prevent a colloid from coming out of suspension.

Emulsion

An emulsion is a mixture of two immiscible (unblendable) substances. One substance (the dispersed phase) is dispersed in the other (the continuous phase). Examples of emulsions include butter and margarine, espresso, mayonnaise, the photo-sensitive side of Photographic film, and cutting fluid for metalworking. In butter and margarine, a continuous lipid phase surrounds droplets of water (water-in-oil emulsion). Emulsification is the process by which emulsions are prepared.

Emulsions tend to have a cloudy appearance, because the many phase interfaces (the boundary between the phases is called the interface) scatter light that passes through the emulsion. Emulsions are unstable and thus do not form spontaneously. Energy input through shaking, stirring, homogenizers, or spray processes are needed to form an emulsion. Over time, emulsions tend to revert to the stable state of oil separated from water. Surface active substances (surfactants) can increase the kinetic stability of emulsions greatly so that, once formed, the emulsion does not change significantly over years of storage.

Homemade oil and vinegar salad dressing is an example of an unstable emulsion that will quickly separate unless shaken continuously. This phenomenon is called coalescence, and happens when small droplets recombine to form bigger ones. Fluid emulsions can also suffer from creaming, the migration of one of the substances to the top of the emulsion under the influence of buoyancy or centripetal force when a centrifuge is used.

Emulsions are part of a more general class of two-phase systems of matter called colloids. Although the terms colloid and emulsion are sometimes used interchangeably, emulsion tends to imply that both the dispersed and the continuous phase are liquid. There are three types of emulsion instability: flocculation, where the particles form clumps; creaming, where the particles concentrate towards the surface of the mixture while staying separated; and breaking, where the particles coalesce and form a layer of liquid.

EMULSIFIER

An emulsifier also known as an emulgent or surfactant is a substance which stabilizes an emulsion. Examples of food emulsifiers are egg yolk (where the main emulsifying chemical is the phospholipid lecithin), and mustard, where a variety of chemicals in the mucilage surrounding the seed hull act as emulsifiers; proteins and low-molecular weight emulsifiers are common as well. In some cases, particles can stabilise emulsions as well through a mechanism called Pickering stabilization. Both mayonnaise and Hollandaise sauce are oil-in-water emulsions stabilized with egg yolk lecithin.

Detergents are another class of surfactant, and will chemically interact with both oil and water, thus stabilising the interface between oil or water droplets in suspension. This principle is exploited in soap to remove grease for the purpose of cleaning. A wide variety of emulsifiers are used in pharmacy to prepare emulsions such as creams and lotions.

Whether an emulsion turns into a water-in-oil emulsion or an oil-in-water emulsion depends on the volume fraction of both phases and on the type of emulsifier. Generally, the Bancroft rule applies: emulsifiers and emulsifying particles tend to promote dispersion of the phase in which they do not dissolve very well; for example, proteins dissolve better in water than in oil and so tend to form oil-in-water emulsions (that is they promote the dispersion of oil droplets throughout a continuous phase of water).

Flocculation

Flocculation refers to a process where a solute comes out of solution in the form of floc or "flakes." The term is also used to refer to the process by which fine particulates are caused to clump together into floc. The floc may then float to the top of the liquid, settle to the bottom of the liquid, or can be readily filtered from the liquid.

In geology, flocculation is a condition in which clays, polymers or other small charged particles become attached and form a fragile structure, a floc. In dispersed clay slurries, flocculation occurs after mechanical agitation ceases and the dispersed clay platelets spontaneously form flocs because of attractions between negative face charges and positive edge charges. In biology the process is used to refer to the asexual aggregation of microorganisms, most commonly brewing yeast at the end of a brew. Flocculation is widely employed in the purification of drinking water as well as sewage treatment and treatment of other industrial wastewater streams.

Flocculants

Flocculants, or flocculating agents, are chemicals that are used to promote flocculation by causing colloids and other suspended particles in liquids to aggregate, forming a floc.

Flocculants are used in water treatment processes to improve the sedimentation or filterability of small particles. For example, a flocculant may be used in swimming pool or drinking water filtration to aid removal of microscopic particles which would otherwise cause the water to be cloudy and which would be difficult or impossible to remove by filtration alone.

Many flocculants are multivalent cations such as aluminium, iron, calcium or magnesium. These positively charged molecules interact with negatively charged particles and molecules to reduce the barriers to aggregation. In addition, many of these chemicals, under appropriate pH and other conditions, react with water to form insoluble hydroxides which, upon precipitating, link together to form long chains or meshes, physically trapping small particles into the larger floc. Long-chain polymer flocculants, such as modified polyacrylamides, are manufactured and sold by the flocculant producing business.

Modified Polyacrylamides can be supplied in dry or liquid form for use in the flocculation process. The most common liquid polyacrylamide is supplied as an emulsion with 10-40% actives and the rest is a carrier fluid, surfactants and latex. Emulsion polymers require activation to invert the emulsion and allow the electrolyte groups to be exposed. Other factors such as pH, temperature, and salinity can induce flocculation or influence flocculation rates.

Mincing

Mincing is a cooking technique in which food ingredients are finely divided. The effect is to create a closely bonded mixture of ingredients and a soft or pasty texture. Flavouring ingredients with spices or condiments such as garlic, ginger, and fresh herbs may be minced to distribute flavour more evenly in a mixture. Additionally bruising of the tissue can release juices and oils to deliver flavours uniformly in a sauce. Mincemeat tarts and Pates employ mincing in the preparation of moldable paste.

Spray Drying

Spray drying is an encapsulation technique employed by the food and pharmaceutical industries. A substance to be encapsulated (the load) and an amphoteric carrier (usually some sort of modified starch) are homogenized as a suspension in water (the slurry). The slurry is then fed into a spray drier, usually a tower heated to temperatures well over the boiling point of water.

As the slurry enters the tower, it is atomized. Partly because of the high surface tension of water and partly because of the hydrophobic/hydrophilic interactions between the amphoteric carrier, the water, and the load, the atomized slurry forms micelles. The small size of the drops (averaging 100 micrometers in diameter) results in a relatively large surface area which dries quickly. As the water dries, the carrier forms a hardened shell around the load.

Load loss is usually a function of molecular weight. That is, ligher molecules tend to boil off in larger quantities at the processing temperatures. Loss is minimized industrially by spraying into taller towers. A larger volume of air has a lower average humidity as the process proceeds. By the osmosis principle, water will be encouraged by entropy to leave the micelles and enter the air. Therefore, the same percentage of water can be dried out of the particles at lower temperatures if larger towers are used.

The application of the spray drying encapsulation technique is to prepare "dehydrated" powders of substances which do not have any water to dehydrate. For example, instant drink mixes are spray dries of the various chemicals which make up the beverage. The technique was once used to remove water from food products; for instance, in the preparation of dehydrated milk. Because the milk was not being encapsulated and because spray drying cause thermal degradation, milk dehydration and similar processes have been replaced by other dehydration techniques. Extreme examples of food processing include the delicate preparation of deadly fugu fish, preparing space food for consumption under zero gravity, winemaking, hot dogs, and chicken nuggets.

YEAST BAKING

In bread production, yeast cells turn carbohydrates into carbon dioxide, which causes the dough to expand or rise, and alcohol, most of which evapourates during baking. The use of potatoes, water from potato boiling, eggs, or sugar in a bread dough accelerates the growth of yeasts. Salt and fats such as butter slow down yeast growth. Baker's yeast comes in two forms. The first form, compressed yeast, is fresh yeast pressed into a square cake. This form perishes quickly, and must be used soon after production in order to maintain the desired effects. Dry yeast is granulated and has a longer shelf life than fresh yeast. In the production of beer or wine, sugar is converted into alcohol by yeast.

A weak solution of water and sugar can be used to determine if yeast is expired. When dissolved in the solution, active yeast will foam and bubble as it digests the sugar and converts it into carbon dioxide. Yeast was first used to bake bread in Egypt (tubular) in approximately the fourth millennium BC. Artifacts have been found that are associated with bread making, as well as drawings that depict bakeries. Prior to the use of yeast in baking, breads were typically unleavened. During this time, bread was seen as a luxury.

Some theories state that yeast was discovered simply by being in the air and coming in contact with the unleavened bread being prepared. Another theory states that ale was used instead of water, and the yeast from the ale caused the bread to rise. In 1859, Louis Pasteur discovered how yeast worked and explained fermentation in the making of beer. Today there are several retailers of baker's yeast, one of the best-known being Fleischmann's Yeast, which was developed in 1868. During World War II Fleischmann's developed active dry yeast, which did not require refrigeration. The company created yeast that would rise twice as fast, cutting down on baking time.

FOOD EXTRUSION

Extrusion has found a great application in food processing. Various products like pastas, breakfast cereals, Fig Newtons, prefab cookie dough, and ready to eat snacks are now manufactured by extrusion. Softer foods such as meringue have long been piped using pastry bags. Extrusion is also used with grains such as wheat, corn, and rice. Extrusion is a manufacturing process used to create long objects of a fixed cross-sectional profile. A material, often in the form of a billet, is pushed and/or drawn through a die of the desired profile shape. Hollow sections are usually extruded by placing a pin or piercing mandrel inside of the die, and in some cases positive pressure is applied to the internal cavities through the pin. Extrusion may be continuous (producing indefinitely long material) or semi-continuous (repeatedly producing many shorter pieces). Some materials are hot drawn whilst others may be cold drawn.

The feedstock may be forced through the die by various methods: by an auger, which can be single or twin screw, powered by an electric motor; by a ram, driven by hydraulic pressure (for steel alloys and titanium alloys for example), oil pressure (for aluminum) or in other specialized processes such as rollers inside a perforated drum for the production of many simultaneous streams of material. Extrusion simulation tools help to understand the extrusion process and to optimize development of tools and products. Commonly extruded materials include; Metals, Polymers, Ceramics, and Foodstuffs.

Extruded Road Marking Compound

"Painted" roadmarkings are often done with extruded two, or three component compounds. Thermoplastics are also common. This is a low pressure, high flow process with very good contour and thickness control. Extrusion has more or less completely replaced the older "sliding mould" method. Benefits are much better economy, higher speed, and general appearance.

THE FOOD PROCESSING INDUSTRY

Meat Packing Industry

The meat packing industry is an industry that handles the slaughtering, processing and distribution of animals such as cattle, pigs, sheep and other livestock. The industry is primarily focused on producing meat for human consumption, but it also yields a variety of by-products including hides, feathers, dried blood, and through the process of rendering, fat such as tallow and protein meals such as meat & bone meal. In the U.S. and some other countries the place where the meat packing is done is called a meat packing plant; in New Zealand, where most of the produce is exported, it is called a freezing works. An abattoir is a place where animals are slaughtered for food.

Because no two animals are the same, the meat packing industry has not been able to automate to the same extent that some other food processors have and remains very labour-intensive. If the meat is to be processed in as cost-effective a manner as possible, labour costs must be minimized by paying the lowest wages possible and maximizing productivity from the workforce. This combined with the nature of the work makes conditions intolerable to many people. In many plants, fewer than one out of ten recruits remains beyond the probationary period.

For this reason, many meat packing plants in the developed world are unionized while those that are not are often prime targets for labour organizers. Relations between management and organized labour in meat packing plants can be strained at the best of times. Strikes and lockouts are fairly common occurrences in the meat packing industry. Because much of the work is relatively unskilled, it is possible to bring in replacement workers so long as such a workforce is available and the laws of the jurisdiction in question allow replacements to be hired. If management does attempt this route, the possibility for violence on the picket line can be great.

The United States meat packing industry held a prominent focus in the 1906 novel The Jungle by Upton Sinclair, which criticized the treatment of workers and the safety of the products themselves. Rendering is an industrial process that converts waste animal tissue into stable, value-added materials. The majority of tissue processed comes from slaughterhouses but also includes restaurant grease and butcher shop trimmings. This material can include the fatty tissue, bones, and offal, as well as entire carcasses of animals condemned at slaughterhouses, and those that have died on farms (deadstock), in transit, etc. The most common animal sources are beef, pork, sheep or poultry.

The rendering process simultaneously dries the material and separates the fat from the bone and protein. A rendering process yields a fat commodity (yellow grease, choice white grease, bleachable fancy tallow, etc.) and a protein meal (meat & bone meal, poultry byproduct meal, etc.). Rendering plants often also handle other materials, such as slaughterhouse blood, feathers and hair, but do so using processes otherwise distinct from true rendering.

Process Variations

The rendering process varies from plant to plant in a number of ways.

1. Whether the end products are to be used as human food is based on the type of raw material and the processing methods.
2. Whether the end products are to be used as animal or pet food
3. The material may be processed wet or dry. In wet processing, water in the form of liquid or steam is added to the material during the rendering process
4. The temperature range used, whether high or low.
5. Processing may be either in discrete batches or in a continuous process.
6. The processing plant may be operated by an independent company that collects the material on

the open market, or by the packing plant that produced the material.

Rendering Processes for Edible Products

Edible rendering processes are basically meat processing operations and produce lard or edible tallow for use in food products. Edible rendering is generally carried out in a continuous process at low temperature (less than the boiling point of water). The process usually consists of finely chopping the edible fat materials (generally fat trimmings from meat cuts), heating them with or without added steam, and then carrying out two or more stages of centrifugal separation. The first stage separates the liquid water and fat mixture from the solids. The second stage further separates the fat from the water. The solids may be used in food products, pet foods, etc, depending on the original materials. The separated fat may be used in food products, or if in surplus, it may be diverted to soap making operations. Most edible rendering is done by meat packing or processing companies.

Rendering Processes for Inedible Products

Materials that for aesthetic or sanitary reasons are not suitable for human food are the feedstocks for inedible rendering processes. Much of the inedible raw material is rendered using the "dry" method. This may be a batch or a continuous process in which the material is heated in a steam jacketed vessel to drive off the moisture and simultaneously release the fat from the fat cells. The material is first ground, then heated to release the fat and drive off the moisture, percolated to drain off the free fat, and then more fat is pressed out of the solids, which at this stage are called "cracklings" or "dry-rendered tankage". The cracklings are further ground to make meat and bone meal.

A variation on a dry process involves finely chopping the material, fluidizing it with hot fat, and then evapourating the mixture in one or more evapourator stages. Some inedible rendering is done using a wet process, which is generally a continuous process similar in some ways to that used for edible materials. The material is heated with added steam and then pressed to remove a water-fat mixture which is then separated into fat, water and fine solids by stages of centrifuging and/ or evapouration. The solids from the press are dried and then ground into meat and bone meal. Most independent renderers process only inedible material.

Benefits of Rendering

After rendering, the materials are much more resistant to spoiling. The fat can be used in animal feed, in soap-making, in candles, as a raw material for biodiesel production, and as a feed-stock for the chemical industry. The bone and protein becomes dry particles known as meat and bone meal. For many years meat and bone meal were fed to cattle. This practice is now prohibited in developed countries because it is believed to be the main route for the spread of BSE (mad-cow disease). Meat and bone meal is still fed to non-ruminant animals in the United States.

Tallow, derived from beef waste, is an important raw material in the steel rolling industry providing the required lubrication as the sheet steel is compressed through the rollers. In the absence of the rendering industry, the cost of waste disposal of waste animal material would be very high and would place a significant economic and environmental burden on areas involved in industrial scale slaughtering.

Economic Impacts

Other major factors which impacted the industry in the 20th century were the popularization of chemical fertilizers, the development of synthetic detergents, the widespread adoption of "boxed beef" in the USA, and the change in consumer eating habits to reject animal fats. In the early 20th century the low cost of synthesis of artificial nitrogen fertilizers undermined the economic use of animal waste to enrich soils. This resulted in the loss of a substantial market for meat by-product solids. But this lost market was replaced by the realisation that these products made good feed for animals. After World War II synthetic detergents came on the scene which eventually displaced soaps for both domestic and industrial washing uses. Thus, in the early 1950's over 50% of the inedible fat market disappeared. Diversion in these materials into animal feeds soon replaced the lost soap market and eventually became the single largest use for inedible fats.

The widespread use of "boxed beef" in which the beef was cut up into consumer portions at the packing plant rather than at the retail level in local butcher shops and markets meant that the fat and meat scrap raw materials for renderers stayed at the packing plants and were rendered there by packer renderers, rather than by the "independent" rendering companies. The rejection of animal fats by diet-conscious consumers led to a surplus of edible fats and their resultant diversion into soapmaking and oleochemicals, displacing inedible fats and contributing to the market volatility of this commodity.

The rendering industry is one of the oldest recycling industries, and made possible the development of a large food industry. The industry takes what would otherwise be waste materials and makes useful products such as fuels, soaps, rubber, plastics, etc. At the same time, rendering solves what would otherwise be a major disposal problem. As an example, the USA recycles more than 21 million metric tons annually of highly perishable and noxious organic matter. In 2004, the U.S. industry produced over 8 million metric tons of products, of which 1.6 million metric tons were exported.

Kitchen Rendering

Rendering involves the melting of a fatty material and removal of the non-fat components. In the kitchen, rendering is used to transform butter into clarified butter or ghee, suet into tallow and pork fat into lard. Unlike raw animal fats, rendered animal fats can be stored for extended periods without

SLAUGHTERHOUSE

The largest slaughterhouse in the world is operated by the Smithfield Packing Company located in Tar Heel, North

Carolina. It is capable of butchering over 30,000 pigs a day. A slaughterhouse, also called an abattoir is a facility where farm animals are killed and processed into meat products. The animals most commonly slaughtered for food are cattle (beef and veal), sheep (lamb and mutton), pigs (pork), poultry, and horses. (Most horse slaughter is in Europe, but horse slaughter also takes place in the USA and Canada and the meat is exported to Europe and Japan).

The design, process, and location of slaughterhouses respond to a variety of concerns. Slaughtering animals on a large scale poses significant logistical problems and public health concerns. Most religions stipulate certain conditions for the slaughter of animals. Public aversion to meat packing, in many cultures, influences the location and practices of slaughterhouses. More recently, animal rights groups have levelled ethical charges at slaughterhouses.

Slaughterhouse Process

The slaughterhouse process differs by species and region, and may be controlled by religious laws such as Kosher and halal laws. A typical procedure follows:

1. Animals are received by truck or rail from a ranch, farm, or feedlot.
2. Animals are herded into holding pens
3. Animals receive a preslaughter inspection.
4. Animals are usually rendered unconscious by stunning or "knocking" using various methods including the use of a captive bolt pistol, breaking the animal's neck or applying an electric shock to the animal's temples. Livestock are also rendered unconscious by CO_2 stunning and by live fire (used at the small locker plants). (This step is prohibited under strict application of Halal and Kashrut codes.)
5. Animals are hung by their hind legs on the processing line.
6. A main artery is cut, the animal's blood drains out and it dies. (Alternatively, this step can be carried

out on a metal tray before the animal is hung on the processing line)

7. The hide/skin/plumage is removed.
8. The carcass is inspected and graded by a government inspector for quality and safety. (This inspection is performed by the Food Safety Inspection Service in the US, and CFIA in Canada.)
9. The internal organs are removed and inspected for internal parasites. The viscera (guts) are separated for inspection from the pluck (heart and lungs), livers are separated for inspection, tongues are dropped or removed from the head and the head is sent down the line on the head hooks or head racks for inspection.
10. The carcass is cut apart and the body parts separated.
11. Meat cuts are quickly chilled to prevent the growth of microorganisms and to reduce meat deterioration while the meat awaits distribution.
12. The remaining carcass may be further processed to extract any residual traces of meat, usually termed mechanically recovered meat, which may be used for human or animal consumption.
13. Waste materials are sent to a rendering plant.
14. The waste water generated by the slaughtering process and the cleaning of the slaughter house is treated in a waste water treatment plant.
15. The meat is transported to distribution centers that distribute to local retail markets.

PIG SLAUGHTERING

Pigs are usually slaughtered after 4-7 months. Pigs intended for pork are usually slaughtered 1-2 months younger than pigs for bacon. The pigs are transported with trucks that have compartments with an individual capacity of 12-15 pigs. On arrival, they are unloaded and driven in lairage pens having a capacity equivalent to a truck compartment. The pigs are held there for 24 hours to recover from fatigue and stress; and they are provided with enough water to flush out intestinal pathogenic bacteria. Moreover, health inspections can be held during that holding period. The live animals are weighed prior to processing so that yield can be accurately determined.

Stunning

Before slaughtering, pigs undergo electrical or carbon dioxide stunning. In the first case, they are stunned using high frequency (50 Hz), low voltage electric current applied by means of two electrodes, which are placed on either side of the brine using tongs. The current induces a state of immediate epilepsy in the brain during which time the animal is unconscious. In the later case, the pigs are passed through a well with a CO_2 and air atmosphere. Legally a minimum of a 70 % concentration of CO_2 by volume is required, but a 90 % concentration is recommended. The pigs are again rendered unconscious due to the acidification of the cerebrospinal fluid upon inhalation of the CO_2. With the CO_2 method "blood splashing" is eliminated, and it also removes the human element required in the electrical stunning. During their state of unconsciousness, the pigs are hoisted onto an overhead rail for slaughtering.

Scalding and Dehairing

Pig carcasses are not skinned after exsanguinations. Instead, the carcasses are dropped into scalding water which loosens the hair for subsequent removal. The carcasses should be kept under water and continually moved and turned for uniform scalding. In large plants, carcasses enter the scalding tub and are carried through the tub by a conveyer moving at the proper speed to allow the proper scalding time. During the hard-hair season (September-November), the water temperature should be 59° to 60°C and the immersion period 4 to 4,5 minutes, while in the easy-hair season (February-March), a temperature of 58°C for 4 minutes is preferable.

In small plants without automation, hair condition is checked periodically during the scalding period. The dehairing process is begun with a dehairing machine, which uses one or more cylinders with metal tipped rubber beaters to scour the outside of the carcasses. Hot water (60°C) is sprayed on the carcasses as they pass through the dehairer moving toward the discharge end. The carcasses are removed from this machine, hand scraped, then hoisted again, hind quarters up. The carcasses are hand-scraped again from the top (hind quarters) down. Any remaining hairs can be removed by singeing with a propane or similar torch. Once the remaining hairs have been singed, the carcasses are scraped a final time and washed thoroughly from the hind feet to the head. Some plants pass the carcasses through a singeing through gas flames

Evisceration

After scalding and dehairing, singeing, or skinning, the head is severed from the backbone at the atlas joint, and the cut is continued through the windpipe and esophagus. The head is inspected, the tongue is dropped, and the head is removed from the carcass. The head is cleaned, washed, and an inspection stamp is applied. Following heading, the carcass is eviscerated. The hams are separated, the sternum is split, the ventral side is opened down the entire length of the carcass, and the abdominal organs are removed. These viscera are received in a moving gut pan to segregate edible (heart, liver) and non edible offal. Intestines are cleaned for sausage casings. The thoracic organs are then freed. Non edible offal is discarded into a barrel to be shipped to the rendering plant.

Cooling

Cutting and deboning are easier to carry out at lower temperature. Therefore, the carcasses are transferred to chill tunnels and chill rooms to cool them down to 0-1°C with air velocity typically 5 to 15 mph, equating to –5°C wind chill, for a 24-hour chill period. For thorough chilling, the inside temperature of the ham should reach at least 3°C. With accelerated (hot) processing, the carcass may be held (tempered) at an intermediate temperature of 16°C for several hours, or be boned immediately. When large numbers of warm carcasses are handled, the chill room is normally precooled to a temperature several degrees below freezing -3°C, bringing the wind chill to -9°C to compensate for the heat from the carcasses

Cutting into Smaller Pieces

The carcasses are processed into 3 cuts of meat (fore-end, middle and hind leg). During further cutting into smaller pieces, the slaughters are assisted in their work by automated transport trays and conveyors. They help in cutting and sorting meat and bone. The products are finally efficiently packaged and stored at low temperature prior to further processing.

POULTRY SLAUGHTERING

Legislation provides for the humane slaughter and pre-slaughter treatment of poultry (turkey, domestic fowl, guinea fowl or goose). On arrival of the transport vehicle into the covered slaughterhouse bay, living birds carried in fixed or loose plastic crates are unloaded and individually hung upside down by the feet on to the shackles from a continuously moving line. The centres of the shackles are approximately 15 cm apart. Ante-mortem inspection is carried out (crates are provided for birds rejected by the inspector).

Slaughter Room

The birds enter the slaughter room through a small narrow opening and are stunned instantaneously. Various types of electrical stunners are used. The birds are stunned either by their heads coming into contact with a 500 V electrified metal slope (wires) or by their heads passing through a 150 V electrically charged water bath. Recent research has shown that it is more humane to kill the birds in the stunner than just to stun them.

Bleeding

Thirty seconds later, the birds are bled automatically or by an operator who severs either the right or left jugular vein at the base of the skull. The birds now pass along a bleeding tunnel for at least 2 minutes for turkeys and at least 90 seconds for domestic fowls. This is to allow the birds to bleed before entering the scalding process. It is estimated that 50 % of the blood is removed.

Scalding

The birds, still suspended from the line, pass through the scald tank in which there is continuously changing water at 50-80°C. The time in the scald should be no more than 2 minutes. This ensures that the skin will be untorn and unblemished. The scalding loosens the feathers for the defeathering process. Sometimes detergents are added to the scald water, making the penetration of the water to the feather follicles much easier.

Defeathering

The birds pass into the defeathering machines, which consist of revolving drums with rubber beaters or discs. The birds are continually flailed or scraped by these, while being sprayed with warm water. The process takes approximately 1 minute. Any feathers still remaining attached are removed by hand. Ducks are often further defeathered by a hot wax process which removes the finer feathers and down. The first post-mortem inspection takes places in this area. Rejected birds are removed from the line. After plucking, the birds are washed by overhead sprays.

Neck Slitting and Foot Removal

A vertical incision is made in the skin on the dorsal surface of the neck to assist in the removal of the crop, oesophagus and trachea at a later stage. The feet are removed automatically by a cutter on the line or by manually operated secateurs. The birds drop on to a conveyor that transfers them though a narrow opening from the "dirty" section of the slaughterhouse into the "clean" section.

Evisceration Line

The birds are rehung by the hocks on to the shackles of the evisceration line. The line runs above a water trough or a mechanical conveyor, which carries away waste materials. Various operations are carried out on this line:

- Venting: Scissors cut a round vent in order to remove the intestines from the carcass. Great care is needed in this important operation as faecal contamination of the carcass, edible offals and operators' hands is to be avoided.
- Drawing: All of the viscera are drawn out of the body cavity, leaving them hanging from the carcass ready for inspection. The drawing is done either by hand or by operators using eviscerating forks or by automatic eviscerating machines.

At this point the inspectors examine the viscera, the body cavity and the carcass generally. Good lighting, properly directed into the body cavity is essential.

- Removal of offals: the edible offals, i.e. the heart, liver and gizzard are removed for further cleaning and washing. The intestines, proventriculus and lungs are discarded into the water through or mechanical conveyor. On some lines a suction tube is then introduced into the body cavity to remove any contamination or portions of lungs remaining.
- Head removal: the heads are generally removed mechanically by traction of a head puller. This also removes the crop, oesophagus and trachea. An inspector or a quality control officer then examines the carcass generally, especially the body cavity.
- Neck removal: the necks are removed by cutting through the vertebrae between the shoulders using automatic or manual secateurs. The necks are classified as part of the edible offal or giblets.
- Line washing: before going into the washing and cooling tanks the birds are spray washed to remove blood and extraneous matter.
- Polyphosphate injection: when polyphosphates are used, they are injected under pressure by guns with two hollow perforated needles. The solution is injected into the breast and sometimes also into the leg

muscles. Up to 5% of the body weight of this permitted additive solution may be injected.

FOOD PRCCESSING THROUGH COOKING METHODS

Steaming

Steaming is a method of cooking using steam. Steaming is a preferred cooking method for health conscious individuals because no cooking oil is needed, thus resulting in a lower fat content. Steaming also results in a more nutritious food than boiling because fewer nutrients are destroyed or leached away into the water (which is usually discarded). It is also easier to avoid burning food when steaming. Steaming works by first boiling water, causing it to evapourate into steam; the steam then carries heat to the food, thus cooking the food.

In western cooking, steaming is most often used to cook vegetables, and only rarely to cook meats. By contrast, vegetables are seldom steamed in Chinese cuisine; vegetables are mostly stir fried or blanched instead. In Chinese cooking, steaming is used to cook many meat dishes, for example, steamed whole fish, steamed pork spare ribs, steamed ground pork or beef patties, steamed chicken, steamed goose etc. Other than meat dishes, many Chinese rice and wheat foods are steamed too. Examples include buns, Chinese steamed cakes etc. Steamed meat dishes (except some dim sum) are less common in Chinese restaurants than in traditional home cooking because meats usually require longer cooking time to steam than to stir fry.

The Chinese chefs developed an efficient method of restaurant cooking: big bamboo steaming baskets, each 1 m (3') in diameter and 10 cm (4") tall, can be stacked up on top of a wok like a chimney. The bottom of each basket is a grid which allows the steam from the wok to rise all the way to the top of the stack. In the kitchen of some dim sum restaurants, a steaming stack can be 20 levels high. The bottom level is removed when done and the entire stack simply shifted downward. This technique ensures a constant supply of freshly steamed dim sum.

Steaming at home can also be done with a wok. A shelf is put on the bottom of the wok, and a small steam basket or a dish of food is put on the shelf. Water is then filled to just below the dish or basket. The water is kept boiling, and a lid is placed over. Most vegetable dishes can be cooked in approximately 5 minutes using this method; most meat dishes, however, take longer than 20 minutes. A common alternative is to put the dish to be steamed on top of rice which is being cooked. A pot of rice which takes about 30 minutes to cook will then be ready at the same time as the steamed food.

Specialized steamers are often available for purchase; however, although they are more convenient, they are not necessarily better. Rice is traditionally steamed in the Lowcountry around Charleston, South Carolina, and specialized rice steamers are a common household cooking vessel in that area, although rather obscure elsewhere. A related technique is enclosing food in a container or material that will release steam when heated, such as clay pot cooking. A kind of steaming can be done outdoors by wrapping meat, poultry, or fish in banana leaves and burying it in hot sand or ash. Another form of outdoor steam cooking is covering a large piece of meat, poultry or fish in wet clay and placing it in a fire.

Double Steaming

Double steaming also called double boiling is a Chinese cooking technique to prepare delicate food such as bird nests, shark fins etc. The food is covered with water and put in a covered ceramic jar. The jar is then steamed for several hours. This technique ensures there is no loss of liquid or moisture (its essences) from the food being cooked, hence it is often used with expensive ingredients like Chinese herbal medicines.

Cantonese calls double steaming dan. Note that the Cantonese usage of this Chinese character deviates from its original meaning which is simmer or stew in Mandarin. This technique is also common in the neighbouring province of Fujian. There is another dessert dish called double steamed frog ovaries in a coconut recommended for women. The

Chinese medicinal ingredients (including hasma), spices, and rock sugar are placed inside a young coconut to soak in the original coconut juice. The filled coconut is then double steamed for several hours. The whole coconut is served whole at the table after dinner. The contents and the inside wall of the coconut are scooped out to be consumed.

Grill (Cooking)

There are multiple varieties of grills, with most falling into one of two categories: gas-fueled and charcoal. There is a great debate over the merits of charcoal or gas for use as the cooking method between grillers. Gas-fueled grills typically use propane (LP) or natural gas (NG) as their fuel source, with gas-flame either cooking food directly or heating grilling elements which in turn radiate the heat necessary to cook food. Gas grills are available in sizes ranging from small, single steak grills up to large, industrial sized restaurant grills which are able to cook enough meat to feed a hundred or more people. Gas grills are designed for either LP or NG, although it is possible to convert a grill from one gas source to another.

Charcoal grills typically use charcoal briquets as their fuel source. The briquets, when burned, will transform into embers radiating the heat necessary to cook food. One may say with certainty that E.G. Kingsford was the prime force behind the American grilling tradition. Kingsford was a relative of Henry Ford who saw that Ford's Model T production lines were producing a large amount of wood scraps that were just being discarded. Kingsford pitched a simple idea to Ford: Set up a charcoal manufacturing facility next to the assembly line and sell the charcoal, with the Ford name, in Ford dealerships. Ford, knowing a good idea when he saw one, immediately implemented Kingsford's idea. After Kingsford's death, the company was renamed Kingsford Charcoal Co. in his honor. Today, Kingsford charcoal is the dominant brand used by charcoal grillers.

Another personality in the charcoal grilling camp is George Stephen. The stereotypical American charcoal grill is a hollow, metal hemisphere with three legs and a small metal disc to catch ash, with a lower grate to hold the charcoal and an upper grate to hold the food to be cooked. George Stephen created the hemispherical grill design, jokingly called "Sputnik" by Stephen's neighbours. Stephen, a welder, worked for Weber Brothers Metal Works, a metal fabrication shop primarily concerned with welding steel spheres together to make buoys.

Stephen was tired of wind blowing ash onto his food when he grilled. One day he had an epiphany: he took the lower half of a buoy, welded three steel legs onto it, and fabricated a shallower hemisphere for use as a lid. He took the results home and within weeks was selling the grills first to his neighbours, then to customers, and finally started the Weber-Stephen Products Company. Weber grills come in many sizes, again, in small 14 inch diameter grills up to a full size 24 inch diameter grill. Grilling is a pervasive tradition in the United States. There are many cook-offs for steak grilling and barbecue (midwestern and southern style) around the United States with serious cash prizes involved in most. Almost all competition grillers use charcoal, most often in large, custom designed brick or steel grills. They can range from a few 55 gallon oil drums sawed lengthwise on their sides to make a lid and grill base, to large, vehicle sized grills made of brick, weighing nearly a ton.

Commonly Grilled Food and Cooking Methods

- Steaks. Pre-heat on high. This way the grill is hot and will scorch the outside of the steak. By the time it is "done" the outside will be blackened (but not burned) and you'll still have some pink in the middle.
- Shrimp. Medium/low heat. Don't overcook.
- Asparagus. Marinate in oil and salt.

CARBONATION AND SUGARCANE PROCESSING

Carbonatation is a chemical reaction where calcium hydroxide reacts with carbon dioxide and forms insoluble calcium carbonate:

$$Ca(OH)_2 + CO_2 \rightarrow CaCO_3 + H_2O$$

Carbonatation is a slow process that occurs in concrete where lime (calcium hydroxide) in the cement reacts with carbon dioxide from the air and forms calcium carbonate. Since carbonatation causes a lower pH (acidic) this may lead to corrosion of the steel reinforcing rods and damage to the construction.

Sugar Refining

The carbonatation process is used in the production of sugar from sugar beet, It is the introduction of milk of lime (calcium hydroxide suspension) and carbon dioxide enriched gas into the "raw juice", the sugar rich liquid prepared from the diffusion stage of the process, to form calcium carbonate and to precipitate and remove impurities. The whole process takes place in "carbonatation tanks" and processing time varies from 20 minutes to an hour.

Carbonatation involves the following effects:

- The increase in alkalinity coagulates proteins in the juice.
- Calcium carbonate absorbs colourants
- Alkalinity destroys some monosaccharide sugars, mostly glucose and fructose

The target is a large particle that naturally settles rapidly to leave a clear juice. The juice at the end is approximately 15 °Bx and 90% sucrose. The pH of the thin juice produced is a balance between removing as much calcium from the solution and the expected pH drop across later processing. If the juice goes acidic in the crystallisation stages then sucrose rapidly breaks down to glucose and fructose; not only do glucose and fructose affect crystallisation but they are melassagenic taking equivalent amounts of sucrose on to the molasses stage.

The carbon dioxide bubbled through the mixture forms calcium carbonate. The non-sugar solids are incorporated into the calcium carbonate particles and removed by natural (or assisted) sedimentation in tanks. There are several systems of carbonatation, named from the companies that first developed them. They differ in how the lime is introduced, the temperature and durations of each stage, and the separation of the solids from the liquid.

- Dorr (also Dorr-Oliver) - a continuous process using two tanks with recycling ("1st carbonatation") to build up particle size for natural flocculation. The recycling ratio is about 7:1. The particles are separated under gravity in a thickening stage in a vessel called a clarifier. The clear juice is then gassed further in another tank ("2nd carbonatation") and filtered. The concentrated mud (underflow) is filtered and/or pressed to recover more liquid. The Dorr process is low in maintenance and man-power but susceptible to frost damaged beet. It is favoured in the UK and the USA.
- DDS (Det Danske Sukkerfabrik - "The Danish Sugarfactory") — multistage process involving pre-liming where the pH of the juice is gradually increased to start precipitation of proteins, followed by addition of further lime and gas. The particles are removed at each stage by filtration.
- RT (Raffinière Tirlemontoise) - another multistage process with a pre-liming stage. Particles also removed by filtration.

Both DDS and RT processes are favoured by European factories. The clear juice from carbonatation is generally known as "thin juice". it may undergo pH adjustment with soda ash and addition of sulphur ("sulphitation") prior to the next stage which is concentration by multiple effect evapouration.

BLANCHING

Blanching is a cooking term that describes a process of food preparation wherein the food substance, usually a vegetable or fruit, is plunged into boiling water, removed after a brief, timed interval and finally plunged into iced water or placed under cold running water (shocked) to halt the cooking process.

Uses of blanching

- Peeling: Blanching loosens the skin on some fruits or nuts, such as onions, tomatoes, plums, peaches, or almonds.
- Flavour: Blanching enhances the flavor of some vegetables, such as broccoli, by releasing bitter acids stored in the cellular structure of the food.
- Appearance: Blanching enhances the colour of some (particularly green) vegetables by releasing gases trapped in the cellular material that obscure the greenness of the chorophyll. Since blanching is done - and halted - quickly, the heat does not have time to break down chlorophyll as well.
- Shelf life: Blanching neutralises bacteria and enzymes present in foods, thus delaying spoilage. This is often done as a preparatory step for freezing vegetables.

Blanching can also describe deep frying in oil at a lower temperature as with the initial cooking of French fries/chips.

Chapter 2

Hospitality and Food Management

HOTEL AND HOSPITALITY

A hotel is an establishment that provides paid lodging, usually on a short-term basis. Hotels often provide a number of additional guest services such as a restaurant, a swimming pool or childcare. Some hotels have conference services and meeting rooms and encourage groups to hold conventions and meetings at their location. Hotels differ from motels in that most motels have drive-up, exterior entrances to the rooms, while hotels tend to have interior entrances to the rooms, which may increase guests' safety and present a more upmarket image.

In Australia, a hotel may also be an establishment that serves alcoholic drinks, and usually meals in a casual setting but which does not necessarily provide accommodation. This type of establishment would more usually be called a pub or bar in other countries. In general use in Australia the terms '"hotel" and pub are usually taken to be synonymous. In India, the word may also refer to a restaurant since the best restaurants were always situated next to a good hotel.

The word hotel derives from the French hôtel, which referred to a French version of a townhouse, not a place offering accommodation (in contemporary usage, hôtel has the meaning of "hotel", and hôtel particulier is used for the old meaning). The French spelling (with the circumflex) was once also used in English, but is now rare. The circumflex replaces the 's' once preceding the 't' in the earlier hostel spelling, which over time received a new, but closely related meaning.

SERVICES AND FACILITIES

Basic accommodation of a room with only a bed, a cupboard, a small table and a washstand has largely been replaced by rooms with en-suite bathrooms and climate control. Other features found may be a telephone, an alarm clock, a TV, and broadband Internet connectivity. Food and drink may be supplied by a mini-bar (which often includes a small refrigerator) containing snacks and drinks (to be paid for on departure), and tea and coffee making facilities (cups, spoons, an electric kettle and sachets containing instant coffee, tea bags, sugar, and creamer or milk).

In the United Kingdom a hotel is required by law to serve food and drinks to all comers within certain stated hours; to avoid this requirement it is not uncommon to come across "private hotels" which are not subject to this requirement. However, in Japan the capsule hotel supplies minimal facilities and room space.

Classification

The cost and quality of hotels are usually indicative of the range and type of services available. Due to the enormous increase in tourism worldwide during the last decades of the 20th century, standards, especially those of smaller establishments, have improved considerably. For the sake of greater comparability, rating systems have been introduced, with the one to five stars classification being most common.

Boutique Hotels

"Boutique Hotel" is a term originating in North America to describe intimate, usually luxurious or quirky hotel environments. Boutique hotels differentiate themselves from larger chain or branded hotels by providing an exceptional and personalized level of accommodation, services and facilities. Boutique hotels are furnished in a themed, stylish and/or aspirational manner. Although usually considerably smaller than a mainstream hotel (ranging from 3 to 100 guest rooms) boutique hotels are generally fitted with telephone and wi-fi Internet connections, honesty bars and often cable/pay TV. Guest services are attended to by 24 hour hotel staff. Many boutique hotels have on site dining facilities, and the majority offer bars and lounges which may also be open to the general public.

Of the total travel market a small percentage are discerning travelers, who place a high importance on privacy, luxury and service delivery. As this market is typically corporate travelers, the market segment is non-seasonal, high-yielding and repeat, and therefore one which boutique hotel operators target as their primary source of income.

Unusual Hotels

Many hotels can be considered destinations in themselves, by dent of unusual features of the lodging and/or its immediate environment:

Treehouse Hotels

Some hotels, such as the Costa Rica Tree House in the Gandoca-Manzanillo Wildlife Refuge, Costa Rica, or Treetops Hotel in Aberdare National Park, Kenya, are built with living trees as structural elements, making them treehouses. The Ariau Towers near Manaus, Brazil is in the middle of the Amazon, on the Rio Negro. Bill Gates even invested and had a suite built there with satellite internet/phone. Another hotel with treehouse units is Bayram's Tree Houses in Olympos, Turkey.

Cave Hotels

Desert Cave Hotel in Coober Pedy, South Australia and the Cuevas Pedro Antonio de Alarcón (named after the author) in Guadix, Spain, as well as several hotels in Cappadocia, Turkey, are notable for being built into natural cave formations, some with rooms underground.

Capsule Hotels

Capsule hotels are a type of economical hotels that are quite common in Japan.

Ice Hotels

Ice hotels, such as the Ice Hotel in Jukkasjärvi, Sweden, melt every spring and are rebuilt out of ice and snow each winter.

Snow Hotels

The Mammut Snow Hotel in Finland is located within the walls of the Kemi snow castle, which is the biggest in the world. It includes The Mammut Snow Hotel, The Castle Courtyard, The Snow Restaurant and a chapel for weddings, etc. Its furnishings and its decorations, such as sculptures, are made of snow and ice. There is snow accommodation also in Lainio Snow Hotel in Lapland (near Ylläs), Finland.

Garden Hotels

Garden hotels, famous for their gardens before they became hotels, includes Gravetye Manor, the home of William Robinson and Cliveden, designed by Charles Barry with a rose garden by Geoffrey Jellicoe.

Underwater Hotels

As of 2005, the only hotel with an underwater room that can be reached without Scuba diving is Utter Inn in Lake Mälaren, Sweden. It only has one room, however, and Jules' Undersea Lodge in Key Largo, Florida, which requires scuba diving, is not much bigger.

Hydropolis is an ambitious project to build a luxury hotel in Dubai, UAE, with 220 suites, all on the bottom of the Persian Gulf, 20 meters (66 feet) below the surface. Its architecture will feature two domes that break the surface and an underwater train tunnel, all made of transparent materials such as glass and acrylic.

Other Unusual Hotels

The Library Hotel in New York City is unique in that its ten floors are arranged according to the Dewey Decimal System. The Rogers Centre, formerly SkyDome, in Toronto, Canada is the only stadium to have a hotel connected to it, with 70 rooms overlooking the field. The Burj al-Arab hotel in Dubai, United Arab Emirates, built on an artificial island, is structured in the shape of a sail of a boat.

HOTEL OCCUPATIONS

The owner, chairman, or CEO of a hotel or hotel group is known as a hotelier. A comfortable room, good food, and a helpful staff can make being away from home an enjoyable experience for both vacationing families and business travellers. While most lodging managers work in traditional hotels and motels, some work in other lodging establishments, such as camps, inns, boardinghouses, dude ranches, and recreational resorts. In full-service hotels, lodging managers help their guests have a pleasant stay by providing many of the comforts of home, including cable television, fitness equipment, and voice mail, as well as specialized services such as health spas. For business travelers, lodging managers often schedule available meeting rooms and electronic equipment, including slide projectors and fax machines.

Lodging managers are responsible for keeping their establishments efficient and profitable. In a small establishment with a limited staff, the manager may oversee all aspects of operations. However, large hotels may employ hundreds of workers, and the general manager usually is aided by a number of assistant managers assigned to the various departments of the operation. In hotels of every size, managerial duties vary significantly by job title.

General managers have overall responsibility for the operation of the hotel. Within guidelines established by the owners of the hotel or executives of the hotel chain, the general manager sets room rates, allocates funds to departments, approves expenditures, and ensures expected standards for guest service, decor, housekeeping, food quality, and banquet operations. Managers who work for chains also may organize and staff a newly built hotel, refurbish an older hotel, or reorganize a hotel or motel that is not operating successfully. In order to fill entry-level service and clerical jobs in hotels, some managers attend career fairs.

Resident or hotel managers are responsible for the day-to-day operations of the property. In larger properties, more than one of these managers may assist the general manager, frequently dividing responsibilities between the food and beverage operations and the rooms or lodging services. At least one manager, either the general manager or a hotel manager, is on call 24 hours a day to resolve problems or emergencies.

Assistant managers help run the day-to-day operations of the hotel. In large hotels, they may be responsible for activities such as personnel, accounting, office administration, marketing and sales, purchasing, security, maintenance, and pool, spa, or recreational facilities. In smaller hotels, these duties may be combined into one position. Assistant managers may adjust charges on a hotel guest's bill when a manager is unavailable.

An Executive Committee made up of a hotel's senior managers advises the general manager, assists in setting hotel policy, coordinates services that cross departmental boundaries, and collabourates on efforts to ensure consistent and efficient guest services throughout the hotel. The Committee may be comprised of the department heads for housekeeping, front office, food and beverage, security, sales and public relations, meetings and conventions, engineering and building maintenance, and human resources. Executive committee members bring a different perspective of guest service to the total management objective reflecting the unique expertise and training of their positions.

Executive housekeepers ensure that guest rooms, meeting and banquet rooms, and public areas are clean, orderly, and well maintained. They also train, schedule, and supervise the work of housekeepers, inspect rooms, and order cleaning supplies.

Front office managers coordinate reservations and room assignments, as well as train and direct the hotel's front desk staff. They ensure that guests are treated courteously, complaints and problems are resolved, and requests for special services are carried out. Front office managers may adjust charges posted on a customer's bill.

Convention services managers coordinate the activities of various departments in larger hotels to accommodate meetings, conventions, and special events. They meet with representatives of groups or organizations to plan the number of rooms to reserve, the desired configuration of the meeting space, and banquet services. During the meeting or event, they resolve unexpected problems and monitor activities to ensure that hotel operations conform to the expectations of the group.

Food and beverage managers oversee all food service operations maintained by the hotel. They coordinate menus with the Executive Chef for the hotel's restaurants, lounges, and room service operations. They supervise the ordering of food and supplies, direct service and maintenance contracts within the kitchens and dining areas, and manage food service budgets.

Catering managers arrange for food service in a hotel's meeting and convention rooms. They coordinate menus and costs for banquets, parties, and events with meeting and convention planners or individual clients. They coordinate staffing needs and arrange schedules with kitchen personnel to ensure appropriate food service.

Sales or marketing directors and public relations directors oversee the advertising and promotion of hotel operations and functions, including lodging and dining specials and special events, such as holiday or seasonal specials. They direct the efforts of their staff to purchase advertising and market their property to organizations or groups seeking a venue for conferences, conventions, business meetings, trade shows, and special events. They also coordinate media relations and answer questions from the press.

Human resources directors manage the personnel functions of a hotel, ensuring that all accounting, payroll, and employee relations matters are handled in compliance with hotel policy and applicable laws. They also oversee hiring practices and standards and ensure that training and promotion programmes reflect appropriate employee development guidelines.

Finance (or revenue) directors monitor room sales and reservations. In addition to overseeing accounting and cash-flow matters at the hotel, they also project occupancy levels, decide which rooms to discount and when to offer rate specials.

Computers are used extensively by lodging managers and their assistants to keep track of guests' bills, reservations, room assignments, meetings, and special events. In addition, computers are used to order food, beverages, and supplies, as well as to prepare reports for hotel owners and top-level managers. Managers work with computer specialists to ensure that the hotel's computer system functions properly. Should the hotel's computer system fail, managers must continue to meet the needs of hotel guests and staff.

Living in Hotels

The American billionaire Howard Hughes lived much of his life in hotels. He moved with his entourage from hotel to hotel and from Beverly Hills to Boston before deciding to move to Las Vegas and become a casino baron. Less than a month after his November 27, 1966 arrival , Hughes made a public offer to buy the Desert Inn. The hotel's 8th floor became the nerve center of his empire and the 9th floor penthouse became Hughes's personal residence. Hughes moved to the Bahamas, Vancouver, London and several other locations — always taking up residence in the top floor penthouse of the hotel. Between 1966 and 1968, he also purchased several other hotel-casinos from the Mafia: Castaways, New Frontier, The Landmark Hotel and Casino, Sands and Silver Slipper.

Coco Chanel made the Hôtel Ritz in Paris her home for more than thirty years, until the day of her death, at 87, in a suite now named "Coco Chanel Suite". King Peter II of Yugoslavia spent much of the Second World War at Claridge's, a hotel in London. His son, Aleksandar Karaðorðeviæ, was born in the hotel. Prince Felix Yusupov lived in the Hotel Vendôme in Paris. Alois Brunner, Austrian Nazi war criminal, is believed to have lived in the Meridian Hotel in Damascus, Syria, under the name Georg Fischer. Sultan Said Bin Taimur of Muscat lived at Dorchester Hotel in London after he was deposed by Qaboos of Oman in 1970, He died in the hotel in 1972. Eleftherios Venizelos, Greek statesman and diplomat, lived in the Hôtel Ritz Paris while he was in exile in France from 1935-1936.

FOOD INDUSTRY

The food industry is the complex, global collective of diverse businesses that together supply much of the food energy consumed by the world population. Only subsistence farmers, those who survive on what they grow, can be considered outside of the scope of the modern food industry.

The food industry includes:

- Regulation: local, regional, national and international rules and regulations for food production and sale, including food quality and food safety, and industry lobbying activities
- Education: academic, vocational, consultancy
- Research and development: food technology
- Manufacturing: agrichemicals, seed, farm machinery and supplies, agricultural construction, etc.
- Agriculture: raising of crops and livestock, seafood
- Food processing: preparation of fresh products for market, manufacture of prepared food products
- Marketing: promotion of generic products (e.g. milk board), new products, public opinion, through advertising, packaging, public relations, etc
- Wholesale and distribution: warehousing, transportation, logistics
- Retail: supermarket chains and independent food stores, direct-to-consumer, restaurant, food services

OVERVIEW

Essentially, the food industry involves the commercial movement of food from field to fork. The modern food industry is the result of technological and cultural changes that have occurred over the last 150 years. Traditionally, over thousands of years, food production was centered around two activities:

1. Labour-intensive agricultural activities, the farming of grain, produce and livestock;
2. Personal food preparation, where individuals and families acquire raw and minimally processed ingredients, and prepare them for their own consumption.

A significant percentage of the population was directly involved in farming, and in the process, many people actually fed themselves, from field to table. By contrast, the modern food industry relies far more on technology, particularly on mechanization and biochemistry, than on human and animal labour. In this way, food is raised, manipulated, preserved and moved around, resulting in a food industry that is to a great degree global in nature, with food and related resources travelling great distances. For example, farm machinery and parts from Europe and agrichemicals from the US may routinely travel to farms in South America, where farm products are raised and shipped to North America for fresh market consumption, or for use in processed foods which may then travel to further points around the world. The point at which foods are gathered and prepared has also become fragmented: much of what we eat has already been assembled for consumption.

This modern food system relies heavily on technology, transportation, management and logistics for physical fulfillment, and on marketing and government regulation for maintaining an efficient consumer market. An incredibly wide range of businesses and individuals are employed by and profit from all aspects of this huge and complex system. A tremendous amount of governmental regulation and administration is also involved in this continual flow of materials, food products, and related information.

DEFINITIONS

Food industry is not a formally defined term, however, it is usually used in a broadly inclusive way to cover all aspects of food production and sale. The Food Standards Agency, a government body in the UK, describes it thus:

"the whole food industry - from farming and food production, packaging and distribution, to retail and catering."

The Economic Research Service of the USDA uses the term food system to describe the same thing:

"The U.S. food system is a complex network of farmers and the industries that link to them. Those links include makers of farm equipment and chemicals as well as firms that provide services to agribusinesses, such as providers of transportation and financial services. The system also includes the food marketing industries that link farms to consumers, and which include food and fiber processors, wholesalers, retailers, and foodservice establishments."

Industry Size

Processed food sales worldwide are approximately US$3.2 trillion (2004). In the U.S., consumers spend approximately US$1 trillion annually for food, or nearly 10 percent of the Gross Domestic Product (GDP). Over 16.5 million people are employed in the food industry.

Agriculture

Agriculture is the process of producing food, feed, fiber and other desired products by the cultivation of certain plants and the raising of domesticated animals (livestock). The practice of agriculture is also known as "farming", while scientists, inventors and others devoted to improving farming methods and implements are also said to be engaged in agriculture. More people in the world are involved in agriculture as their primary economic activity than in any other, yet it only accounts for four percent of the world's GDP.

Wholesale and Distribution

A vast global transportation network is required by the food industry in order to connect its numerous parts. These include suppliers, manufacturers, warehousing, retailers and the end consumers.

Retail

With populations around the world concentrating in urban areas, food buying is increasingly removed from all aspects food production. This is a relatively recent development, taking place mainly over the last 50 years. The supermarket is a defining retail element of the food industry, where tens of thousands of products are gathered in one location, in continuous, year-round supply.

Food preparation is another area where change in recent decades has been dramatic. Today, two food industry sectors are in apparent competition for the retail food dollar. The grocery industry sell fresh and largely raw products for consumers to use as ingredients in home cooking. The food service industry offers prepared food, either as finished products, or as partially prepared components for final "assembly".

FOOD INDUSTRY TECHNOLOGIES

Sophisticated technologies define modern food production. They include many areas. Agricultural machinery, originally led by the tractor, has practically eliminated human labour in many areas of production. Biotechnology is driving much change, in areas as diverse as agrichemicals, plant breeding and food processing. Many other areas of technology are also involved, to the point where it is hard to find an area that does not have a direct impact on the food industry. Computer technology is also a central force, with computer networks and specialized software providing the support infrastructure to allow global movement of the myriad components involved.

Marketing

As consumers grow increasingly removed from food production, the role of product creation, advertising, publicity become the primary vehicles for information about food. With processed food as the dominant category, marketers have almost infinite possibilities in product creation. The smooth flow of international trade is critical to the functioning of the modern food industry. Government regulations have to be synchronized to some greater degree to allow this.

Labour and Education

Until the last 100 years, agriculture was labour intensive. Farming was a common occupation. Food production flowed from millions of farms. Farmers, largely trained from generation to generation, carried on the family business. That situation has changed dramatically. In North America, over 50% of the population were farm families only a few decades ago; now, that figure is around 1-2%, and some 80% of the population lives in cities. The food industry as a complex whole requires an incredibly wide range of skills. Several hundred occupation types exist within the food industry.

Research and Development

Research in agricultural and food processing technologies happens in great part in university research environments. Projects are often funded by companies from the food industry. There is therefore a direct relationship between the academic and commercial sectors, as far as scientific research.

Prominent Food Companies

Monsanto is a leading producer of pesticide, seeds, and other farming products. Both Archer Daniels Midland and Cargill process grain into animal feed and a diverse group of products. ADM also provides agricultural storage and transportation services, while Cargill operates a finance wing.

Bunge is a global soybean exporter and is also involved in food processing, grain trading, and fertilizer. Dole Food Company is the world's largest fruit company. Chiquita

Brands International, another US based fruit company, is the leading distributor of bananas in the United States. Sunkist Growers, Incorporated is a U.S. based grower's cooperative. Tyson Foods is the world's largest processor and marketer of chicken and the largest beef exporter from the United States. Smithfield is the world's largest pork processor and hog producer.

Nestlé is the world's largest food and beverage company. The Altria Group owns 88.1% of Kraft Foods, the largest U.S. based food and beverage company. Unilever is an Anglo-Dutch company that owns many of the world's consumer product brands in foods and beverages.

A BRIEF HISTORY OF FOOD

Food in America

It was not the last time cannibalism would be resorted to in America. Later Virginians wanted to grow a profitable crop; they tried sugar but the climate was too cold. They settled on tobacco. Soon tobacco was bringing in so much money that people planted it on any available land—they ripped up their gardens, even grew it between graves. But who would hoe and harvest these thousands of acres of tobacco? The Native Americans who didn't die of Old World diseases refused to do it. African slaves were too expensive, although some arrived in 1619. England had the perfect labour force: a surplus of poor, desperate young men in their late teens and early twenties. They signed an indenture— a contract—giving them a free trip to America and free room and board in exchange for four to six years of work. Then they were supposed to get their freedom, tools, corn, and land of their own—something they had zero chance of getting in England. The person who hired the indentured servant and paid for his trip received free labour and fifty acres of land. It was a sweetheart deal all around. Most of these young men didn't live four years after they got to America. They died from dysentery, typhoid, malaria. The ones who did live found that there was only one woman for every six men. And soon the best land was in huge plantations owned by a few wealthy men who also had all the political power. In 1676, when former indentured servants couldn't get land, women, or the vote, they went on a rampage. Bacon's Rebellion ended with Jamestown burned and more than 20 former indentured servants hanged. Planters wanted a labour force they could control, not these Englishmen who used violence to get their rights. In 1698, when England ended the Royal African Company's monopoly on the slave trade, anyone with a ship could get into the slave trade. With competition, the price of slaves dropped. Now it was affordable to own Africans and profitable to sell them.

The Carolinas and Rice

At about the same time, the English established a colony south of Virginia—Carolina, named after King Charles II. Many of the settlers were from Barbados. They intended to grow food for the Caribbean sugar plantations and to export more expensive items, but after failing at wine, olive oil, and silk, they decided on rice as their staple crop. Rice requires skilled labour; Africans had this skill. They were also immune to malaria, and weren't Christian, so according to the Christian world at that time, they could be enslaved for the rest of their lives. The settlers also imported the Barbados slave code, with punishments that escalated from whipping to facial mutilation and sometimes death, which the code said was the slave's fault for forcing his master to discipline him. Charleston, South Carolina, became the primary port through which slaves entered the United States. By 1710, black slaves outnumbered white settlers in the coastal regions of the area that became South Carolina.

In spite of the conditions under which the slaves were brought to America, some of their African cuisine and culture survived. This influenced how cooking developed in the American South, since they were the cooks. Along with their knowledge of rice cultivation, cooking, and storage, they brought yams, okra, watermelon, and their love of fried food. They also brought back foodstuffs that had been taken from the New World to Africa, like the chile pepper and the peanut, and their word for it—goober. They brought the banjo and the drum and the music that would become jazz. New England:"Almost Beyond Believing"2 In 1620, Pilgrims—Protestants who wanted to be allowed to worship without being persecuted—landed at Plymouth, Massachusetts. Before they went ashore, the men on the ship entered into an agreement. The Mayflower Compact was the first constitution in America. Only one paragraph long, it sets forth an important principle: that all would be equal and work together as a community. The Pilgrims, and the Puritans who settled the Massachusetts Bay Colony in Boston ten years later, had their work cut out for them.

These were people used to living in towns. They didn't know how to hunt or fish or farm. But they didn't like many of the strange plants and animals in North America anyway—those huge quahog clams, the slimy steamers. And the codfish and lobsters were bigger than they were, sometimes six feet long. They wouldn't eat them at first, even after the Indians showed them how. But with the help of the native tribes, the Pilgrims survived their first year and had a celebration. Thanksgiving Foods "The turkey is certainly one of the most delightful presents which the New World has made to the Old." Most of the foods Americans eat at Thanksgiving dinner now are native to the Americas: turkey, cranberry sauce, mashed potatoes, sweet potatoes, corn-bread stuffing, pumpkin pie. In French the word for turkey is dinde, short for poulet d'inde, which means "chicken from India," because the French, like other Europeans, thought the turkey was from the Indies. Geese, ducks, and other wild fowl were abundant only during certain seasons in the New World, but turkeys don't migrate, so they were available all year. And they had an instinct that helped humans: when one turkey was shot, the others froze in place. It was easy to kill a dozen turkeys in a morning. Nobody ever called anybody a turkey and meant it as a compliment.

Cranberries and blueberries, both members of the heather family and both native to New England, were more than food in sauce and pies. Mashed and mixed with sour milk, they were used as paint. That is why the colours most often associated with colonial American buildings are muted cranberry and milky purple-gray. Although pumpkin was widely used in the colonies, recipes for pumpkin pie didn't appear in print until the first American cookbook, written by Amelia Simmons in 1796. She called it "pompkin" and gave two different versions. Both had pumpkin, ginger, and eggs, but one used cream and sugar, the other milk and molasses. One used the Old World spices mace and nutmeg, the other New World allspice.

The Codfish

The staple "crop" in the Massachusetts Bay Colony was the codfish, Gadus morhua. What sugar was to the Caribbean and tobacco was to the Food Fable squanto and fish fertilizer Contrary to what American myth has long held, it is quite unlikely that alewives or other fish were uses as fertilizer in Indian fields, notwithstanding the legendary role of the Pilgrims' friend Squanto in teaching colonists this practice. Squanto probably learned the technique while being held captive in Europe, and if any Indians used it in New England, they did so in an extremely limited area. Having no easy way to transport large amounts of fish from river to field, and preferring quite sensibly to avoid such back-breaking work, Indians simply abandoned their fields when the soil lost its fertility. Fertilizing fields with fish, as the English eventually did, seemed to Indians a wholly unnecessary labour.

Chesapeake, Cod was to Massachusetts

There were millions off the coast, north to Newfoundland and Labrador. Once it was salted and dried, cod was stiff as a board and could be stacked and shipped like lumber. It was also almost 80 percent protein. In this form it made its way to Europe: bacalà in Italy, bacalao in Spain, bacalhau in Portugal. According to historian Mark Kurlansky, by the middle of the 16th century, "60 percent of all fish eaten in Europe was cod." It was the perfect food for Lent. The best grade was sent to

Spain; the worst fed the slaves in the West Indies. It could also be bartered for slaves in Africa. Shipbuilders got rich because of cod, too. The cod was so important to the economy of Massachusetts that a large carved wooden cod hangs in the statehouse in Boston. Fifty-one Pilgrim men, women, and children hosted ninety men of the Wampanoag tribe and their chief, Massasoit. It was in the fall, to celebrate the good harvest of corn (wheat and barley weren't as successful). The celebration lasted three days. There were "wild fowl" and five deer. The idea of a national day of thanks was raised in the late 1700s with the first president, George Washington, who proposed November 26 as the date. Nothing came of it until the 1850s, when magazine journalist Sarah Josepha Hale rallied the women of America to pressure the president for a national holiday. In 1863, the third year of the Civil War, President Lincoln declared that the last Thursday in November should be a day of giving thanks. It was the same year that Lincoln issued the Emancipation Proclamation freeing the slaves, and made his speech at the battlefield in Gettysburg, Pennsylvania, in which he said these famous words: "that government of the people, by the people, for the people, shall not perish from the earth."

In 1939, President Franklin D. Roosevelt wanted to extend the Christmas shopping season to give the economy a boost and help it recover from the depression. He moved Thanksgiving one week earlier. Congress objected. The president and Congress did a tug-of-war over the date until 1941, when it was settled: Thanksgiving is the fourth Thursday in November. In 1970, Wampanoag leader Wampsutta (Anglo name: Frank James) was invited to speak at the Thanksgiving celebration at Plymouth, Massachusetts. When word got out that his speech was about the oppression of Native Americans, the invitation was revoked. He gave his speech anyway, in front of the statue of Massasoit, overlooking the replica of the Mayflower. That was the first Native American National Day of Mourning for the culture, the religion, and the lives and lands of their ancestors. Maple Syrup: Tapping the Sap of the

Sugar Tree "Maple Moon" was what Native Americans called the time in the spring when the sap started to flow in the sugar maple tree, Acer saccharum.

Just as the grapevine was a symbol of resurrection for the ancient Greeks, so the maple was for Native Americans. Flowing sap meant the end of winter and the rebirth of nature. The Iroquois performed a religious ritual, a maple dance, to pray for warm weather and plenty of sap. According to legend, an Iroquois chief pulled his tomahawk out of a tree where he had thrown it the night before and went off to hunt. In the meantime, the weather turned warm and sap oozed into a container left by accident at the base of the tree. On her way to get water for cooking, his wife saw the container of liquid and used that instead; everyone agreed it was much better than water.8 Seventeenth-century European writers give Native Americans full credit for knowing how to make maple syrup and sugar, but in the 18th century, Europeans started to claim that they taught the Indians. As historians Helen and Scott Nearing have pointed out, language is on the side of the tribes. All their words for maple syrup translate as "drawn from wood," "sap flows fast," "our own tree," while they called white sugar "French snow"—a clear indication of its origin.

Maple sugar was a primary food in Native American cooking; among some tribes it was the only condiment. It replaced salt, which they did not like, and it was used to season dried cornmeal porridge, mixed with bear fat as a sauce for roasted venison, sprinkled on boiled fish, and eaten with berries or all by itself, a pound a day. It was reconstituted into a sweet drink that was used in ceremonies, along with tobacco smoked in the peace pipe. Women boiled the sap from maple, walnut, hickory, box elder, butternut, birch, and sycamore trees down to sugar crystals, which was difficult because before Europeans came, they had no metal pots. Their vessels were made of birch bark or gourds which held between one and two gallons and could not be placed directly over fire. Instead, they dropped heated stones into the liquid until it boiled, which involved continuously taking out cool stones and replacing them with hot ones. These small amounts of liquid were then poured into hundred-gallon moose-skin vats. It is not surprising that the Indians began to trade for metal pots and utensils as soon as the Europeans introduced them. Another way to process the syrup was to let it freeze at night, then scrape the ice off the top. This required several nights until just syrup was left. Maple sugar that was to be used for gifts was poured into molds that one European described as shaped like "bear's paws, flowers, stars, small animals, and other figures, just like our gingerbread-bakers at fairs."

The American Culinary Tradition: Pocket Soup and Johnnycake American cooking developed along two parallel lines. In the South, where slave labour did the kitchen work, cooking could take more time. Labour-intensive cooking, such as barbecue, could be done by slaves. Barbecue needed a great deal of preparation. Either beef or pork had to be properly butchered and marinated. Then the fire had to reach just the right temperature, and the meat had to be added. The fire had to be carefully watched and the temperature maintained. This required a great deal of labour. However, pit cooking developed differently in New England, in the form of the clambake. There, a fire was allowed to burn down in a pit; then clams, lobsters, and corn were buried under wet seaweed and left to steam for several hours. No labour was necessary to prepare the food before or after it was placed in the pit, except to dig it out. American cooking in the North arose from the middle-class necessity of doing a great deal of work as quickly as possible. They invented shortcuts and new ways to preserve foods. Two examples are pocket soup and johnnycake. Travel was not easy in the colonies. Roads were poor or nonexistent, and there was no guarantee that travelers would be able to find food when they needed it. Sailors, too, appreciated a bit of home. Pocket soup, also known as portable soup, was the solution.

This was an early bouillon cube—soup cooked down until it was a condensed gelatinous mass, then cut into small cubes and dried for ten days. Dropped into a cup of water, it reconstituted into soup. Johnnycake or journey cake was a cornmeal cake that would keep without becoming moldy or disintegrating. Another example of New England fast food was hasty pudding, made famous in the song "Yankee Doodle" (and in the name of a Harvard University club). This was cornmeal—called Indian or "Injun" meal—or rye meal cooked on top of the stove, not baked, so it was ready in half an hour. This is a long time by today's microwave standards, but the baking times for regular cornmeal pudding recipes in American Cookery range from one and a half hours to two and a half hours. Sara Josepha Hale's recipes for cornmeal pudding require three to four hours of cooking, even those that are boiled. What makes hasty pudding hasty is that the meal is soaked first and added a bit at a time, and the pudding is boiled and stirred constantly. In this cooking technique, it resembles polenta. Cobbler, Slump, Grunt, Dumpling, Crumble, and Crisp Just as regional cooking developed according to the kind of produce and labour available in each area, different areas had different names for the same food.

For example, in most of the country, a cobbler is chopped, sweetened fruit with a sweet biscuit dough baked on top. The exception is New England, where it is called a slump, with the further exception of Cape Cod, where it is called a grunt. Other combinations of fruit and dough are a dumpling, pieces of fruit or a whole fruit, like an apple, wrapped in a pastry square and baked. A crumble is a mixture of flour, butter, sugar, and seasonings like cinnamon and nutmeg crumbled over chopped fruit and then baked. A crumble is different from a crisp because a crisp has more butter, which makes the topping crisper. The topping on a crisp sometimes includes oats. Brown Betty, Sally Lunn, and Anadama Women, perhaps cooks, have left their names on various foods but not much other information.

Brown Betty is a thrifty New England Buona Forchetta's Anadama Bread 1 large or 2 small loaves 2 cups water 11D 2 teaspoons salt 1D 2 cup stone-ground yellow cornmeal 3 tablespoons melted unsalted butter or olive oil 1D 4 cup honey or dark molasses 2 tablespoons active dry yeast 1D 2 cup lukewarm water (85° to 95°F) 5 to 6 cups unbleached bread flour In a large pot, bring the water and salt to a boil over medium-high heat. With a wire whisk, slowly stir the cornmeal into the water, making sure it does not lump. When it has thickened, remove it from the heat and stir in oil or butter and honey or molasses. Transfer to a large mixing bowl and let cool completely. Dissolve the yeast in the lukewarm water. Stir into the cornmeal mixture. Stir in the flour, a cup or so at a time, mixing well as you go to incorporate it. This will form a firm dough that should not be too dry. When the dough pulls away from the sides of the bowl, stir well a few more times, rub oil on your hands, and transfer the dough to a clean oiled bowl.

Same-day method: Cover the bowl with plastic wrap and let the dough rise in a warm place until doubled in volume, about 1 hour. Proceed with the shaping instructions. Overnight method: Cover the bowl and refrigerate overnight. The dough will rise in the refrigerator and acquire flavor from the slower yeast action. Remove the dough 3 hours before shaping and let stand, covered, in a warm place. Proceed with shaping instructions. To shape into loaves: Preheat the oven to 500°F. Oil one seasoned nonstick, ovenproof 9-inch skillet or two 5-inch skillets. Shape the dough into 1 large or 2 small round loaves. Place the loaf or loaves in the oiled pan or pans and let rise for about 40 minutes or until doubled. Brush the tops of the loaves with olive oil, if desired.

To Bake Loaves

Place the bread in the oven and reduce the oven temperature to 400°F. Bake for about 40 minutes or until nicely browned and loaf sounds hollow when tapped with your finger. Remove the loaf from a pan and cool on a wire rack. dessert that layers leftover bread with fruit, usually apples, and is baked. It isn't a bread pudding because it lacks eggs to make the custard binder. Sally Lunn is a very light, yeast-risen egg bread. Anadama is supposedly named after Anna, who kept cooking only one thing— a cornmeal and molasses bread—until her husband finally burst out, "Anna, damn her!" Suzanne Dunaway's Buona Forchetta Bakery in southern California makes an updated version of this bread.

Beer is a Good Family Drink

As food historian John Hull Brown points out in Early American Beverages, men, women, and children in colonial America drank alcoholic beverages. Beer, familiar from England, was the earliest drink in the colonies. Women were the brewers; they made beer from nearly anything that grew. They made vegetable beers from corn, tomatoes, potatoes, turnips, pumpkins, and Jerusalem artichokes. They made tree beers from the bark of birch, spruce, and sassafras, and from maple sap. Fruit-based beers were brewed from persimmons, lemons, and raisins. There were herb beers using wintergreen, and spice beers made of ginger, allspice, and cinnamon. Even flowers became beer: rose beer. There was molasses beer. They made their ale two barrels at a time, from 8 or 9 bushels of malt, 12 pounds of hops, 5 quarts of yeast, and 72 gallons of water.13 And, of course, just as in ancient Egypt, once they had beer they had leavening for bread, either from the beer itself or from the "leavins"—the dregs. They also distilled "spirituous waters" and cordials using spices from the Middle East like coriander, cardamom, and anise seed, and the stones of apricots, peaches, and cherries.

Wine was made from ginger, currants, and cherries, but sweet wines, sack, and Madeira were imported. Later, the Scots-Irish brewed whiskey from corn, barley, or oats. Colonial Americans drank hard cider distilled from apples, peachy made from peaches, and perry made from pears. The colonists liked to dress up their alcoholic beverages with cream, sugar, eggs, mace, and nutmeg—like eggnog. "Kill-Devil" Rum, Stonewall, Bogus, and Flip Rum, distilled in New England after 1670, was cheap and available. It was called by a variety of names—rhum, rumbullion, rumbooze— and used in a variety of mixtures: stonewall, which was cider and rum; bogus, which was unsweetened beer and rum; blackstrap, made with molasses and rum; and flip, a popular drink that appears at least as far back as 1690 in New England. Here's one way to make it. Punch, with its five ingredients of tea, arrack, sugar, lemons, and water, arrived from India via the British East India Company. New Englanders added a sixth ingredient, and rum punch was born. Life was good to New Englanders; they could expect to live ten years longer than if they had stayed in old England. But since they attributed their longer life to drinking alcohol, it became difficult to enforce laws restricting its intake.

Life was longer, but food preparation was still difficult and time consuming. Before the modern stove with a cooktop and an oven was invented in the mid-19th century, most cooking was done with the quadriceps, because it involved long hours of squatting to stir foods in front of the open hearth. A stool or rocking chair could be pulled up next to the fire, but it still involved long hours next to open flames. On wealthy southern plantations, meats were hung in a separate smokehouse.

The Golden Age of the Netherlands

Between England's colonies in New England and the Chesapeake was the Dutch colony of New Netherland. The Dutch knew that they would have to entice people from other countries to settle New Netherland, because the Dutch people, prosperous and free to practice the religion of their choice, had no reason to leave their own country. The Dutch settlers who did go to New Netherland found oak trees that grew seventy feet high and made logs that burned hot and bright for hours. As in the Netherlands, bread was a staple in New Nether- land, but it was baked at home. The Netherlands was urbanized, so commercial bakers made bread, but parts of the colony were very sparsely populated, so it was necessary for people to have their own brick ovens built into the wall next to the fireplace. American ingredients like corn and pumpkin found their way into standard Dutch recipes like pancakes. Bread was more than food in the Dutch colony; it was a trade item so much sought after by the Native Americans— especially white breads and sweet cakes—that by 1649 there were laws against making bread to trade with the Indians.

New Netherland was just a small part of a vast Dutch empire. The Dutch replaced the Italians—the Medicis of Florence and the Venetians—as the international bankers, and the world banking center moved to the Netherlands. The Dutch dominated or controlled the world shipping trade in spices, sugar, coffee, slaves, precious gems, and grain. The Dutch fleet of 10,000 ships also delivered oil, wine, and salt from Portugal, Spain, and France to northern Europe, and gold and silver from New World mines to Old World vaults. One of the reasons the Netherlands rose to power was that it was unique—a unified, religiously tolerant republic. During the 16th century, while the European monarchies fought with the Church and within their own countries over religion (and in some places killed a greater percentage of the population than the Black Death had), the Netherlands was open for business. Many of the Jews who had been driven out of Spain by the Inquisition went north to the hospitable Protestant Netherlands and contributed their knowledge of banking and business to an already flourishing economy. The stock exchange, called the bourse (French for "purse"), was created in Amsterdam in the middle of the 16th century. In 1609, the Bank of Amsterdam opened. It had an international money exchange, it used the system of writing checks invented by the Arabs in the Middle Ages, and the Dutch government guaranteed the safety of deposits—something not available in the United States until 1933. The Dutch florin was accepted as payment all over the world, much as the American dollar is today.

"God Made the World, but the Dutch Made Holland"19 Dutch life was tied to the sea and was a constant battle with it. The Dutch invented windmills to pump water out of the fields and reclaim land from the sea, and dikes, walls to hold back the sea. Much of Dutch food and industry centered around the sea. Twenty-five percent of the Dutch population was connected to the herring industry, from fishing and selling to preserving by smoking, salting, and pickling.

In a time when the economy of other European countries was suffering, the Dutch were extremely prosperous, with a large middle class and a high standard of living. Dutch virtues were cleanliness and thrift. Every morning, Dutch housewives washed not only their own stoops but also the public sidewalks in front of their houses. They lived and ate well. At fish markets, the Dutch bought only live fish. They threw away dead fish, as well as mackerel and red mullet. Even workers could afford meat, cheese, and butter, and the urban poor were provided for in poorhouses that had been recycled from monasteries or convents when the Netherlands converted to Protestant from Catholic. Sailors on warships were fed a 4,800-calorie-per-day diet of mutton, beef, pork, smoked ham, bread, beans, peas, and smoked and pickled fish, much of it herring. They were a country that grew no grain and made no wine, but they controlled trade from the breadbasket of Europe, the countries around the Baltic Sea.

"French haute cuisine did not appear until a century later and then showed little Italian influence; and there is no evidence that Catherine's cooks had any impact on French cooking in the early 16th century." Catherine supposedly introduced frozen ices, artichokes, parsley, and the fork to France. Wheaton says further that Catherine didn't have much power at court because she didn't have children for 14 years; because her husband was not supposed to become king, but his brother died; and because her husband's mistress set court fashions. There was a dramatic shift in French cuisine in the middle of the 17th century. In 1651, a French chef named La Varenne published a cookbook called Le Cuisinier françois—The French Cook. As Anne Willan, who has named her cooking school in France after him, pointed out, Le Cuisinier françois "is a seminal work; it marks the end of medieval cooking and the beginning of haute cuisine."

More fresh fruits and vegetables appear in these recipes, because they are more readily available and because gardening had advanced considerably, especially among the upper classes. However, there were still not many foods from the New World. La Varenne used the foods that were trendy among the French nobility, like peas, lettuce, and artichokes. People had to have peas. Woe to the host who served asparagus instead, although asparagus could be served disguised as peas. Le Pastissier is the first thorough pastry cookbook, with precise, clear instructions and definitions of weights and measures, perhaps the influence of the Scientific Revolution that was then taking place in Europe. However, Willan thinks that Le Pastissier was probably not written by La Varenne or was written by him and an anonymous Italian pastry chef, because Italian pastry chefs were the best in the world at that time. Also, cooking and pastry were two separate professions. In any case, it is sophisticated—there are fifteen varieties of marzipan. It also has the first cakelike biscuit recipes.

PACKAGING AND LABELING OF FOOD

Packaging is the enclosing of a physical object, typically a product that requires protection from tampering. Labelling refers to any written or graphic communications on the packaging or on a separate but associated label.

The Purpose of Packaging and Labels

Packaging and labeling have seven objectives:

- Protection against physical impact on object - The objects enclosed in the package may require protection from, among other things, damage caused by physical force, rain, heat, cold, sunlight, pressure, airborne contamination, automated handling devices, or any combination of one or more of these.
- Protection against dust and dirt - In a modern supply chain products are subject to different environments. They start packed in boxes and stacked on a pallet. In about 80% the products end up in a distribution center for commissioning and fine distribution to the store where the product will be sold.

During this period the physical protection also applies to dust and dirt that can easily settle on the consumer packaging. Especially products packed in plastic containers like shampoos, detergents and ketchups due to static charging easily attract dust and dirt. As a consumer we don't want to get dirty hands when picking up a product from the shelf. Transportation packaging keeps our products clean and neat till the shelf and so helps cut cleaning costs on the shopfloor.

- Agglomeration - Small objects are typically grouped together in one package for reasons of efficiency. For example, a single box of 1000 pencils requires less physical handling than 1000 single pencils. Alternatively, bulk commodities (such as salt) can be divided into packages that are a more suitable size for individual households.
- Information transmission - Information on how to use, transport, or dispose of the product is often contained on the package or label. An example is pharmaceutical products, where some types of information are required by governments.
- Marketing - The packaging and labels can be used by marketers to encourage potential buyers to purchase the product. Package design has been an important and constantly evolving phenomenon for dozens of years.
- Reducing theft - Some packages are made larger than they need to be so as to make theft more difficult. An example is software packages that typically contain only a single disc even though they are large enough to contain dozens of discs. These packages may also be deliberately difficult to open, to hamper thieves from removing their contents without drawing notice. Packages also provide opportunities to include anti-theft devices, such as dye-packs or electronic article surveillance tags, that can be activated or detected by devices at exit points and require specialized tools to deactivate. Using packaging in this way is a common tactic for loss prevention.
- Prevention of pilferage and tampering - Products are exposed to many contacts in the supply chain. Persons

handling could steal products (pilferage), replace full products with empty ones or add unwanted contaminants to the contents (tampering). Packaging that cannot be re-closed or gets physically damaged (shows signs of opening) is very helpful in the prevention of these acts. The flaps of corrugated and cardboard boxes are therefore glued in such a way that any opening irreversibly damages them. The overpackaging of certain objects has led to a phenomenon known as wrap rage.

Packaging Types

The above materials are fashioned into different types of packages and containers such as:

- Aseptic packages
- Bags
- Bales
- Blister packs
- Bottles
- Boxes
- Cans
- Cartons
- Envelopes
- Flexible packaging
- Molded Pulp
- Pallets
- Wrappers

There are also special containers that combine different technologies for maximum durability:

- Bags-In-Boxes (used for soft drink syrup and other liquid products)
- Wine box (used for wine)

Symbols Used in Labels

Many symbols for package labelling are internationally standardized, the purpose being to minimize the loss in goods shipping and receiving. Three of them are very common and are recognized almost everywhere in the world.

Packaging Machines

Packaging machines are of the following main types:

- Horizontal form fill and seal machines
- Vertical form fill and seal machines
- Cartoning machines
- Case Packing machines
- Palletizing machines
- Bottling machines
- Induction Sealing or cap sealing machine

FOOD LABELLING REGULATIONS

The law on food labelling is multifaceted and is spread over many reforms and parliamentary acts, making the subject complex. However, there are general laws which should be implied on any food product:

- Name – This must also inform the customer the nature of the product. It may also be necessary to attach a description to the product name. However, there are certain generic names which must be only used for their conventional uses, for example: Muesli, Coffee, prawns.
- Ingredients – All ingredients of the food must be stated under the heading Ingredients and must be stated in descending weight. Moreover, certain ingredients must be identified by a specific name, such as preservatives must be identified as 'Preservatives', and then identified by its standardised European serial number, e.g. sodium nitrate or E250.
- Nutritional Information – Although it is not a legal requirement to declare Nutritional Information on the

product, if the manufacturer makes claims that the product is 'Low in Sugar', it must be supported with nutritional information (normally in tabulated form). However, as a rule it is recommended to declare nutritional information as consumers more than ever are investgating this information before making a purchase. Moreover, there are two European nutritional labelling standards which must be adhered to if nutritional information is shown.

- Medicinal or Nutritional Claims – Medicinal and Nutritional claims are tightly regulated, some are only allowed under certain conditions while others are not authorised at all. For example, presenting claims the food product can treat, prevent or cure diseases or other 'adverse conditions' are prohibited. While claiming the food is reduced in fat or rich in vitamins require the food to meet compulsory standards and grades, in addition, the terms must be used in a form specified in regulations.
- Date Tagging – There are two types of date tagging:
  - Use by Date – 'Use by Date' must be followed by a day or month which the product must be consumed by. To be employed on perishable foods that usually would be kept cold, for example, fish, meat, dairy products and 'ready to eat' salads.
  - Best Before Date – 'Best Before Date is used as an indicator of when the product will begin to degrade from optimal quality: this includes when the food becomes stale, begins to taste 'off' or decays, rots or goes mouldy. There are also regulations on which type of best before date must be applied:
    - Best before + Day for foods with a shelf life of up to 3 months.
    - Best before end + Month for foods with more than a 3 month shelf life.

- Best before end + Year for food with more than an 18 month shelf life.

- Storage Conditions – If there are any particular storage conditions for the product to maintain its shelf life, these must be pointed out. However, as a rule it is recommended to always describe the necessary storage conditions for a food product.
- Business Name and Address – In addition to the business name and address, it is necessary to indicate the manufacturer or packager, if independent to the main business and the seller established within the European Union.
- Place of Origin – The food is required to specify its place of origin, especially if the name or trademark is misleading.
- Instruction for Use – This is only necessary if it is not obvious how to use or prepare the product, in which case the consumer's own initiative must be used.
- Presentation – The label must be legible and easy to read, also it must be written in English, however, the manufacturer may also include other languages.
- Lot Mark or Batch Code – It must be possible to identify individual batches with a lot mark or batch code - the code must be prefixed with the letter 'L' if it can not be distinguish from other codes, however, the date mark can be used as a lot mark. Manufacturers must bear in mind that the smaller the size of a batch, the smaller financial consequences in the case of a product recall.
- Sectioning – All of the following must be in the same field of vision:
  - Product name
  - Date mark
  - Weight
  - Quantity
  - Alcohol strength (if applicable).

However, there are many other Laws and European regulations for different types of food products.

FOOD STORAGE

Food storage is both a traditional domestic skill and is important industrially. Food is stored by almost every human society and by many animals. Storing of food has several main purposes:

- Preparation for periods of scarcity or famine
- Taking advantage of short term surplus of food as at harvest time
- Enabling a better balanced diet throughout the year
- Preparing for special events and celebrations
- Planning for catastrophe or emergency
- Protection against predators or others

Grain

Grain is stored in rigid sealed containers to prevent ingress of moisture or attack by vermin. For domestic quantities metal cans are used (in the USA the smallest practical grain storage uses closed-top #10 metal cans).

Storage in grain sacks is not effective. Mold and pests destroy a 25kg cloth sack of grain in a year — even if stored off the ground in a dry area. On the ground or damp concrete, the time is as little as three days, and the grain might have to be dried before it can be milled. Food stored under unsuitable conditions should not be purchased or used because of risk of spoilage. To test whether grain is still good, sprout some. If it sprouts, it is still good, but if not, it should not be eaten. It may take up to a week for grains to sprout. When in doubt, throw it out.

Meat

Unpreserved meat has only a relatively short life in storage. Pork should be eaten within one day but beef and venison improve with up to 5 days storage in a cold room. Dry aging techniques are sometimes used to tenderize specialty gourmet meats by hanging them in carefully controlled environments for up to 21 days. Semi-dried meats like salamis and country style hams are processed first with salt, smoke, sugar, or acid, or other "cures" then hung in cool dry storage for extended periods, sometimes exceeding a year.

Fish and Shellfish

It is unsafe to store fish or shellfish without preservation. Fresh shellfish and whitefish should be eaten within a few hours of harvesting.

Use of Stored Food

Guidance for surviving emergency conditions in many parts of the world recommends acquiring a limited range of grains (usually corn, wheat and beans supplemented with oil, dried milk, and vitamins) and then preparing them in simple ways for long-term survival. This may not be wholly practical because of appetite exhaustion. An unvarying diet of staples prepared in the same way causes most people to eat less. Garden-grown fruits and vegetables, freeze-dried, canned, and fresh-baked foods are essential supplements to such a programme.

A special virtue of home stored foods is their low cost. Costs of dry bulk foods (before preparation) are often less than 1/4 of convenience and fresh foods purchased at supermarkets.

COMMERCIAL FOOD STORAGE

Grain and beans are stored in tall grain elevators, almost always at a rail head near the point of production. The grain is shipped to a final user in hopper cars. In the former Soviet Union, where harvest was poorly controlled, grain was often irradiated at the point of production to suppress mold and insects. In the U.S., threshing and drying is performed in the field, and transport is nearly sterile and in large containers that effectively suppress pest access, so irradiation is not required.

Fresh fruits and vegetables are either packed in plastic cups in cardboard boxes for fresh premium markets, or placed in large plastic tubs for sauce and soup processors. Fruits and vegetables are usually refrigerated at the earliest possible moment, and even so have a shelf life of two weeks or less. There is a thriving but small market in bulk vegetables and convenience foods for campers.

In the USA meat animals are usually transported live, slaughtered at a major distribution point, hung and transported for two days to a week in refrigerated rail cars, and then butchered and sold locally. Before refrigerated rail cars, meat had to be transported live, and this placed its cost so high that only farmers and the wealthy could afford it every day. In Europe much meat is transported live and slaughtered close to the point of sale. In much of Africa and Asia most meat is for local populations is reared, slaughtered and eaten locally which is believed to be much less stressful for the animals involved and requires very little meat storage capacity. In Australia and New Zealand where a large proportion of meat production is for export meat is stored in very large freezer plants before being shipped overseas in freezer ships.

FOOD STORAGE: REFRIGERATOR AND FREEZER

Storage does not improve the quality of any food. The quality of a food will also not decrease significantly during storage as long as the food is stored properly and used within the recommended time frame.

Quality is not the same as safety. A poor-quality food may be safe, such as overripe fruit or soured pasteurized milk. An unsafe food may have good quality in terms of appearance and taste, but have a high (unsafe) bacterial count. For example, cooked chicken may be placed on a plate that held the raw chicken and become contaminated. (The raw chicken juices may contain salmonella bacteria.) The goal of home food storage is to provide both safe and high-quality foods.

Maintaining a food's quality depends on several factors: the quality of the raw product; the procedures used during processing; the way the food is stored; and the length of storage. The recommended storage time takes these factors into consideration. Since bacteria frequently get into food through careless food handling, keep everything — hands, refrigerator, freezer and storage containers — clean.

Selection Guidelines

To help assure quality, some products have "open dates" on the package. Product dating is optional on most products. Dates may also be "coded" by the manufacturer and only understood by them. The most commonly used open dates are:

Sell-by Date: This is the last recommended day of sale, but allows for home storage and use. The date is given after the statement, "Sell by (a date)." Breads and baked goods may have "sell-by dates."

Use-by Date: Tells how long the product will retain top quality after you buy it. You will find this date after the statement, "Use by." Some packaged goods have "use-by dates."

Expiration Date: This is the last day the product should be used or eaten. You may find this date after the statement, "Do not use after (date)." Eggs may have "expiration dates."

Pack Date: Canned or packaged foods may have dates that tell you when the product was processed. This does not tell how long the food will be good.

These are guidelines; if a food is not properly handled, its storage life will be shortened. Follow these tips for purchasing top-quality foods that have been handled safely.

- Look for packages of food that are not torn or broken.
- Refrigerated food should feel cold (less than 45 °F) and frozen food should be frozen solid. Purchase these foods last.
- When shopping, place packaged raw meat, poultry and fish in plastic bags and keep from contact with other foods.
- Take perishable foods home quickly to refrigerate. If travel time will exceed one hour, pack fresh meats in a cooler with ice and keep in the passenger area of the car in warm weather.

- At home, refrigerate perishable food immediately. The "Danger Zone" for most food is between 40 to 140 °F. Bacteria grow most rapidly in this range of temperatures, doubling in number in as little as 20 minutes.

Storage Guidelines

For best results in maintaining product quality practice the rule: First In, First Out. This means you use the oldest products first and the newest products later. A good practice in the home is to place the newly purchased products in back of the same products already on the shelf. It may help to write purchase dates on products without "open dates" on the package. Follow recommended storage times for the refrigerator and freezer.

Freezer

- Keep freezer temperature at or below 0 °F. A good indication of proper temperature is that ice cream will be frozen solid.
- Use moisture-proof, freezer-weight wrap. Examples are foil, freezer bags and freezer paper. Label and date all packages.
- Food stored beyond the recommended time will be safe to eat, but eating quality (flavor and texture) and nutritive value will be less.
- Keep an inventory of freezer contents.

Refrigerator

- Use a thermometer to check that temperature remains between 34 and 40 °F at all times. Avoid frequently opening the refrigerator door, especially in hot weather.
- Wrapping perishable food prevents the loss of flavour and the mixing of flavour and odours.
- Raw meat, fish, poultry, shucked shellfish and shrimp should be wrapped securely so they do not leak and contaminate other foods. Place the store packages in

a leak-proof plastic bag or place the package on a plate to contain any juices. Clean up leaks with warm soapy water and sanitize with a solution of 1 teaspoon chlorine bleach to 1 quart water.

- Cooked meats and leftovers should be tightly wrapped to prevent drying out.
- Avoid cross contamination of other foods in the refrigerator by live shellfish.
- Do not store live shellfish in water or in an air-tight container where they could suffocate and die. Store in a shallow dish covered with damp paper towels. Discard shellfish that has died in storage.

Chapter 3

Food Safety and Management

FREEZING AND FOOD SAFETY

Food safety is a matter that affects anyone who eats food. Whether or not a person consciously thinks about food safety before eating a meal, a host of other people have thought about the safety of that food, from farmers to scientists to company presidents to federal government officials and sanitarians. This chapter serves as a broad introduction to food safety and the concerns facing those who work with food. A history of food safety concentrates on scientific discoveries from the 1600s to modern times. The chapter ends with a look at food preservation techniques that humankind has practiced over the millennia to make food safer. These techniques range from the earliest methods of drying to newer high-tech methods such as food irradiation, and newer lower-tech methods such as using natural antimicrobials. Foods in the freezer are they safe? Every year, thousands of callers to the USDA Meat and Poultry Hotline aren't sure about the safety of items stored in their own home freezers. The confusion seems to be based on the fact that few people understand how freezing protects food. Here is some information on how to freeze food safely and how long to keep it.

What can you Freeze?

You can freeze almost any food. Some exceptions are canned food or eggs in shells. However, once the food (such as a ham) is out of the can, you may freeze it. Being able to freeze food and being pleased with the quality after defrosting are two different things. Some foods simply don't freeze well. Examples are mayonnaise, cream sauce and lettuce. Raw meat and poultry maintain their quality longer than their cooked counterparts because moisture is lost during cooking.

Is Frozen Food Safe?

Food stored constantly at 0 °F will always be safe. Only the quality suffers with lengthy freezer storage. Freezing keeps food safe by slowing the movement of molecules, causing microbes to enter a dormant stage. Freezing preserves food for extended periods because it prevents the growth of microorganisms that cause both food spoilage and food borne illness.

Does Freezing Destroy Bacteria and Parasites?

Freezing to 0 °F inactivates any microbes bacteria, yeasts and molds present in food. Once thawed, however, these microbes can again become active, multiplying under the right conditions to levels that can lead to food borne illness. Since they will then grow at about the same rate as microorganisms on fresh food, you must handle thawed items as you would any perishable food. Trichina and other parasites can be destroyed by sub-zero freezing temperatures. However, very strict government-supervised conditions must be met. It is not recommended to rely on home freezing to destroy trichina. Thorough cooking will destroy all parasites.

Freshness and Quality

Freshness and quality at the time of freezing affect the condition of frozen foods. If frozen at peak quality, foods emerge tasting better than foods frozen near the end of their useful life. So freeze items you won't use quickly sooner rather than later. Store all foods at 0° F or lower to retain vitamin content, colour, flavor and texture.

Nutrient Retention

The freezing process itself does not destroy nutrients. In meat and poultry products, there is little change in nutrient value during freezer storage.

Enzymes

Enzyme activity can lead to the deterioration of food quality. Enzymes present in animals, vegetables and fruit promote chemical reactions, such as ripening. Freezing only slows the enzyme activity that takes place in foods. It does not halt these reactions which continue after harvesting. Enzyme activity does not harm frozen meats or fish and is neutralized by the acids in frozen fruits. But most vegetables that freeze well are low acid and require a brief, partial cooking to prevent deterioration. This is called "blanching." For successful freezing, blanch or partially cook vegetables in boiling water or in a microwave oven. Then rapidly chill the vegetables prior to freezing and storage. Consult a cookbook for timing.

Packaging

Proper packaging helps maintain quality and prevent "freezer burn." It is safe to freeze meat or poultry directly in its supermarket wrapping but this type of wrap is permeable to air. Unless you will be using the food in a month or two, overwrap these packages as you would any food for long-term storage using airtight heavy-duty foil, (freezer) plastic wrap or freezer paper, or place the package inside a (freezer) plastic bag. Use these materials or airtight freezer containers to repackage family packs into smaller amounts. It is not necessary to rinse meat and poultry before freezing. Freeze unopened vacuum packages as is. If you notice that a package has accidentally been torn or has opened while food is in the freezer, the food is still safe to use; merely overwrap or rewrap it.

Freezer Burn

Freezer burn does not make food unsafe, merely dry in spots. It appears as grayish-brown leathery spots and is caused by air reaching the surface of the food. Cut freezer-burned portions away either before or after cooking the food. Heavily freezer-burned foods may have to be discarded for quality reasons.

Colour Changes

Colour changes can occur in frozen foods. The bright red colour of meat as purchased usually turns dark or pale brown depending on its variety. This may be due to lack of oxygen, freezer burn or abnormally long storage. Freezing doesn't usually cause colour changes in poultry. However, the bones and the meat near them can become dark. Bone darkening results when pigment seeps through the porous bones of young poultry into the surrounding tissues when the poultry meat is frozen and thawed. The dulling of colour in frozen vegetables and cooked foods is usually the result of excessive drying due to improper packaging or over-lengthy storage.

Freeze Rapidly

Freeze food as fast as possible to maintain its quality. Rapid freezing prevents undesirable large ice crystals from forming throughout the product because the molecules don't have time to take their positions in the characteristic six-sided snowflake. Slow freezing creates large, disruptive ice crystals. During thawing, they damage the cells and dissolve emulsions. This causes meat to "drip" – lose juiciness. Emulsions such as mayonnaise or cream will separate and appear curdled. Ideally, a food 2-inches thick should freeze completely in about 2 hours. If your home freezer has a "quick-freeze" shelf, use it. Never stack packages to be frozen. Instead, spread them out in one layer on various shelves, stacking them only after frozen solid.

Refrigerator - Freezers

If a refrigerator freezing compartment can't maintain zero degrees or if the door is opened frequently, use it for short-term food storage. Eat those foods as soon as possible for best quality. Use a free-standing freezer set at 0° F or below for long-term storage of frozen foods. Keep a thermometer in your freezing compartment or freezer to check the temperature. This is important if you experience power-out or mechanical problems. Because freezing keeps food safe almost indefinitely, recommended storage times are for quality only. Refer to the freezer storage chart at the end of this document, which lists optimum freezing times for best quality. If a food is not listed on the chart, you may determine its quality after defrosting. First check the odor. Some foods will develop a rancid or off odor when frozen too long and should be discarded. Some may not look picture perfect or be of high enough quality to serve alone but may be edible; use them to make soups or stews. Cook raw food and if you like the taste and texture, use it.

Safe Defrosting

Never defrost foods in a garage, basement, car, dishwasher or plastic garbage bag; out on the kitchen counter, outdoors or on the porch. These methods can leave your foods unsafe to eat. There are three safe ways to defrost food: in the refrigerator, in cold water, or in the microwave. It's best to plan ahead for slow, safe thawing in the refrigerator. Small items may defrost overnight; most foods require a day or two. And large items like turkeys may take longer, approximately one day for each 5 pounds of weight. For faster defrosting, place food in a leak proof plastic bag and immerse it in cold water. (If the bag leaks, bacteria from the air or surrounding environment could be introduced into the food. Tissues can also absorb water like a sponge, resulting in a watery product.) Check the water frequently to be sure it stays cold. Change the water every 30 minutes. After thawing, cook immediately. When microwave-defrosting food, plan to cook it immediately after thawing because some areas of the food may become warm and begin to cook during microwaving.

Refreezing

Once food is thawed in the refrigerator, it is safe to refreeze it without cooking, although there may be a loss of quality due to the moisture lost through defrosting. After cooking raw foods which were previously frozen, it is safe to freeze the cooked foods. If previously cooked foods are thawed in the refrigerator, you may refreeze the unused portion. If you purchase previously frozen meat, poultry or fish at a retail store, you can refreeze if it has been handled properly.

Cooking Frozen Foods

Raw or cooked meat, poultry or casseroles can be cooked or reheated from the frozen state. However, it will take approximately one and a half times the usual cooking time for food which has been thawed. Remember to discard any wrapping or absorbent paper from meat or poultry. When cooking whole poultry, remove the giblet pack from the cavity as soon as you can loosen it. Cook the giblets separately. Read the label on USDA-inspected frozen meat and poultry products. Some, such as pre-stuffed whole birds, must be cooked from the frozen state to ensure a safely cooked product.

A Brief History of Food Safety

Very little about food borne illness or food safety is found in historical records. Scientists did not begin to understand bacteria, and their relationship to disease, until the late nineteenth century. People did recognize that food spoils, but the reasons for that and the potential for becoming ill from food were not known. Perhaps the absence of food safety from historical chronicles is an indication that it was less of a concern than were other problems in the past. Even early food regulations were not aimed at making food safer, but rather at preventing economic fraud. So, a history of food safety really does not exist, but numerous discoveries, inventions, and regulations have led to the present knowledge and state of affairs in food safety.

Food preservation methods such as drying, smoking, freezing, marinating, salting, and pickling had their beginnings thousands of years ago. Whether these methods were employed solely to keep food for later use, to improve flavor, or for other reasons is not known. But they also had the effect of keeping food safer. Even cooking can be viewed as an ancient method of making food safer. The Chinese Confucian Analects of 500 B.C.E. warned against consumption of sour rice, spoiled fish or flesh, food kept too long or insufficiently cooked food. The Chinese disliked eating uncooked food believing, "Anything boiled or cooked cannot be poisonous."

Among the earliest of food safety manuals was one published in China in the year 2 (Needham 1962). It is possible that the practice of drinking tea originated because tea required using hot water, which would make it safer than using unheated contaminated water (Trager 1995). Doubtless other cultures in antiquity, while oblivious to the causes or prevention of foodborne disease, experienced it and prescribed methods to avoid it.

Early scientists grappled with the nature of disease and bacteria, which would set the stage for later discoveries. Much of the present knowledge about pathogens that cause food borne illness is built on a foundation of scientific discoveries spanning back over three centuries. Aristotle (384–322 B.C.E.) and his Greek philosopher/scientist predecessors believed in the spontaneous generation of organisms—that insects and animals arose spontaneously from soil, plants, or other species of animals. Francisco Redi, an Italian physician and poet, set out to disprove this theory in 1668. He believed that maggots did not arise spontaneously in meat, which challenged the common wisdom of the day. He prepared eight flasks with meat in them; four sealed and four left open to the air. No flies could land on the meat in the sealed flasks, thus no maggots grew. The clear conclusion was that maggots did not form by spontaneous generation, but that flies laid eggs that were too small to be seen.

This, however, was not enough to convince skeptics. Italian biologist Lazzaro Spallanzani in 1768 disproved the spontaneous generation theory. Even though Redi proved that insects did not arise from spontaneous generation, scientists still believed that microorganisms did. In his experiments, Spallanzani boiled solutions that would normally breed microorganisms for prolonged periods of time, which killed any microorganisms that might be in the solution, on the walls of the flask, or in the air inside the flask. Then he sealed the flasks to prevent any new spores or microorganisms from entering. No microorganisms grew no matter how long he left them standing. The fact that no new microorganisms appeared meant that there was no spontaneous generation.

The discovery of bacteria in the late nineteenth century, the increased understanding of bacteria's role in disease, and the realization that there is a connection between human diseases and animal diseases led to the ideas that cleanliness is important and that unsanitary conditions can contribute to disease. In 1847 Hungarian physician Ignaz Semmelweiss wondered why women who bore their children in hospitals died of fever during childbirth, while those who gave birth at home usually did not. Noting that doctors went straight from the operating room to labouring mothers, he concluded that the doctors themselves were carrying disease to the women from the dissecting room. In those days the doctors didn't wash their hands, but wiped them on their aprons, which were already coated with body fluids. Semmelweiss ran experiments in which he had the doctors wash their hands with soap and water, and then rinse them in a chlorinated lime solution before entering the maternity wards.

Death rates plummeted from 10 percent to 1.5 percent, only to climb again when the experiments were discontinued. Thereafter, he forced doctors to wash their hands before treating patients. Unfortunately, the validity of his work was not recognized at the time. His colleagues greeted his theory with ridicule, refusing to believe that their own hands were a vehicle for disease. Instead they attributed the deaths to a phenomenon arising from the "combustible" nature of the pregnant women. Historians attribute Semmelweiss's eventual despondency to the ridicule of his theories and attacks on his character. He was committed to an insane asylum, where he died of blood poisoning. Lack of personal hygiene remains one of the main causes of food borne illness 150 years later.

In a classic case of epidemiologic sleuthing, Dr. John Snow demonstrated in 1848 how cholera spread throughout London. He noticed that people who obtained their water from a particular well were more likely to become ill than those drawing their water from another well. He persuaded city officials to remove the pump handle from that particular well, which forced inhabitants to draw water from another well. The number of cholera cases dropped immediately. Louis Pasteur further elucidated the linkage among spoilage, disease, and microorganisms with his work on fermentation and pasteurization in the 1860s and 1870s. In 1872 German scientist Ferdinand Julius Cohn published a three-volume treatise on bacteria, and essentially founded the science of bacteriology. He was the first to attempt to classify bacteria into genera and species, and the first to describe bacterial spores. But this new field of bacteriology needed bacteria on which to conduct experiments and to study. It took Robert Koch in the 1880s to perfect the process of growing pure strains of bacteria in the labouratory.

At first he used flat glass slides to grow the bacteria. His assistant, Julius Richard Petri, suggested using shallow glass dishes with covers, now commonly called Petri dishes. Koch also established strict criteria for showing that a specific microbe causes a specific disease. These are now known as Koch's Postulates. Using these criteria scientists can identify bacteria that cause a number of diseases, including food borne diseases. In 1947 Joshua Lederberg and Edward Lawrie Tatum discovered that bacteria reproduce sexually, and opened up a whole new field of bacterial genetics.

Even though Anthony van Leeuwenhook, a Dutch biologist and microscopist, had improved the microscope to the degree that small microscopic organisms could be seen for the first time as far back as 1673, the discovery of food borne disease-causing microorganisms developed slowly. In 1835 James Paget and Richard Owen described the parasite Trichinella spiralis for the first time. German pathologists Friedrich Albert von Zenker and Rudolph Virchow were the first to note the clinical symptoms of trichinosis in 1860. However, the association between trichinosis and the parasite Trichinella spiralis was not realized until much later. In 1855 the non-pathogenic form of Escherichia coli was discovered. It later became a major research tool for biotechnology. Englishman William Taylor showed in 1857 that milk can transmit typhoid fever. In1885 USDA veterinarian Daniel

Salmon described a microorganism that caused gastroenteritis with fever when ingested in contaminated food.

The bacteria were eventually named Salmonellae. August Gärtner, a German scientist, was the first to isolate Bacillus enteritidis from a case of food poisoning in 1888. The case was the result of a cow with diarrhea slaughtered for meat; 57 people who ate the meat become ill (Satin 1999). Emilie Pierre-Mare van Ermengem, a Belgian bacteriologist, was the first to isolate the bacterium that causes botulism, Clostridium botulinum, in 1895. The case concerned an uncooked, salted ham served at a wake in Belgium. Twenty-three people became ill; three died. Van Ermengem isolated C. botulinum from both the ham and one of the victim's intestines. He demonstrated that the organism grows in an oxygen-free environment, and that it produces a toxin that causes the illness. In a perhaps overzealous use of the scientific method, M.A. Barber demonstrated that Staphylococcus aureus causes food poisoning.

He became ill after each of three visits to a farm in the Philippines in 1914. Suspecting cream from a cow with an udder infection, Barber took home two bottles of cream, let them sit out for five hours, drank some of the cream, and became ill two hours later with the same symptoms he experienced on the farm. He isolated a bacterium from the milk, placed it in a germ-free container of milk, waited a while, and then convinced two hapless volunteers to drink the milk with him. They all became ill with the same symptoms (Asimov 1972). In 1945 Clostridium perfringens was first recognized as a cause of foodborne illness. It wasn't until the years between 1975 and 1985 that some of today's major foodborne pathogens—Campylobacter jejuni, Yersinia enterocolitica, Escherichia coli O157:H7, and Vibrio cholerae—were first recognized.

FOOD PRESERVATION

Since the earliest times humankind has searched for ways to make the food supply safer and to make food last longer.

Without the use of some preservation technique, the natural microorganisms that are present everywhere in the environment will grow and multiply in foods. Preservation aims either to destroy or inhibit the growth of harmful microorganisms in food by making an environment unsuitable for them. The earliest recorded instances of food preservation date back to ancient Egypt and the drying of grains and subsequent storage in sealed silos.

The stored grain could be kept for several years to insure against famine in case the Nile River flooded. People in many parts of the world developed techniques for drying and smoking foods as far back as 6000 B.C.E. Microorganisms need water to carry out their metabolic processes. Many preservation techniques that are familiar to us, such as drying, smoking, and salting, seek to reduce available water in a product. Freezing foods and making foods more acidic through fermentation and pickling also inhibit microorganism growth. Salting was so important in Roman life that Roman soldiers received "salarium," or salt, as payment. This is the origin of today's term "salary."

Large-scale deployment of armed forces led to the need for more advanced methods of food preservation to keep food safe for troops in the field. Napoleon's realization that armies do indeed travel on their stomach caused him to offer a prize for an improved food preservation method. In response to this need, Nicolas Appert, a French candy maker, developed a process by which he placed food in bottles, sealed the bottles, and then heated them for hours in boiling water. When Appert published his method in 1810 he had no knowledge of bacteria. It took another 50 years and Louis Pasteur to elucidate the relationship between microorganisms and the spoilage of food. What Appert developed is essentially the process for canning food. Over 28 the years, food scientists have made many improvements in the canning process, but the basic idea of using high heat remains the same. As testimony to the durability of canned foods, a can of meat from Captain Parry's 1824 expedition to the Northwest Passage opened 114 years later in 1938 was still perfectly safe and edible.

Most American homes have a device that is extremely useful for keeping foods safe—the refrigerator. Although refrigeration was developed in the early 1800s, refrigerators were not readily available for home use until the 1930s. Most pathogenic bacteria do not grow at all, or grow very slowly, at refrigerated temperatures. However, spoilage bacteria, those that cause food to smell or taste bad, can grow in the refrigerator. While spoilage bacteria cause foods to become of unacceptable quality, they do not cause illness. Spoilage bacteria serve a good purpose in that they prevent people from eating food that may contain harmful bacteria.

Freezing, except in cold climates, did not fully develop until the 1950s. Freezing keeps food safe by slowing the movement of molecules, causing microbes to enter a dormant stage. Freezing preserves food for extended periods of time because it prevents the growth of microorganisms that cause both food spoilage and foodborne illness; so frozen food is theoretically safe forever. The quality of frozen food, however, diminishes quickly with time. For example, when air reaches the surface of food, it causes dry grayish-brown leathery spots to appear. A turkey kept in the freezer for 10 years would be perfectly safe, but may be dried to little more than skin and bones. One can only wonder about the quality of the meal served in 1799 by William Buckland, dean of Westminster, England, who reportedly served his unsuspecting dinner guests meat from a recently discovered frozen mammoth that was 100,000 years old.

A method of making food safer that is well-known and accepted today is pasteurization. Pasteurization is the process of heating foods to a temperature for a designated period of time to destroy disease-causing and/or food spoilage bacteria. The amount of time the product is heated depends on the temperature; higher temperatures require less time. It is different from sterilization in that some spoilage bacteria survive. Pasteurization takes its name from its inventor, Louis Pasteur. The most familiar pasteurized product in the United States is milk. Before milk was routinely pasteurized it spread tuberculosis, brucellosis, typhoid fever, diphtheria, and scarlet fever. Pasteurized milk made its debut in the United States in the 1880s, but took 30 years to gain full acceptance. Milk is not the only pasteurized food product available in grocery stores.

In the mid-1990s there were several high-publicity foodborne illness outbreaks traced back to unpasteurized juice. Now, 98 percent of all juices in the United States are pasteurized. Eggs are another product that has benefited from pasteurization. While estimates are that Salmonella enteritidis infects only one in 20,000 eggs, with a production rate of almost 60 billion eggs per year, that still leaves close to three million infected eggs. Egg products, which are eggs removed from their shells for use in processed foods and available in liquid, frozen, and dried forms, must be pasteurized by law. The latest product to undergo pasteurization is intact shell eggs. Shell eggs are pasteurized with a combination water bath and hot air treatment under relatively low temperatures but longer times so that the nature of the egg does not change.

A newer form of pasteurization is called ultrahigh temperature (UHT) pasteurization. The amount of bacteria killed with a heat method such as pasteurization depends on how high the temperature is, and how long the food is held at that temperature. For instance, heating to a lower temperature requires that the food be held at the low temperature for a longer time. But using very high heat means that the food can be kept at that heat for a shorter time. UHT pasteurization takes advantage of this principle by using a very high temperature for a very short time. This provides an almost sterile product with an increased shelf life, but without significant changes in colour, flavor, or texture of the food. Many countries use UHT for processing milk, which allows consumers to purchase cartons of milk that do not need refrigeration.

Preservation techniques that limit the availability of water, such as drying, salting, and smoking, and those that use heat, such as canning and pasteurization, dramatically alter the nature of the food itself. These processes degrade the colour, flavor, texture, and nutrients in food. Today's consumers want their food to appear fresh and natural, as close to just-picked or just-slaughtered as possible. They don't want preservatives and other chemicals added to their foods, and at the same time they want convenience. But not many American consumers are willing to shop for fresh produce or meats every day. A number of new techniques are in use or in development that try to meet this demand for food with fresher, more natural qualities. There are several methods of applying electricity instead of heat to pasteurize food; these techniques are referred to as cold pasteurization. Irradiation, ohmic heating, and high-intensity pulsed electric fields are some of these technologies.

One of the earliest examples of applying electricity to foods is ohmic heating. In this process, a continuous electric current, which generates heat, is passed through the food. Experiments with ohmic heating began in the early 1900s. This method of processing is useful for viscous liquids and foods containing particles. High-intensity pulsed electric fields (PEF) is another emerging nonthermal technique. Unlike ohmic heating, PEF does not cause an increase in the temperature of food. PEF involves applying a short burst of high voltage to a food placed between two electrodes, which destroys bacterial cell membranes. This process has the potential to be used on juices, cream soups, milk, and egg products—all products in which heat produces undesirable changes.

Food irradiation is another technology to make food safe that, like canning, got its start in feeding the military. After World War II, the U.S. Army began experiments irradiating fresh foods for troops in the field. All irradiation is energy moving through space in invisible waves. The length of the wave determines the nature of the energy. As the wavelength gets shorter, the energy of the wave increases. Microwaves have a relatively long wavelength, so they have lower energy that is strong enough to move molecules and cause heat through friction, but not strong enough to structurally change atoms in the molecules. Ionizing radiation has a shorter wavelength and therefore higher energy—enough energy to change atoms by knocking electrons from them to form ions, but not enough energy to split atoms and cause exposed objects to become radioactive. Food irradiation exposes foods to very high-energy, short-length invisible waves. Depending on the dose, irradiation performs different functions.

Low doses delay ripening and sprouting in fresh fruits and vegetables, and control insects and parasites in foods. Medium doses extend the shelf life of foods and reduce both spoilage and pathogenic microorganisms by damaging the genetic material of bacteria so they can no longer survive or multiply. High doses disinfect certain food ingredients, such as spices, and sterilize meat, poultry, seafood, and prepared foods. NASA began irradiating foods for astronauts in 1972; a case of foodborne illness while in space could be deadly, since no medical care would be available. Similarly, some hospitals use irradiated foods to feed their more susceptible patients.

Irradiation is regulated in the United States as a food additive, therefore FDA approves the process. Each new food is approved separately with a specific dosage level. After FDA grants approval, guidelines are established. USDA writes the guidelines for irradiation of meat and poultry products. The latest approval for irradiation in the United States was granted in 2000 for eggs. A petition is pending for permission to irradiate ready-to-eat meat and poultry products. Foods that are irradiated must display the radura and the words "treated with radiation" or "treated by irradiation." Although 40 countries currently permit irradiation of food, its usage has been slow to catch on in the United States.

This is mainly due to high start-up costs and to fears about consumer acceptance of the process. When the technology was new, many thought irradiation meant the food would be radioactive. As consumers have become more educated, they have realized that is not the case. Opponents of irradiation argue that irradiating foods produces chemical changes in the food. Proponents of the technology answer that these same chemical changes occur when food is cooked. Recent outbreaks of E. coli O157:H7, Listeria, and other bacteria are creating a demand for irradiated products. Irradiated foods also retain their texture, colour, and taste better than do foods that are preserved by heat treatments.

Applying high pressure uniformly throughout a food product is another method of nonthermal food preservation. This inactivates microorganisms, spores, and undesirable enzymes, and increases the shelf life of foods. Japan is a leader in this technology. Although this method was initially studied at the end of the nineteenth century, consumer demand has caused renewed interest in commercializing the process. Jams made by high-pressure processing retain the taste and colour of fresh fruit, unlike conventionally cooked jams. High-pressure processing is currently used in yogurts, salad dressings, and citrus juices. It has the potential to be used for minimally processed meat and fish products, convenience foods with long shelf lives and fresh and natural colours, and frozen foods with improved quality. The major drawback to this method is that it is costly to implement. Future usage will depend on how much the consumer is willing to pay for more natural food.

Modified atmosphere packaging (MAP) is a process in which oxygen is removed from a food package and other gases, usually carbon dioxide and/or nitrogen, are added. Vacuum-packaging, in which oxygen is removed but no other gases are added is also a type of MAP. The role of oxygen in food is that of a spoiler, one that causes degradation and spoilage of foods. Thus eliminating or reducing the amount of oxygen in a package prolongs the shelf life of the product. Examples of MAP products are fresh-cut produce, ready-to-eat salads, fresh pasta, lunch meats, and other meat products. These are the convenience food products that consumers want. However, from a food safety standpoint, there are some dangers with MAP products.

Because lack of oxygen suppresses most spoilage bacteria in MAP products, the odors that would normally warn consumers that a food is spoiled are not present. There are some pathogenic bacteria, notably C. botulinum, that do not need oxygen to survive. Without the competition for food and water from spoilage bacteria, these bacteria can thrive. Manufacturers combat this by adding other gases such as carbon dioxide, which lowers the pH; decreasing the available water in a food; adding salt; and keeping the temperature low. It is important for consumers to understand that these types of products must be kept at the proper temperatures to keep them safe.

Ultraviolet (UV) radiation is the major bacteria-destroying factor in sunlight. Scientists are using UV light to kill pathogenic microorganisms. The most prevalent use of this technology is to kill pathogens in water systems. It is environmentally friendly, safe, more cost-effective than chlorination, and doesn't affect the taste of water as chlorination does. One problem with this technique is that it doesn't penetrate substances very deeply, so action is limited to the surface. At high doses products develop off flavors and odors, but at low doses it can extend the shelf life of foods without damaging quality. It is used in dairy plants, in meat and vegetable processing plants, in the ice cream industry, and to sterilize packaging materials.

As consumers have become chemical- and preservative-phobic, food preservation using natural antimicrobials has evolved. This concept involves a more natural and milder alternative to making food safer. By their very nature of being milder, natural antimicrobials by themselves are not sufficient to control pathogens. However, when used in combination with other food preservation methods they can improve the safety of foods without the use of traditional chemical preservatives such as sorbate or benzoate, which consumers no longer consider natural and healthy. Nature contains many antimicrobial compounds.

Those used in food processing are derived from either plants or microorganisms. Spices and herbs have long been used to inhibit yeasts, bacteria, and molds. However, the spices and herbs themselves are less effective than the active ingredients such as essential oils, organic acids, and phenols found in them. Scientists are working to more actively exploit these active ingredients rather than using the whole spice or herb. As part of their life cycle, microorganisms produce compounds that affect the growth of other microorganisms around them. Many of these compounds inhibit microbial growth to increase the competitive edge of the producing organism. Lactic acid bacteria are the most important of these natural antimicrobials. Lactic acid bacteria have been used for centuries in fermentation, cheeses, and sausages. Many natural antimicrobials also have the advantage of being regulated as generally recognized as safe (GRAS) substances.

PASTEURIZATION

Pasteurization is the process of heating food for the purpose of killing harmful organisms such as bacteria, viruses, protozoa, molds, and yeasts. The process was named after its inventor, French scientist Louis Pasteur. The first pasteurization test was completed by Pasteur and Claude Bernard on April 20, 1862. Unlike sterilization, pasteurization is not intended to kill all micro-organisms (pathenogenic) in the food. Instead, pasteurization aims to achieve a "log reduction" in the number of viable organisms, reducing their number so they are unlikely to cause disease (assuming the pasteurized product is refrigerated and consumed before its expiration date). Commercial scale sterilization of food is not common, because it adversely affects the taste and quality of the product.

Milk Pasteurization

Pasteurization is typically associated with milk, first suggested by Franz von Soxhlet in 1886. There are two widely used methods to pasteurize milk: high temperature/short time (HTST), and ultra-high temperature (UHT). HTST is by far the most common method (except in Europe where UHT is more common). Milk simply labeled "pasteurized" is usually treated with the HTST method, whereas milk labeled "ultra-pasteurized" or simply "UHT" must be treated with the UHT method. HTST involves holding the milk at a temperature of 72 °C (161.5 °F) for at least 15 seconds. UHT involves holding the milk at a temperature of 138 °C (280 °F) for at least two seconds.

Pasteurization methods are usually standardized and controlled by national food safety agencies (such as the USDA in the United States and the Food Standards Agency in the United Kingdom). These agencies require milk to be HTST pasteurized in order to qualify for the "pasteurized" label. There are different standards for different dairy products, depending on the fat content and the intended usage. For example, the pasteurization standards for cream differ from the standards for fluid milk, and the standards for pasteurizing cheese are designed to preserve the phosphatase enzyme, which aids in cutting the cheese.

The HTST pasteurization standard was designed to achieve a 5-log reduction (0.00001 times the original) in the number of viable microorganisms in milk. This is considered adequate for destroying almost all yeasts, mold, and common spoilage bacteria and also to ensure adequate destruction of common pathogenic heat-resistant organisms (including particularly Mycobacterium tuberculosis, which causes tuberculosis and Coxiella burnetii, which causes Q fever). HTST pasteurization processes must be designed so that the milk is heated evenly, and no part of the milk is subject to a shorter time or a lower temperature.

HTST pasteurized milk typically has a refrigerated shelf life of two to three weeks, whereas ultra pasteurized milk can last much longer when refrigerated, sometimes two to three months. When UHT pasteurization is combined with sterile handling and container technology, it can even be stored unrefrigerated for long periods of time.

Alternative Milk Pasteurization

In addition to the standard HTST and UHT pasteurization standards, there are other lesser-known pasteurization techniques. The first technique, called "batch pasteurization", involves heating large batches of milk to a lower temperature, typically 68 °C (155 °F). The other technique is called higher-heat/shorter time (HHST), and it lies somewhere between HTST and UHT in terms of time and temperature. Pasteurization causes some irreversible and some temporary denaturization of the proteins in milk.

In most legislations, double pasteurization is not considered pasteurized. A heat treatment at a lower temperature or for a shorter time is sometimes performed. Possibly, such milk could be called "raw milk" or, confusingly, "unpasteurized milk". It cannot be called "pasteurized", even though a significant number of pathogens are destroyed during the process.

Raw Milk

In recent years, there has been some consumer interest in raw milk products, due to perceived health benefits. Advocates of raw milk maintain, correctly, that some components survive in milk that has not been pasteurized. Specifically, raw milk contains immunoglobulins and the enzymes lipase and phosphatase, which are inactivated by heat. Raw milk also contains vitamin B6 of which up to 20% may be lost on heat treatment. It is also claimed to contain beneficial bacteria which aid digestion and boost immunity.Commercial distribution of packaged raw milk is not allowed in most US states. Drinking raw (untreated) milk or eating raw milk products is "like playing Russian roulette with your health," says John Sheehan, director of the Food and Drug Administration's Division of Dairy and Egg Safety. "We see a number of cases of food borne illness every year related to the consumption of raw milk."

More than 300 people in the United States (approximately 1 in a million) got sick from drinking raw milk or eating cheese made from raw milk in 2001, and nearly 200 became ill from these products in 2002, according to the Centers for Disease Control and Prevention. Raw milk may harbor a host of disease-causing organisms (pathogens), such as the bacteria campylobacter, escherichia, listeria, salmonella, yersinia, and brucella. Common symptoms of foodborne illness from many of these types of bacteria include diarrhea, stomach cramps, fever, headache, vomiting, and exhaustion. Most healthy people recover from foodborne illness within a short period of time, but others may have symptoms that are chronic, severe, or life-threatening.

People with weakened immune systems, such as elderly people, children, and those with certain diseases or conditions, are most at risk for severe infections from pathogens that may be present in raw milk. In pregnant women, Listeria monocytogenes-caused illness can result in miscarriage, fetal death, or illness or death of a newborn infant, and Escherichia coli infection has been linked to hemolytic uremic syndrome, a condition that can cause kidney failure and death. Some of the diseases that pasteurization can prevent are tuberculosis, diphtheria, polio, salmonellosis, strep throat, scarlet fever, and typhoid fever. In fact, some doctors suggest that babies and breast-feeding mothers avoid all but UHT pasteurized dairy products. In regions including Africa and South Asian countries, it is common to boil milk after it is harvested. This intense heating greatly changes the flavor of milk, which the respective people are accustomed to.

Standards of Milk Pasteurization

Milk pasteurization has been subject to increasing scrutiny in recent years, due to the discovery of pathogens that are both widespread and heat resistant (able to survive pasteurization in significant numbers). Researchers have developed more sensitive diagnostics, such as real-time PCR and improved culture methods that have enabled them to identify pathogens in pasteurized milk. One bacterium in particular, the organism Mycobacterium avium subspecies paratuberculosis (MAP), which causes Johne's disease in cattle and is suspected of causing at least some Crohn's disease in humans, has been found to survive pasteurisation in retail milk in the U.S., the UK, Greece, and the Czech Republic. The food safety authorities in the UK have decided to re-evaluate pasteurisation standards in light of the MAP results and other evidence of harmful, pasteurisation-resistant pathogens.

The USDA (which is responsible for setting pasteurisation standards in the U.S.) has not re-evaluated their position on pasteurisation adequacy. They do not dispute the studies, which are at this point accepted by the scientific community, but maintain that the presence of MAP in retail pasteurized milk must be due to post-pasteurisation contamination. However, some researchers within the Food and Drug Administration, which is responsible for food safety in the U.S., have begun pushing for a re-evaluation of these results. There is a small but growing body of criticism directed at these agencies by Crohn's disease sufferers, scientists, and doctors. Some have suggested that the U.S. dairy industry has been successful in suppressing the agencies' response to a potential health crisis, for fear of consumer panic which would lead to a decrease in milk consumption. It is worth noting that while MAP has not been definitely proven to be harmful in humans, all other mycobacteria are pathogenic, and it has been definitively shown to cause disease in cattle and other ruminants.

A newer method called flash pasteurization involves shorter exposure to higher temperatures, and is claimed to be better for preserving colour and taste in some products. The term cold pasteurization is used sometimes for the use of ionizing radiation or other means (e.g. chemical) to kill bacteria in food. Food irradiation is also sometimes called "electronic pasteurisation".

Pasteurised Products

Products that can be pasteurized :

- eggs
- sports drinks
- canned food
- water
- juice
- honey
- apple cider

Flash Pasteurization

Flash pasteurization is a method of heat pasteurization of perishable beverages like milk, fruit and vegetable juices, and beer. It is done prior to filling into containers in order to kill spoilage microorganisms, as an effort to make the products safer and to extend their shelf life. The liquid moves in a controlled, continuous flow while subjected to temperatures of 71.5°C (160°F) to 74°C (165°F), for about 15 to 30 seconds, a ratio expressed as pasteurisation units.

The process is more prevalent in Europe and Asia than in North America. The benefits of the process involve maintaining colour and flavor while killing potentially harmful bacteria. Juice company Odwalla moved from non-pasteurised to flash-pasteurised juices in 1996 after tainted unpasteurized apple juice sickened many children and killed one.

Cold Pasteurization

Cold Pasteurization is the process of exposing food to ionizing radiation in order to disinfest, sanitize, sterilize, or preserve food. It is, like most technology involving ionizing radiation, the subject of some controversy regarding its safety. This process is used on other things as well, such as medical hardware. This process is known as Food Irradiation. By irradiating food, depending on the dose, some or all of the microbes, fungi, viruses or insects present are killed. This prolongs the life of the food in cases where microbial spoilage is the limiting factor in shelf life. Some foods (e.g., herbs and spices) are irradiated at such high doses (5 kilograys or more) that they are partially sterilized. It has also been shown that irradiation can delay the ripening or sprouting of fruits and vegetables and replace the need for pesticides.

The United Nations Environmental Programme passed the Montreal Protocol on Substances that deplete the Ozone Layer banning amongst other substances all non-critical uses of methyl bromide, the most common fumigant for post-harvest quarantine treatment of fruit. Although in theory still permitted for quarantine applications, prices of the fumigant have increased dramatically as a consequence. Some governments and corporations think that irradiation is a legitimate replacement for such fumigants and in consequence some large agricultural nations of the world are currently building irradiation facilities for fresh fruit, although the food industry has been slow to adopt this technology on any large scale. The United States Department of Agriculture has approved irradiation technology as an alternative treatment for fruits and vegetables that are considered hosts to a number of fruit flies and seed weevils. The United Nations Food and Agricultural Organization (FAO) have passed a motion to support this step committing the member states to implement this technology for their national phytosanitary programmes.

NANOTECH RESEARCH FOR FOOD INDUSTRY

Discoveries in nanotechnology are affecting a range of aspects in the food industry, from food safety to the molecular synthesis of new products and ingredients, according to a survey of current research by scientists. The four major areas in food production that may benefit from nanotechnology development are microscale and nanoscale processing, product development, and methods and instrumentation design for improved safety and biosecurity, the scientists say in an article published in the current issue of the Journal of Food Science.

"The fact that systems with structural features on the nanoscale have physical, chemical, and biological properties substantially different from their macroscopic counterparts is changing the understanding of biological and physical phenomena in food systems," they say. Nanotechnology, which deals with controlling matter at near-atomic scales to produce unique or enhanced materials, products and devices, has been touted as the next revolution in many industries, including food manufacturing and packaging. Yet the public's concerns have been raised that nanostructured materials could potentially lead to unforeseen health or environmental hazards.

In the food area fears arise over the unknown consequences of digesting nano-scale particles designed to behave in specific way in the body. In the article scientists Jochen Weiss, Paul Takhistov, and Julian McClements give an overview of the current state of nanotechnology research in the food industry, providing processors with a heads up of the probable changes that may come their way in the sector.

"Strategies to apply nanoscience to the food industry are quite different from these more traditional applications of nanotechnology," the scientists noted. " Food processing is a multitechnological manufacturing industry involving a wide variety of raw materials, high biosafety requirements, and well-regulated technological processes." The potential benefits of nanotechnology have been recognized by many industries, and commercial products are already being manufactured, such as in the microelectronics, aerospace, and pharmaceutical industries. Developments in these industries are driven by fundamental and applied research in physics, chemistry, biology, engineering, and materials science.

In contrast, applications of nanotechnology within the food industry are rather limited, the scientists say. Production of nanoscale structures for use in food science and technology therefore frequently relies on an in-depth understanding of thermodynamically driven self-assembly processes, write the scientists. They suggest areas of current research that could prove useful for the food sector in the near future include the molecular design of protective surface systems, surface engineering, and various methods of manufacturing, such as electrospinning and nanofiltration.

Other areas where nanotechnology has the potential to impact food and agricultural systems include security, disease-treatment delivery methods, tools for molecular and cellular biology, materials for pathogen detection, and the protection of the environment. Such examples include the use of nanotechnology for achieving further advancements in the security of manufacturing, processing, and shipping of food products through sensors for pathogen and contaminant detection. Devices to maintain historical environmental records of a particular product and tracking of individual shipments could also be developed, they suggest. Other nanotechnology developments are systems to provide the integration of sensing, localization, reporting, and remote control of products, and transportation, and the encapsulation and delivery mechanisms for functional ingredients to their specific site of action.

The influence of the material properties of foods at the nanoscale level on their bioavailability and nutritional value has been highlighted by at least two studies. In addition, other scientists have investigated the relationship between the morphology of food materials and their bulk physicochemical properties. Such studies include ones on biopolymers in solutions, gels, and films. One study found functional nanostructures can incorporate individual biological molecules, which is useful in the development of biosensors that can use natural sugars or proteins as target-recognition groups.

"In summary, there are a large number of potential applications of nanotechnology within the food industry; however, many of these may be difficult to adopt commercially because they are either too expensive or too impractical to implement on an industrial scale," the scientists concluded. However a limited number of nanotechnology applications may have commercial potential in the near future. Most likely, the limited application of nanotechnology to the food industry will change as nanofabrication technologies become more cost-effective, they suggest. Such areas include the development of functional ingredients such as drugs, vitamins, antimicrobials, antioxidants, flavorings, colourants, and preservatives.

Association colloids could be another fertile area for commercialisation. Association colloids include surfactant micelles, vesicles, bilayers, reverse micelles, and liquid crystals — used for many years to encapsulate and deliver polar, nonpolar, or amphiphilic functional ingredients. Nano-emulsions such as the use of high-pressure valve homogenizers or microfluidizers could be used to incorporate functional food components within the droplets, the interfacial region, or the continuous phase.

"While it is difficult to engineer the interfaces to be completely impermeable to compounds in the bulk phase that may interact with the encapsulated compounds, the rate of permeation can often be significantly reduced, thus increasing the kinetic stability of the bioactives," the scientists stated. Nanostructured multiple emulsions can be another area of work, used to create delivery systems with novel encapsulation and delivery properties. The most common examples of this are oil-in-water-in-oil and water-in-oil-in-water emulsions. For example, a nanostructured emulsion would consist of nanometer-sized water droplets or reverse micelles contained within larger oil droplets that are dispersed within an aqueous continuous phase.

Functional food components could be encapsulated within the inner water phase, the oil phase, or the outer water phase, thereby making it possible to develop a single delivery system that contains multiple functional components. The technology could be used to separate aqueous phase components that might adversely react with each other if they were present in the same aqueous phase. It could also be used to protect and release an aqueous phase component trapped within the inner water droplets to a specific site such as the mouth, stomach, or small intestine, they suggest.

Another area for commercialisation is the use of nanostructured multilayer emulsions. Recent studies show that the use of multilayer emulsions can create novel delivery systems, they stated. Such systems typically consist of oil droplets at the core surrounded by a shell of nanometer thick layers. The shell is comprised of different polyelectrolytes. Under certain circumstances, emulsions containing oil droplets surrounded by multilayer interfaces have been found to have better stability against environmental stresses than conventional oil-in-water emulsions with single-layer interfaces.

THERMAL PROCESSING

Thermal processing is the primary method for both adding value and ensuring microbial safety of meat and poultry products. Although numerous technologies (e.g., irradiation, ultra high pressure, pulsed electric fields) loom on the horizon for the broader food industry, the application of heat will certainly continue as the dominant means to impart desirable characteristics, add economic value, and ensure product safety. Additionally, major shifts in consumer demand and regulatory burden are increasing the importance of thermal processing in all of these areas.

Growth in the fully-cooked market sector and evolving regulations are creating a need for better information related to thermal inactivation of pathogens in meat and poultry products. Regulatory changes are shifting the burden to processors to ensure, through scientific rationale, that a new or modified process meets lethality performance standards. Although product and process parameters are known to affect thermal resistance of bacteria, most reported information is from labouratory studies that encompass a limited range of conditions. In most cases, the validity of this information for commercial processes is uncertain.

In this context we can highlight three questions. (1) why thermal processing and microbial inactivation are increasingly important issues to the meat and poultry industry, (2) what is currently known about thermal inactivation of pathogens in meat and poultry products, and (3) what information and tools are urgently needed to meet pathogen lethality standards in commercial cooking systems.

Market Evolution

Consumers increasingly want convenient, easy-to-prepare entrees, and this demand is likely to be reflected in continued rapid growth in the fully cooked, ready-to-eat meat and poultry market segment. Given $90 billion in U.S.-wide annual sales of all meat and poultry (AMI, 2000), any improvements in margin by value-added processing have the potential for significant returns to the industry and to the overall economy. Therefore, it is in the industry's best interest to respond in timely and creative ways to meet this need. Clearly, any growth in this market will depend on the design, operation, and improvement of thermal processing systems for manufacturing these products. However, novel product and process development will ultimately be inhibited if processors are unable to meet new food safety requirements that govern these activities.

In terms of regulatory pressures, there is an evolving shift from a command-and-control paradigm (i.e., meeting specific endpoint temperatures) to lethality performance standards. This shift is evident in one final rule and one currently proposed rule. The 1999 rule changes specified lethality performance standards for cooked and roast beef and cooked poultry products, but continued to provide only time-temperature specifications for cooked patties. The amended regulations state that any process producing ready-to-eat, whole -muscle products must achieve 6.5-log10 or 7.0-log10 reduction in Salmonella for whole -muscle beef or poultry, respectively. Processors are no longer held to specific endpoint temperatures; however, they "must validate new or altered process schedules by scientifically supportable means".

The currently proposed rule changes extend this general approach to essentially all ready-to-eat products containing meat or poultry. The 1999 rule changes mentioned above do allow for processing within "safe harbor" guidelines (i.e., specified time -temperature combinations), and draft compliance guidelines have been published for certain common products covered by the currently proposed changes . However, there are two major and foreseeable problems. First, it is unlikely that compliance guidelines will be published for every affected product, particularly niche specialty and ethnic products, thereby implicitly leaving many processors (probably those with the least likelihood of having in-house capacity to address the issue) without "safe harbors" and forcing them to prove that their processes meet the lethality performance standards.

Secondly, the current evolutionary shift of the microbial safety burden for ready-to-eat products to processors may likely foreshadow a more complete change, given that there are no guarantees that the "safe harbor" guidelines will remain in place indefinitely. Although the new regulatory paradigm creates greater opportunities for customized processes, it clearly puts significant pressure on the industry to document process lethality for any new product or process. Unfortunately, the current state -of-knowledge is insufficient for reliable lethality predictions in commercial processes. Challenge studies (i.e., inoculation of real products with target organisms) are impossible in commercial facilities, where pathogens cannot be brought on site.

Additionally, existing pathogen inactivation models have been developed primarily with model products in labouratory conditions and therefore are not necessarily valid for conditions occurring in many commercial processes. Therefore, "scientifically supportable means" do not currently exist for reliable and robust predictions of thermal process lethality in this industry. Obviously, it is common knowledge that heat kills bacteria. However, when evaluating process lethality, it is essential to understand the wide range of both product and process parameters, beyond just temperature, that affect the process outcome. Thermal inactivation of bacteria is affected by numerous intrinsic factors. In general, resistance is higher in meat products than in buffer solutions, peptone - agar, or other model media. In any medium, there is typically an optimal pH for maximum bacterial heat resistance.

Water activity (and/or moisture content) of the product is widely known to be a controlling factor in microbial growth; however, its effect on thermal inactivation is less obvious, but extremely important. Salmonella survivors on the surfaces of fully-cooked, dry roasted beef and suggested that thermal resistance was enhanced by the reduction in water activity near the meat surface. However, very few studies have quantified the effects of moisture content or aw on microbial inactivation. Studies clearly showed that intrinsic properties of the product have a significant impact on the heat resistance of bacteria. Nevertheless, most literature on the inactivation of food borne pathogens is based on studies conducted with liquid media, meat slurries, or external inoculation of meat. For example, most of the published inactivation data for Listeria were developed with liquid media. Although several of the studies documented some effect of product parameters on thermal inactivation, none quantitatively modeled the relationships between those parameters and pathogen inactivation rates.

Although product factors, such as pH, fat content, and water activity, all have an effect on thermal resistance of pathogens, the environmental conditions during thermal processing typically become the predominant factors controlling the inactivation rate, even overriding expected intrinsic effects. Let us consider process factors to be those parameters that can be controlled either by the process design or operation, such as heating (e.g., air) temperature, cooking time, humidity, and heating (or cooling) rates. With the exception of heating temperature and time, far less is known about the effects of environmental conditions on thermal inactivation, as relevant to commercial processes.

These effects can be either immediate or delayed, as occurs when bacteria exhibit stress-induced tolerances to heat. For example, although the effects of water activity on thermal resistance have been described, water activity is an intrinsic property of the product, reflecting the equilibrium vapour pressure over the product at a specified temperature. In a commercial impingement oven, high air velocities create a very small boundary layer around the product, so that the micro-environmental conditions around the product in the oven are essentially controlled by the oven conditions (i.e., temperature and humidity).

Therefore, it may be the case that any inactivation mechanism for a pathogen cell at or near the surface of the product is thereby controlled more by the oven humidity than by the water activity of the supporting medium (i.e., the meat product). We are currently attempting to test this question by breaking it into its two parts (product vs. process conditions). In a study that varied ground turkey moisture content from 71 to 76% and tested thermal resistances of Salmonella in that medium, we can find no significant moisture effects when the samples were sealed in plastic pouches and heated in an isothermal water bath at 55 to 65 degree C, so that the chemical potential of the water in the sample reflected only the product properties. We can currently conduct analogous tests in a controlled air heating system, so that the water status around the sample reflects the oven conditions (i.e., humidity), rather than the product conditions.

Additionally, there is sufficient evidence to suggest that thermal inactivation of pathogens in food systems is a path-dependent process. In other words, past handling and treatment of a contaminated sample affects thermal resistance of those pathogens in future processes. For example, Stephens et al. (1994) tested the effects of heating rate on thermal inactivation of Listeria monocytogenes in tryptic phosphate broth. Contrary to the basic assumption behind kinetic -based modeling, bacterial inactivation decreased significantly for heating rates below 5 degree C/min, with deviations as high as 105-fold when comparing expected to observed survivor ratios. They did not, however, explicitly incorporate this effect into predictive models for inactivation, nor did they test it in meat or poultry products. Obviously, the importance of the heating rate effect depends on the type of thermal process and would be more relevant to slow cooking procedures than to rapid cooking, as might typically occur in an impingement oven.

Clearly, both product and process parameters have significant effects on the thermal resistance of pathogens in meat and poultry products. However, mere knowledge that these effects exist is insufficient to aid a processor in designing, operating, or evaluating the efficacy of a thermal process, in terms of the relevant lethality performance standards. Quantitative analysis requires either direct measurement via inoculated challenge studies (relevant only for validating existing processes) or validated models that can predict the lethality outcome for specified product and process conditions (relevant for either designing new processes or evaluating existing ones).

Because commercial cooking systems create complex conditions around the product, with varying temperature, humidity, airflow, etc., scale -up of labouratory-based inactivation data to commercial-scale processes, without evidence that the data account for all of the relevant process parameters, can be a dangerous leap. Pilot-scale challenge studies in systems that simulate the full-scale process are desirable; however, because most industry pilot-scale facilities are used primarily for product/ process development activities, the introduction of pathogens into those environments is impossible. Therefore, inoculated challenge studies are rarely an option in evaluating process lethality, particularly for new or modified processes. Because of the impracticality of challenge studies, the processor is left with predictive models as the primary means for evaluating and documenting process lethality. The rest of this section outlines just the basics behind quantitative microbiology and what is needed before these techniques will be universally applicable to thermal processes in the meat and poultry industry.

MICROBIAL MODELING

The purpose of modeling is to reduce biological, chemical, and physical phenomena to systems of mathematical equations. A model must describe the phenomena of interest with sufficient accuracy to enable the necessary design, operation, or management decisions without requiring actual testing that is either too expensive, too time consuming, unsafe, or all of the above. The most important point about predictive models is that they must be validated by testing on data independent of those used to create the model before they can be used for prediction of future results.

In terms of basic microbial modeling methods, there have been several recent reviews. Whiting and Buchanan (1993) classified models into three types: primary, secondary, and tertiary - where primary models describe changes in microbial populations with time, secondary models describe the relationships between the primary model parameters and various environmental conditions (such as temperature, pH, and water activity), and tertiary models are computer tools that integrate the primary and secondary models into user-friendly units. Whiting (1995) noted that most current primary and secondary models are merely descriptive, so that there remains a need for models based on physicochemical, physiological, or biochemical mechanisms. Additionally, Buchanan (1993) and Whiting (1995) both stated that there are insufficient data on the effects of non-thermal factors (e.g., pH and water activity) on bacterial inactivation.

In general, most previous studies have assumed first-order kinetics for primary models of thermal inactivation. However, Peleg and Cole (1998) challenged this assumption by proposing that any non linearity observed in semi logarithmic survival curves is due to a distribution of heat resistances among individual organisms, rather than to mixed populations or experimental artifacts, as is typically assumed. They tested their methodology by modeling the population of resistances from a variety of published inactivation studies, using a Weibull distribution for their calculations. They illustrated several important implications of this approach. First of all, the determination of model parameters by regressing linearized data may not be sensitive to the detailed shape of the population distribution; therefore, non-linear regression is more desirable. Additionally, they noted that first-order models have previously included the effects of intrinsic factors as influencing only the rate constant, k, while these factors may also influence the shape of the survival curves. In order to include this effect in an inactivation model, it is therefore necessary to describe it in terms of changes in the distribution of the population's resistance.

Modeling and Validation

It is typically assumed that inactivation models can be applied to a real thermal process by dividing the process into a series of small time steps, and then computing the cumulative inactivation by stepping through these time steps and recalculating the survivors after each interval. Although their model was a significant contribution, temperature was the only transient variable included. They noted that there still is a need to include the influence of water activity, which also varies during dynamic thermal processes.

With respect to tertiary inactivation models, the compliance guidelines for the new FSIS regulations specifically refer to the USDA-ARS Pathogen Modeling Programme thereby inferring that this tool could be used to relate cooking parameters to pathogen lethality. Another example is the AMI Process Lethality Spreadsheet. Both tools are excellent examples of tertiary inactivation models (simple to use, user-friendly, Windows-based); however, both have a number of limitations relevant to the real thermal processes.

First, the current version of PMP does not include primary models for thermal inactivation of Salmonella, nor does either model include secondary models that relate important product and process conditions (e.g., fat content, humidity) to inactivation. Both assume first- order inactivation kinetics, which ignore any lag or tailing phenomena that can be important, in terms of resistant sub-populations. Additionally, neither model accounts for temperature and moisture gradients that occur in real food products and therefore cause "lethality profiles" within a meat product. Consequently, there is still a need to further extend the methods of quantitative microbiology by coupling the inactivation models with validated process (heat and mass transfer) models to evaluate the lethality of commercial cooking systems.

The general observation that current microbial inactivation models fail to account for all of the factors relevant to commercial thermal processes is certainly of no comfort to an industry that is increasingly being compelled to verify and prove that cooking systems are meeting lethality performance standards. There is a significant need for user-friendly, publicly available, validated models that would allow a user to enter the product conditions (size, shape, composition, initial temperature) and process parameters (equipment specifications, such as temperature, time, air velocity, humidity, etc., for each stage of a multi-stage process) and get back a prediction of product temperature profiles, cooking yield, and pathogen inactivation. Such a tool could ultimately be used to design and control multi-stage processes to ensure that the lethality performance standard is met while simultaneously optimizing cooking yield and product quality. Such models are under development for certain specific processes, such as contact frying and convection cooking but much more work is needed for the continuous -flow operations used in typical process plants.

In the meantime, processors should be cautious in applying simple D and Z values to integrated time temperature histories from process data. Minimally, they should be aware of the medium and heating conditions used to generate the inactivation parameters, and recognize whether their processes differ from those conditions in significant ways, such as product composition or process humidity. Even though under-cooking in food manufacturing facilities is not currently causing widespread food safety problems, continued development of new products and processes (and the ongoing regulatory changes) necessitate a proactive stance in ensuring proper evaluation of thermal process lethality.

Product Quality

Thermal technologies have long been at the heart of food processing. The application of heat is both an important method of preserving foods and a means of developing texture, flavour and colour. An essential issue for food manufacturers is the effective application of thermal technologies to achieve these objectives without damaging other desirable sensory and nutritional qualities in a food product. New packaging media such as flexible trays, pouches, and glass containers have superceded traditional canning with great results. The availability of such packaging opportunities has created the demand for products of more challenging theological behaviour that may contain differing degrees of particulate material and hence the need for new designs of heat exchanger. While the primary concern of food manufacturers is the production of safe foods, there is little market for low quality foods no matter how safe they are. The need to maximize process efficiency and final product quality has led to a number of new developments, including refinements in existing technologies and the emergence of new "minimal" techniques. Thermal Technologies in Food Processing reviews all these key developments and looks at future trends, providing an invaluable resource for all food processors. Thermal technologies have long been at the heart of food processing. Hear application is both an important methods of food preservation as well as a means of developing texture, flavour and colour.

ER or ohmic heating is a promising technique for thermal processing of particulate foods. Theoretically, it is possible for food particulates with uniform electrical conductivity to heat evenly. The establishment of an approved process would be simplified because the liquid temperature could be used for lethality calculations. A project was developed the multipoint (MP) probe and advanced the development of liquid crystal (LC) sheets and magnetic resonance imaging (MRI). They were capable of measuring 1-, 2- and 3-dimensional temperature profiles, respectively. The development of the MRI for temperature measurement was not finished while the other two were completed and are being used in various applications. Studies on tortuousity, shadowing effects and convection were conducted to understand safety factor in ER processing. Results showed that in food systems consisting of solids from various materials, shadowing effects could make the cold spot develop in solids with high electrical conductivity. This is an important finding since the rule of thumb in ER processing is that the cold spot develops in components with low electrical conductivity. A study on the effects of no, free and forced convections and conductivity ratios showed that the location of the cold spot (between solid and liquid) was not affected by convection but rather by conductivity ratio.

Mycotoxins are a chemically diverse group of secondary metabolites produced by fungi. They are responsible for significant financial losses for the food industry and pose a threat to human and animal health. The objectives of this project were to:

1. Study the effects of processing/chemical treatments on fumonisin in corn-based food and patulin in apple cider/juice,
2. Participate in surveys for fumonisin and patulin in food,
3. Correlate apple quality with patulin levels in juice/cider, and
4. Determine the effects of washing treatments on patulin levels in cider made from contaminated apples.

We found that fumonisin is fairly heat stable under most conditions encountered during thermal processing (e.g. boiling, retorting, baking and frying) but may be destroyed during extrusion cooking. Adding glucose to contaminated corn grits enhanced destruction of fumonisin during extrusion. In dry milling experiments, fumonisin tended to concentrate in bran, germ and fine fractions of naturally contaminated corn. Work on the stability of patulin has shown that the compound is stable under pasteurization temperatures/times. However, addition of ascorbic acid to juice may result in losses of patulin.

Surveys conducted of corn-based foods and apple juices/ciders purchased in the Chicago area indicated that most foods contained low levels of fumonisin or patulin. High levels of fumonisin were found in samples of blue and high-lysine corn meal. Several lots of a generic brand of apple juice contained high levels of patulin. In several experiments, we found that cider made from dropped apples had significantly higher patulin levels than cider pressed from tree-picked fruit.

Washing the dropped apples with water and chlorine solution before pressing, appeared to lower patulin levels in the cider. More work is needed understand the effects of processing on mycotoxins and to identify methods for reducing mycotoxin levels in food.

Bacteria along with fat, protein and other debris form a persistent biofilm on food contact surfaces which are not normally removed by routine cleaning. Currently high temperature chlorinated water is used widely in the food industry to sanitize processing equipment or processing lines. Although this technique is generally effective there are disadvantages associated with it, including a concern that more resistant and virulent strains of bacteria are emerging because disinfectants and sanitizers (such as chlorine) have been used repeatedly. In June 1997, the Electric Power Research Institute Expert Panel submitted a petition to FDA proposing that the uses of ozone should be considered as GRAS (generally recognized as safe). The potential of ozone has been shown to be an effective replacement for chlorine to sanitize food contact surfaces.

A concentration as low as 0.1PPM effectively removes high organic content biofilms on the food contact surfaces. Ozone was shown to be a more powerful disinfectant than chlorine. Some limited labouratory work has been conducted on the use of ozone as a sanitizer against biofilms on stainless steel plates with pure non-pathogen cultures. There is no further information about the efficacy of ozone with food pathogens on different material surfaces. Furthermore no work has been undertaken to date to evaluate the effects of temperature, pH, contact time, quality of surface, food soils, and background microflora on bacteria removal. There is also a lack of adequate information on corrosion data on the effect of ozone on food contact surface materials. It is the purpose of this study to provide the basis for the effective and safe utilization of ozone as a replacement for chlorine. The application of ozone sanitation is now gaining interest by food industry.

Various research reports have raised concerns about the public health protection provided by the current 60-day aging period in the manufacture of hard cheeses made with unpasteurized milk. Salmonella typhimurium, Listeria monocytogenes, and Escherichia (E.) coli O157:H7 have been shown to survive aging for 5 to 15 months. The purpose of this study is to investigate the adequacy of the 60-day minimum aging to eliminate the foodborne pathogens. Even at the 101 inoculation level into raw milk, E. coli O157:H7 populations increased by 1 to 2 logs at the milling and pressing steps. Populations of E. coli O157:H7 in cheese aged for 60 days at 7°C were reduced by less than 1 log. This population increase during cheese making, and decrease during the 60 days aging resulted in no net change. After 300 days, no growth of E. coli O157:H7 was seen on the plates after either pre-enrichment or enrichment.

The evaluation of the adequacy of the minimum aging period of hard cheeses made from milk thermalized to eliminate food pathogens was not completed because of need to decontaminate the pilot plant before extensive remodeling of the Biocontainment Pilot Plant (BCPP) could begin. The validation of techniques to monitor and control the processing conditions used in the manufacture of hard cheeses will be conducted as a regulatory review of computer records documenting the steps of cheese making.

The Federal Register (April 24, 1 998) reported several cases of illness resulting from consumption of various types of juices, mostly unpasteurized apple cider. UV light disinfection is a nonthermal process which involves the exposure of pathogenic microorganisms light radiation, between 200-400 nm. UV light inactivates microorganisms by attacking their DNA, which renders them incapable of reproduction. A big obstacle in the application of UV light processing in fruit juices is the low transmittance at the UV range. For UV processing to be effective, the required dosage at specified wavelength must be delivered. A major focus of this project is to develop protocols to validate the UV dose for destruction of pathogens. Effectiveness of UV light against target pathogens and surrogates will be evaluated using a continuous type UV reactor. Chemical actinometry will be used to measure radiation dose in juices subjected to UV radiation. Natural components of juice will be monitored for suitability to use as radiation markers.

Degradative photochemical reactions, such as browning and vitamin deterioration, will be studied in juices subjected to UV processing. Investigators also plan to submit a proposal for external funding at a later date. The most effective wavelength for disinfection is about 254 nm and it is usually produced using low pressure mercury lamps. However, the use of broader band light sources, i.e. medium pressure mercury lamps, which produces UV light at the range of 200-400 nm has been found effective against microorganisms that require high dosage for inactivation, e.g. cryptosporidium.

Some magnetic materials create temperature dependent magnetic fields that penetrate conducting materials. By measuring the size of the surrounding magnetic fields, one can determine the temperature of the magnet without contact to the magnet or an object that contains the magnet. Since the magnet can be small and is a solid piece of material it has several advantages, 1) the electronics do not need to travel with the magnet through harsh environments, 2) the magnet can be placed in suspended solids with minimal effect on their motion. The remaining part of the magnetic thermometer consists of a magnetometer that is consistent with the working environment. The magnetometer needs to account for the velocity, position and orientation of the magnet when these quantities are unknown. The result is that by simply moving the magnet past the sensor the temperature of the magnet is determined.

At the NCFST a prototype magnetic thermometer has been built to measure temperatures in objects moving through 2" or smaller pipes. The prototype has worked successfully in industrial environments but its performance must be improved. Because of the necessity to have product flow into and out of the sensor, interference can never be perfectly shielded. However, there are ways to improve the shielding and the measurement=s immunity to external noise. The magnetic shield can be lengthened and a second layer can be added. By changing the triggering method and data analysis, one can reduce the effect of unshielded signals as well. This should help the system measure smaller magnetic particles or similar sized particles at increased distances. This project should develop a system that would be compatible with other applications as well.

Mycotoxins are a chemically diverse group of secondary metabolites produced by fungi. They are responsible for significant financial losses for the food industry. Mycotoxins pose a threat to human and animal health, and the determination of methods for reducing the mycotoxin content of food is desirable. In addition, there is a need to develop a data base on the occurrence and levels of mycotoxins in processed food. In the past, work done at the NCFST has mainly focused on the effects of thermal processing and chemical treatments on fumonisin in corn products. More work is needed understand the effects of processing on mycotoxins and to identify methods for reducing mycotoxin levels in food. Little is known about the effects of thermal processing on moniliformin, zearalenone and other mycotoxins. Although there have been some reports on the destruction of aflatoxin and other mycotoxins with gamma irradiation, little is know about the effects of electron beam irradiation in combination with chemical treatments on mycotoxin. Finally, more work is needed to determine if patulin levels can be used to predict the microbial quality of apple cider and other juices.

Gamma irradiation did not affect the IR spectra of pure colourant and PS test specimens measured in a range of 550-4000 wavenumbers. Qualitatively, the HS/GC/MS results suggest that irradiation did not generate new chemicals. Volatiles detected in irradiated test specimens (PS sheets and colourants) are alcohols, aldehydes, ketones, aromatic and aliphatic hydrocarbons that are unique to either PS or each colourant. Volatiles detected in pure colourant (100%) were not detected in coloured PS specimens. Amounts of PS solids migrating in 10 and 50% ethanol food simulating solvents were in a range of 0.0035 - 0.013% (w/w) based on polymer weight. Total polymer dissolution followed by precipitation of PS with methanol and analysis of the extract by HPLC-PDA showed the extraction of typical residuals from PS and other unidentified chemicals. Regardless of irradiation, addition of each colourant reduced concentrations of phenol, benzaldehyde, and acetophenone in the extracts. Irradiation increased the concentrations of other chemicals but had no effect on styrene.

The uncertain association of Mycobacterium paratuberculosis (MpT) with Crohn's disease prompted this study to determine the incidence and concentration of MpT in raw milk. The objectives of this project were to determine the concentration of MpT in raw milk from commercial tankers and evaluate the adequacy of conventional pasteurization to inactivate MpT. Over the course of 11 months in 2002, MpT was found to be present in 32 out of 405 samples (8%). Of those, 30 were positive on Harold's egg yolk medium. The range of concentration of MpT was from .008 to <1.0 cfu per milliliter. In no case did the concentration ever exceed 1 cfu per milliliter. The number of MpT present in bulk tanker raw milk is important because this serves as the initial bioburden present before pasteurization. The effectiveness of conventional pasteurization time/temperature conditions for the inactivation of MpT in milk has been called into question, primarily by researchers in the United Kingdom where pasteurization treatment times have been extended to 25 seconds holding at temperature. The results from this study suggest that conventional pasteurization (72° for 15 seconds) should be adequate to control the bioburden of incoming raw tanker milk.

A standard test method involving biofilm formation by various bacteria on various surfaces in a rotating disk reactor has been tested and validated. Attachment to various types of surfaces including stainless steel, polycarbonate, polyvinyl chloride and glass by various microorganisms under wet and dry conditions has been studied and compared. Using a biosensor manufactured by ST Microelectronics, bacteria attached to stainless steel, glass, polycarbonate, and polyvinyl chloride have been detected.

SHELF LIFE OF FOOD

Shelf life is that length of time that food, drink, medicine and other perishable items are given before they are considered unsuitable for sale or consumption. In some regions, a best before, use by or freshness date is required on packaged perishable foods. Shelf life is different from expiration date; the former relates to food quality, the latter to food safety. A food that has passed its shelf life is still safe, but optimal quality is no longer guaranteed. In most food stores, shelf life is maximised by using stock rotation, which involves moving products with the earliest sell by date to the front of the shelf, meaning that most shoppers will pick them up first and so getting them out of the store. This is important, as some stores can be fined for selling out of date products, and most if not all will have to mark such products down as wasted, leading to a loss of profit.

Shelf life is most influenced by five primary events: light transmission, gas transmission, heat transmission, humidity transmission, or mechanical stresses. Product quality is often mathematically modelled around a single parameter: the concentration of a chemical compound, a microbiological index, or a physical parameter. Under some circumstances, the shelf life is critical to health. Some medicines begin to deteriorate (e.g. in potency) or begin to accumulate toxic breakdown products immediately after manufacture or packaging. Depending on the material involved, this can be dangerous to life. Bacterial contaminants are ubiquitous, and foods left unused too long will often acquire substantial amounts of bacterial colonies and become dangerous to eat. Food poisoning is the result, and can be fatal. Some companies use induction sealing to assist in the extension of the shelf life of their products.

Temperature Control

Nearly all chemical reactions will occur (at various rates depending on the individual nature of the reaction) at common temperatures. Examples are the breakdown of many chemical explosives into more unstable compounds. Nitroglycerine is notorious. Old explosives are thus more dangerous (i.e., liable to explode without warning) than recently manufactured explosives. Rubber products also degrade as sulphur bonds induced during vulcanization revert; this is why old rubber bands and other rubber products soften and get sticky as they age.

These breakdown processes characteristically happen more quickly at higher temperatures. The usually quoted rule of thumb is that chemical reactions double their rate for every 10 degree Celsius increase in temperature (because of activation energy barriers). However, as with all rules of thumb, there are many caveats and assumptions. The rule of thumb is only true for reactions with activation energy values around 50kJ/mol. This observation, taken from a limited interpretation of the Arrhenius equation, has been grossly misused in food shelf-life testing, and has led to an incorrect belief that "triple time" can be simulated by increasing the temperature by 15 degrees Celsius. e.g. Storing a product for one month at 35 degrees Celsius simulates three months at 20 degrees Celsius.

The same is true, to a point, of the chemical reactions of life. In the particular case of bacteria and fungi, the reactions needed to feed and reproduce increase at higher temperatures, up to the point that the proteins and other compounds in their cells themselves begin to breakdown so quickly that they cannot be replaced. It is the reason high temperatures kill bacteria and other micro organisms; 'tissue' breakdown reactions reach such rates that they cannot be compensated for and the cell dies. On the other hand, 'elevated' temperatures short of these result in increased growth and reproduction; if the organism is harmful, perhaps to dangerous levels. Just as temperature increase speeds up reactions, temperature decreases reduce them. Therefore, to make explosives stable longer, or keep rubber bands springy, or force bacteria to slow down their growth, they can be cooled. This is the reason shelf life is generally extended by refrigeration and the reason some medicines must be refrigerated; the breakdown reaction paths at room temperature are so rapid the medicine becomes unusable very quickly. Only refrigeration keeps them potent long enough to be practical.

Best Before

Best before is sometimes indicated on food and drink wrappers, followed by a date, and is intended to indicate the date before which the supplier intended the food should be consumed. The term best before is similarly used to indicate the date by which the item will have outlived its shelf life, and is intended to ensure that customers will not unwittingly purchase or eat stale food. Sometimes the packaging process involves using pre-printed labels, making it impractical to write the best before date in a clearly visible location. In this case, a term like best before see bottom or best before see lid might be printed on the label and the date marked in a different location as indicated.

Use By

Generally, foods that have a use by date written on the packaging must not be eaten after it has expired. This is because such foods usually go bad quickly and may be injurious to health if spoiled. It is also important to follow storage instructions carefully for these foods (for example, product must be refrigerated). Foods that have a best before date are usually safe to eat after the date has passed, although they are likely to have deteriorated either in flavour, texture, appearance or nutrition.

Sell by- Display Until

These dates are intended to help keep track of the stock in stores. Food that has passed its sell by or display until date, but is still within its use by / best before will still be edible, assuming it has been stored correctly. It is common practice in large stores to throw away such food, as it makes the stock control process easier. It also reduces the risk of customers buying food without looking at the date, only to find out the next day that they cannot use it. Most stores will rotate stock by moving the products with the earliest dates to the front of shelving units, which allows them to be sold first and saving them from having to be either marked down or thrown away, both of which contribute to a loss of profit.

Mark-downs

It is also common for food approaching the use by date to be marked down for quick sale, with greater reductions the closer to the use by date it gets. A freshness date is the date used in the American brewing industry to indicate either the date the beer was bottled or the date before which the beer should be consumed. Beer is perishable. It can be affected by light, air, or the action of bacteria. Although beer is not legally mandated in the USA to have a shelf life, freshness dates serve much the same purpose and are a marketing tool.

Freshness Dates

The Boston Beer Company, maker of Samuel Adams, was among the first to start adding freshness dates to their product line in 1985. For ten years there was a slow growth in brewers adding freshness dates to their beer. The practice rapidly grew in popularity after the Anheuser-Busch company's heavily marketed "Born-On dates" starting in 1996. Many other brewers have started adding freshness dates to their products, but there is no standard for what the date means. For some companies, the date on the bottle or can will be the date that the beer was bottled; others have the date by which the beer should be consumed.

MICROBES IN FOOD

In reality, microbes grow very well in the natural world and they often grow in places where we would rather they didnt. They grow on our bodies and cause disease. They damage crops during transport and grow in our food, making it inedible. They create holes by growing inside pipes and contribute to rust on cars. We are in a constant battle to keep microorganisms at bay. The application of knowledge about microbial growth and how to control it has dramatically helped human society. In this chapter we will look at the methods used to influence the population of microbes, with specific examples of how they are employed.

The object of microbial control can range from complete eradication of microorganisms to the mere inhibition of their growth, and the goal of the treatment will influence the control method chosen. Sterilization is the complete removal of all life forms from a given area (note that this includes viruses even though they are not really living). Treatments causing sterilization tend to be drastic and can sometimes alter the chemistry of the object being treated. Items that need to be sterile before use include medical instruments, syringes, bandages, fermentation vessels, culture media, and some kinds of food. Contamination of these items with any type of organism would be deleterious, either causing infection or unreliable research results. The next level down from sterilization is the selective removal of a subset of microbes.

In many cases only certain microbes are damaging to an item and more gentle treatments can be used to eliminate only these harmful microbes without killing everything. A good example of this is heat treatment of milk. Treatment of milk at 72 C for 15 seconds (or 66 C for 30 minutes), termed pasteurization, will kill common pathogens transmitted in milk, including tuberculosis bacilli, E. coli and Salmonella enterica strains. While many harmless bacteria are not killed by this treatment, their elimination it is not necessary. Finally, sometimes it is sufficient to inhibit microbial growth in a sample, without killing any of them. Breads contain preservatives such as sodium benzoate that inhibit the growth of molds and lengthen the shelf life of the product. The mold spores find their way onto the bread after baking, but cannot grow as quickly due to the preservative.

METHODS TO CONTROL MICROBES

High Temperature

High temperature kills by causing lyses of the membrane or denaturation of critical enzymes. Two methods of providing heat are generally used. Dry heat involves incubation in an oven-like environment, while moist heat utilizes steam under pressure, and the latter is more effective. Water has a very high heat capacity (ability to carry heat) and moist air is capable of holding more heat than dry air. Moist heat is therefore more effective because it increases the rate of heat penetration into a substance. With dry heat a higher temperature or longer time of exposure is necessary to obtain the same amount of killing as that seen with moist heat.

If you have ever used a wet oven mitt to grab a hot pan you know how much more readily heat travels in a moist environment. In either case, at temperatures above the lethal limit for a bacterial strain, cell population decrease from heating follows a first-order exponential pattern. Because of this experimental pattern, the initial number of bacteria in a sample will affect the time necessary to eliminate that population from the sample. The goal of a heat treatment is to bring the target population down to some acceptable level. In addition, each species of microbe also has its own characteristic resistance to heat, with some bacteria being much more heat tolerant than others.

A final factor influencing the effectiveness of a heat treatment is the composition of the environment surrounding the microbe. High salt and acidic environments increase the rate of killing at a given temperature due to the damaging effects salt and acid have on the cell. Conversely, fats and proteins in a solution have a protective effect. Because of all these mitigating factors on the effectiveness of heat treatment, determining the success of a given treatment on a given type of sample must be done empirically, that is by experimentation.

Rate of Death of Heat Treatment

When trying to develop an effective heat treatment for a food or culture medium it is often necessary to quantitatively determine the rate of death. One of the best methods for achieving this goal is through the determination of decimal reduction times (or D value). The decimal reduction time is a measure of the heat sensitivity of a microbe and is defined as the length of time it takes for the viable population to decrease 10 fold at a given temperature. D can be determined by incubating a culture at a lethal temperature and periodically determining the number of surviving microbes in the sample by viable plate count. The log of the viable plate count is plotted against time and a straight line is drawn through the points. The negative reciprocal of the slope (-1/slope) of the line is the decimal reduction time. This value is only valid for the microbe under study, at that temperature and in the medium used. In a typical experiment, the D value at a series of temperatures is determined. Any change in sample conditions will require an additional D value analysis. Once a D value is determined it is possible to estimate how long a sample must be heated at a certain temperature to destroy a known population of cells.

Determining the D value at a large number of temperatures for any sample is tedious and the concept of thermal death time (TDT) and the Z value was developed to allow prediction of D values at any lethal temperature. The TDT is the time it takes for a population of cells to reach 10^0 (effectively zero) at a given temperature. This can be determined by multiplying the $\log_{10}$ of an initial cell population by the D value or by determining the X intercept from a D-value experiment. Once several TDTs have been determined for at least three temperatures, the Z value can be obtained.

The Z value measures the sensitivity of a microbe to a change in temperature and is defined as the amount of temperature increase necessary to decrease the TDT ten-fold. To determine the Z value for a microbe, the TDT is plotted (on a log scale) against its temperature and a line is drawn through the points. The Z value is the negative reciprocal of the slope of the line. With a Z value in hand, it is possible to predict the microbes death rate in the specific medium at any lethal temperature. D values, TDT and Z values are very useful in the food industry, where one wants the treatment to appropriately reduce the microbial population with minimum negative effect on the food itself.

Types of Heat Treatments

One of the most ancient methods of killing microorganisms is incineration. This typically destroys all living things as well as the sample that contains them. Incineration was used in the past to prevent the spread of infectious disease. During the black plague of the 14th century, it was a common practice to burn the corpses of those who succumbed to the illness, sometimes with all their possessions. The burning of houses and possessions is no longer common due to its destructive nature, but during some outbreaks of highly infectious disease, it is still very effective. Also, incineration is still legally required for the disposal of body parts as well as animals suspected of being infected with anthrax.

Another historical method of sterilization was repeated boiling also known as Tyndallization. Boiling a solution for 30 minutes at room temperature will kill most vegetative cells, but not bacterial endospores. In Tyndallization the boiled medium is cooled, incubated for a period of hours and then boiled again and this cycle is repeated three times. During the cooling periods, the endospores usually germinate and turn into heat-sensitive vegetative cells. Subsequent rounds of heating then kill these cells. More than two rounds of heating are necessary to insure that all spores have germinated. Tyndallization was often used to sterilize media before the invention of the autoclave (described below). It has the drawback that it is time consuming and the growth of germinated spores can alter the medium, possibly making it unsuitable for its intended purpose.

The most common method of sterilization currently used in labouratories and hospitals is autoclaving, which is basically a sophisticated pressure cooker. This employs stream under pressure to raise the temperature to 121 C at 15-17 psi for at least 15 minutes. At this elevated temperature all living cells, including endospores and viruses, are killed. Large liquid volumes and some types of medium need longer autoclaving times to insure complete elimination of microbes. One of the most hardy endospore-forming microorganisms is Bacillus stearothermophilus, which contains spores that can maintain viability for about 13 minutes at 121C. It can therefore be used as a standard bioassay to verify that an autoclave is working properly.

Autoclaves are simply steel chambers with pipes for entrance and exit of gas. During sterilization, the autoclave is filled with steam to a pressure of 15-17 psi, resulting in a temperature of 121C. The autoclave is an old, large autoclave still in service in the Bacteriology Department at the University of Wisconsin-Madison. Dry heat in an oven can also be used to kill microbes. Obviously this treatment will not work for liquid items since they will reach a maximum of 100 C, but for non-liquid items that do not melt at the oven temperature (160-170 C or above), it can be effective. Items such as metal and glass can be sterilized in this manner, however these treatments can ruin some items. For example surgical instruments loose sharpness when treated in this manner.

One problem with all of these high-temperature methods is that they can drastically alter the composition of the sample due to the breakdown of heat-labile components. In some cases alternatives to high temperature must be found to preserve the integrity of the item. For foods this often means treatment at lower temperatures since most food does not need to be sterile. The first and still most common method is pasteurization, named after the great microbiologist Louis Pasteur. Originally developed to prevent the spoilage of wine, it is commonly used for milk, and eliminates the transmission of Coxiella burnetti, Mycobacterium tuberculosis, Brucella, Staphylococcus, Salmonella and E. coli strain O157:H7. In the original batch pasteurization method, the food was heated at 66 C for 30 minutes, but most modern applications use flash pasteurization, which is a treatment at 71 C for 15 seconds. The shorter incubation time allows for easier automation and less damage to food during processing. Also, the higher temperature is more effective at killing Coxiella burnetti. Pasteurization not only eliminates pathogens, but also greatly decreases the number of spoilage organisms. Pasteurization is used extensively in treating many other food products including beer, wine, yogurt, juices and cheese.

In microbiology labouratories, heat sensitive compounds are often necessary additions to culture media preparations. Unlike the case with foods, it is possible to easily separate heat sensitive compounds from the rest of the medium by simply not adding them initially. Heat sensitive compounds are treated separately, using some low-temperature sterilization method, and added back to the medium aseptically after it is autoclaved and cooled. In this way the heat-labile components are undamaged, yet medium containing them can still be made sterile.

Low Temperature

Low temperature slows the rate of all chemical reactions, including those catalyzed by enzymes and it also decreases the fluidity of the cell membrane. Freezing the membrane thus prevents much of cellular metabolism by preventing enzymes in the membrane from functioning properly. Refrigerator temperatures (4 C) prevent the growth of many bacteria, extending the shelf life of many products. However, there are a large number of microorganisms still capable of slow growth at 4C and these will eventually spoil foods. Refrigeration merely slows down the process of spoilage. Freezing a sample at or below 20 C stops all microbial growth. Low temperature, even freezing, is not damaging to most microorganisms and, when brought up to suitable temperatures, the microbes will begin growing again. In fact, microorganisms are well preserved in liquid nitrogen (-196C) and this is a common method of preserving bacterial strains in research labouratories.

Chapter 4

Food Preservation

FERMENTATION

The food that enters the alimentary canal reaches the small intestines and the large bowel i.e., the .ascending, transverse, and descending colon Segmoid flexure and colon. We all learn from Physiology that the food we take undergoes many changes through the action on it of the secretions from various glands imbedded in the mucus membrane at various places from the mouth to the colon. When the body does not perform its natural functions owing to one or other of numerous causes, there will be excessive or meagre secretions and at times a dearth of such fluid; and digestion is consequently rendered imperfect. The undigested food-mass is deposited in the latter portions of the bowels and putrefies in a short time, giving rise to fermentation for reasons which will be explained later on. This fermented matter is foreign to the system and is referred to as foreign matter by Leuis Kuhne.

Foreign matter enters the body as solids generally mixed up in food, as liquids in the form of dissolved impurities in water or other beverages, and as gases in the form of foul air breathed in through the nose. A healthy body is endowed with the capacity to reject and throw out all the internal impurities. This the body can do only when it is not hindered by improper and unnatural methods of living.

Before entering into the discussion of the prevention of fermentation, let us deal with the primary causes of fermentation apart from human digestion. Fermentation is the result of the decomposition of any matter, organic or inorganic, when it loses its internal vitality, viz., life. This we can see when we put toddy in a pot. The toddy gradually decomposes and begins to ferment and occupies more space. During the process the fermented substance rises to the top of the pot and sometimes overflows from the sides of the vessel. Similarly, fallen leaves, plucked vegetables, and dead bodies of animals decompose and ferment if they are merely left in a place for a sufficient length of time.

As long as there is life in any organism, it will have animation, As soon as the organism is severed from its life-supplying connection, it gradually loses its vitality and decays and id finally decomposed. Let us now examine how the stage of fermentation is reached by gradation. Take for instance, the case of a flower or a fruit. The former shows visible changes more rapidly than the latter on account of its tender existence. Immediately after severance from the stem of the tree it loses its brightness and fragrance and finally fades and is decomposed. If the same is put in strong sunlight, the process quickens and the final stage is reached in a proportionately short time. If it is thrown into fire, the decay is immediate which is quite visible to the naked eye.

Now we have to consider other changes such as chemical alterations that undergo during the process of combustion. Elementary Chemistry teaches us that, when two congenial elements are brought together and heat is applied to them, a new compound different from the original elements is formed. The properties of the new compound are quite different from the properties of the combining elements.

In the process of cooking we observe that even fresh vegetables and live animals immediately lose their vitality. This is evidence to prove that fire in an active state destroys life. The process of cooking various articles in combination gives rise to countless compounds with the production of a large quantity of heat. Nobody knows except by surmise that these new compounds are proper and suitable for human consumption and are conducive to the building and growth of the human tissue structures.

We see in the outer world that all dead matter decomposes under heat. One may safely assume even without special knowledge that similar changes do occur in the human body with the animal heat that is always available. We know that dead solid substances such as metal pieces are thrown out by the digestive apparatus at the expense of the internal nerve energy. When the decomposed fluid and semi-solid matter and. the compounds formed by the various vegetable and food substances produced through heat enter the human digestive canal, it is not possible to estimate the exact amount of nerve energy that is required to propel and expel these substances as well as the toxins formed from the system.

This investigation reveals to us the reason for the decay and fall in average human life from a hundred to the present average of twenty-two years and it is no other than the eating of articles cooked on fire. With the process of digestion and evacuation of dead matter the whole secret of disease and nervous expenditure is intertwined.

The daily amount of nervous expenditure in the extraneous digestion and expulsion of the inert mass of the residue in the colon totals to nearly more than half or three-fourths of human life. Thus it can be clearly deduced that man's fall in his average life from hundred to twenty-two years is due to the above-mentioned cause.

Coming to the vitamin theory we meet with the various vitamins, such as A, B, C, D_f E, etc., that are said to exist in fresh leaves, vegetables, fruits and germinated seedlings. The propounders of the "Vitamin Theory" clearly state that these vitamins, L a, live atoms die under strong heat. But the eminent scientists and nutrition experts of the present day are still under, the delusion that Vitamins exist when slow heat is applied. This delusion is due more to the innate human weakness not to throw off the customary belief in old superstitions and orthodox theories.

A close examination of the statement of experts that life particles still remain after a slight heat, though appealing at the outset, is incorrect in the result. This is because heat kills life and changes the original elements. Take for instance the case of a snake whose head is crushed. Though a greater portion of the body has lost its life, the last portion of the tail shows signs of life by its movement for a short time. From this it cannot be inferred that the whole body is as efficient with life and vigour as when the snake was alive and unhurt. In the case of vegetables too, they are not as efficient after being plucked from the tree as they were when they were suspending from the branches. The moment they are detached, they gradually lose vitality and finally decay and fire destroys the little vitality that is still remaining.

Some of the up-to-date scientific writers state that grape sugar is formed in vegetables when gentle heat is applied to them. What really happens is the natural evapouration of the proper proportions of water and other substances and the consequent deposit of the sugary (starchy) matter in a concentrated form stuck up in the charred and dead cellular structure of the vegetable on account of the heat. Concentrated and crystalline deposits like essences act powerfully and present a great deal of resistance during the process of digestion as the particles are thickset and innumerable. In fresh vegetables this sugar and sweetness is imperceptible as it is evenly distributed along the whole uncontaminated fluid and other substances in the structure.

Grape sugar is naturally formed in fruits when they pass from the hard raw green stage to the soft ripe stage with yellow or red colour beautiful to look at. This process is only possible when the unripe fruit hangs from the tender stem that supports it. Through the action of sun's light the sour green fruit gradually attains maturity changing its green colour and acid smell and taste to a beautiful yellow and red colour with a nice sweet flavour. Even fruits are ripened by fruit-sellers by artificial heat, by shutting them in closed places with dry leaves or hay. In such cases though flavour and colour are attained to a certain degree they are not equal to the fruit that ripens and falls from the tree by itself. Most of the fruits become rotten in the process of artificial ripening. When left to nature all fruits mature and fall one by one till the last fruit is ripe and falls.

The theory of grape-sugar formation in the case of vegetables is inaccurate because no vegetable attains sweetness if it is allowed to remain on the tree to the last. In such cases most of the vegetables not only lose the little sweetness which they possess in the green stage but also form a hard shelly coating with fibrous matter containing detached hard seeds inside. Some vegetables become red and flabby and fall off from the tree, dropping hard seeds. This evidence is enough to show that vegetables are fit to be eaten only when they are green and tender and fruit when they are fully ripe. If heat is applied to live vegetables, they become a dead mass liable to fermentation Our readers should remember that the vitamin extracts and essences advertised by chemists have really no value as they are dead matter liable to fermentation. They should closely scrutinize these before they venture on the purchase of such stored drugs.

The full vitamin benefit is derived only when we eat food stuffs, fresh and uncooked.

The following chapters deal with the method of shifting men from the variegated cooked delicious dishes to the equally good, and delicious uncooked food combinations, gradually leading them to natural mono-diet. Readers need not be afraid that they should become austere ascetics and sages at the mention of mono-diet. As the body increases in efficiency, the consumption of food quantity gradually diminishes and hence change from cooked to uncooked food will itself automatically lead to the final goal. Those who desire an easy happy-going life may safely enjoy the combinations of uncooked vegetable food and maintain their vigorous health during their lives.

FOOD

Food is the main source of the supply of nutrition to the bodies of all living beings. The purpose of this nutrition is to enable the body to discharge its various functions, both voluntary and involuntary. As long as these duties are performed, it is immaterial in which way food is consumed. To understand the right way we have to observe living creatures leading a natural life. Just as an artist traces carefully the direction of each line, shade and light from the object placed and posed before him on a pedestal, an observer of nature should draw his inferences from the living volumes of the library before him. The volumes here are the bodies of all animals. The matter is their movements, habits, and other details which the observer can read for himself. The library is the whole universe before him. The reader is the observer himself. By constant and minute observation, one can realize for himself the dictates of the supreme Almighty or Nature, as he may prefer to call it. Such close observation reveals to us that all animals in nature consume the food procurable in nature without making any changes or combinations of them. The deduction from this is that man also should blindly copy the method adopted by animals. The result will be perfect happiness and bliss enjoyed by his fellow creature.

Again, all animals, whether they eat plants, meat, or fruit, take their food when it (food) has life. A cow which lives on grass bites a portion of the vigorous tender grass growing on a pasture land or on the side of a hill. A tiger catches its prey and sucks its life blood before the heart of the animal actually ceases to beat. A parrot perches on a stem and selects a ripe fruit, while the sap of the tree is being conveyed to it from the root through the trunk, the branch, and the slender stem supporting the fruit. In all these cases we understand the secret of the enjoyment of vigorous life and health of all those used for food.

The effects of this method of eating may now be examined. The food, as it enters the mouth automatically undergoes various changes by the secretions of the glands in the different parks of the alimentary canal. The nutrition is separated and finds its way to the minute cell structures and enlivens them- Similarly, the wastes from the minute cells in the remote and intricate parts of the body automatically find their way into their drainage channels, and finally reach the purifying blood that surrounds the lungs. By the action of respiration and the law of diffusion, the impurities that empty from the Superior Vena Gava are here burnt and scarlet blood is thrown into the Abrta by the strong muscular action of the heart. When we eat natural products full of living substances, a similar procesl of digestion and elimination results. As stated in the New Science of Healing the use of water or toilet paper for cleaning the anus after evacuation becomes superfluous in a few days after one resorts to the natural method of living.

The various food dishes of the different nations of the Globe consist of cereals, vegetables, diary products and flesh. Physiologists say that starches, proteids, carbohydrates, and fats are required for the building of tissues and the well-being of man. It is clear that all the required physiological substances are derived from the cereals, vegetables and fruits which form the dietary of Nations. Among the food grains soma are starchy and some are proteins. All grains such as rice, wheat, maize, cholam etc which can be boiled and cooked and which can be made into bread after being powdered are the main sources of starch, while all the pulse grains, such as Bengal gram, green gram and red gram etc., serve as sources for proteid supply in the body. Carbohydrates are derived from the cellular structure of the vegetables and fruits. Nuts supply fats to the human body. From dairy products and flesh of animals proteins and fats go to the human tissues. The required sugar passes to the human body from the fruits. In the succeeding paras it will be shown that dairy products and animal flesh are sources of deposit of foreign matter and consequent irritation and stimulation.

According to the structure and disposition of man, he is erect and is balanced on his two legs with his head topmost, supported on the spinal column which is attached to the pelvic girdle supported on the thigh bones. Both the arms swing from the ends of the shoulder hones attached to the back of the arms by means of muscles, the ribs sweep from the spinal column on the back to the breast flat bone in the front, making a peculiar conical cage for the support of the heart and lungs and main arteries. Of the two mechanisms the lungs may be called an air-pump and the heart a fluid pump. According to a recent writer the lungs are a pump and the heart a valve of that pump. Whatever it may be, a regular automatic pumping system is going on from the birth to the last breath of animal life on account of the air pressure outside.

The conical portion of the bony cage is upward and attached to the two cross-bones on each side with the breast flat bone in the middle. The feet and the lower legs suspend from the lower heads of the thigh bones. From the bony structure and the long bones of the fingers and from, the soft nails man is able only to collect fruits, seeds and other vegetable products. The arrangement of his teeth clearly shows that they are fit for cutting and tearing vegetable products only. Again, his long alimentary canal is an evidence of the slow process of digestion. The nails of all flesh eating animals are sharp, curved and hard. Their teeth are long, pointed at the top and broad below, quite contrary to the teeth of human beings. The digestive canal is very short and helps the rapid evacuation of the fleshy diet.

Now, if flesh is passed through the long alimentary tract of man, it decomposes and begins to ferment at every bend and pouch of the tract because flesh is dead matter and cannot be eaten without being cooked with various condimental combinations. All cooked matter committed to fire is a dead mass requires rapid elimination from the system. For this purpose the long alimentary tract is an, uncongenial for it to go through. For all the above reasons flesh is not a natural food for man.

Regarding milk, a close examination of the sucking of infants and babies of the mammal class reveals how milk should be drunk. As soon as the milk is milched from the udder of animals, infinite microscopic microbes are said to instantaneously infest the raw milk. Doctors recommend boiling to kill these minute micro-organisms. Along with the decay of the organisms the life particles in the milk also become dead, converting the whole quantity into a life-less substance liable to fermentation. During the process of sucking of infants the life particles and the corpuscles in the milk enter the alimentary tract without coming into contact with the outside air. The whole substance undergoes various digestive changes in the alimentary tract of the child and coincides completely with the living corpuscles and atoms in the blood of the infant. During this process the digestion will be complete and elimination automatic without any remnants.

In nature milk is only intended as food for the young of animals for a limited period only, i. e., till they are able to chew hard foods and digest them. This period varies with different animals. In the case of man it cannot be more than two, or three years, though in some exceptional cases a few children suck till they are seven years old. But the late sucking is a superfluity to the child due to the abnormal living of the child and the mother. It must be seen as to what happens when the milk of one animal is drunk by another. This is rarely the case in nature except in the case of man who can subdue and wield every other creature in the creation on account of his superior intellect. Apart from all scientific pronouncements a common sense scrutiny will show that the milk is only a changed form of the_ blood of that species.

The blood of an animal contains the substances conducive to the growth and building of the tissue structures of the animal. From the blood, the essence to form the foetus of that special animal is formed. It is clear that the substances in the milk of a particular animal are only useful for the special class of that young. For instance, in human milk all the substances that go to form the soft skin, soft nails, long hairs and other various peculiar tissues are in it, while animal milk supplies substances that go to form the thick skin, the hard and long horns, the short and bristly hair and the hard hoofs. If we try to rear the young of any animal with human milk, the awkwardness will be clearly seen. First of all, the quantity secreted from the human breast is quite insufficient for the young of any animal. Even supposing a large quantity is procured by collecting from a number of human mothers; the young of animals gradually famish and die. This is a clear proof that human milk cannot maintain the lives of young animals.

It must now be shown how man is thriving by milching, boiling, and drinking the milk of other animals. When man drinks the milk of other animals, it is clear that it is a hard and indigestible dose to the human stomach. Just as all indigestible substances are enshrouded in the mucous waste of the body which sticks up in the most narrow parts of the human alimentary, respiratory, land circulatory tracts and expelled from the system with great struggle and nervous expenditure. The phrase " Foreign matter" of Kuhne may safely be identified with the mucus in the system, which we link to the pulse-diagnosis in Ayurveda. Thus it is found that the milk of animals is not good to t£e human system but is an irritant which causes great friction, lessening the nervous energy in the human system. Man after becoming an adult or even after passing the stage of weaning abhors sucking from the breast or tasting human milk. There is no reason why he should like the secretion from the udders of lower animals.

The examination of this secretion clearly shows the wisdom of Nature's frugality. When the woman's menstrual periods cease along with the growth of the foetus, the formation of milk, which is the nutrition for the foetus, begins to tickle and accumulate in the mammary glands of the breast. Though milk is the nutrition to the foetus, it really contains the bodily wastes of the animal organism which are periodically thrown out from the body. It is a wonder how man who dislikes secretions, emanations, and wastes of his own body likes and consumes as food the detestable wastes of inferior animals. When a great amount of energy is required to expel the poisons and the wastes formed during tte process of digestion, tissue construction, and destruction in the human body itself, just conjecture how muck more additional nervous energy is required to drive off the animals' wastes and secretions in milk and fleshy food-stuffs consumed by man.

From all the above arguments it can be-gathered that milk is not only unfit to be in the human dietary but it is an item that should be entirely effaced from our menu and is an article to be avoided completely. When milk is said to contain bodily wastes in its composition, it can be conjectured how many more poisonous waste are in mutton and flesh. It is pronounced in a recent work that milk and eggs are sources for the formation of the mucus which sticks and clogs the entire tubular human system. When milk is tabooed as a food article even in the raw state, it is much more objectionable to use milk or dairy products obtained from boiling. Each time heat is applied, the remaining life particles are lost and more dead matter is formed. Thus both milk and flesh are unfit for human consumption for the reasons stated above.

After eliminating milk and flesh from the dietary, proper substances from natural foods -should be substituted in their place by substituting nutritious and strong foods such as nuts pulpy fruits and roots.

FOOD CHEMISTRY

Food is made up of chemicals that include primarily water, proteins, lipids, carbohydrates and minerals. The major components that are altered by processing include proteins, lipids and carbohydrates. The chemical nature of foods is important in two ways in respect to food processing:

- Food chemicals are altered by processing and these changes results in changes in the characteristics of the food and consumer acceptance of the product.
- Because of the lability of some food chemicals, the parameters used in food processing, such as temperature and shear, are limited to achieve minimal changes in the characteristics of the food and to maximize consumer acceptance.

Minimal processing results in the least change in the chemicals of food, provide the highest quality and result in foods with a very short shelf-life. As processing is performed to extent shelf-life (drying, canning), there is more chemical change and loss of perceived quality.

pH

The pH of foods (negative log of the hydrogen ion concentration) is important both in respect to the flavor, texture and food safety. The FDA generally regards foods with a pH of less than 4.6 to be of less concern from a microbiological view point.

Water

Water is an important component of foods, which influences textural properties and the extent to which the food may be subjected to microbial spoilage. Removing water through concentration, drying or freezing reduces the "free" water and prevents microbial growth.

Water activity is a measure of free (unbound) water available for chemical and biological activity.

A_w = vapour pressure of food product at a specified temperature vapour pressure of pure water

Generally bacterial require a water activity of >0.9 to growth and most yeasts and molds are inhibited by a water activity of <0.7. The FDA considers that a A_w <0.85 to control the outgrowth of pathogenic bacteria. It is well to remember that moisture migrates from high to low water activity. Materials that are water soluble are call hydrophilic and those that are not water soluble are called hydrophobic.

The three components of food that have the greatest effect on the characteristics of processed foods are lipids (fats and oils), carbohydrates (sugars, starches and gums) and proteins. In addition, minerals are important in that they modify the functional properties of proteins. Vitamins influence the process of foods because they may be lost through the action of heat, light or oxygen.

Lipids

May be classified as fats (solid at room temperature) or oils (liquid) at room temperature and contain a mixture of water insoluble components – the primary one being a triglyceride. A triglyceride contains 3 fatty acids that are esterified to the 3 hydroxy alcohol – glycerol. Fatty acids have the general formula:

R-COOH

with the R group containing carbon C and hydrogen H. If the carbon atoms are bond together with a single bond C-C, the compound is saturated. If the carbon atoms are bound together with a double bond C=C, the compound is unsaturated. Fatty acids that are unsaturated can react with oxygen to product undesirable off flavors.

Triglycerides that contain mostly unsaturated fatty acids are oils and triglycerides that contain mostly unsaturated fatty acids are fats. Generally oils, because of the higher level of unsaturated fatty acids will oxidize over time. Protection against oxidation can involved: a) use of antioxidants, b) free radical quenchers - oxygen scavengers and c) packing in light protective packages and/or oxygen free packaging. Hydrogenation (addition of hydrogen and removal of double bonds) is used to covert vegetable oils into semi-solid or solid fats to be used as ingredients in baked goods. These partially hydrogenated products are less susceptible to oxidation than the original oils.

Some lipids, such as phospholipids and mono- and di glycerides are used as emulsifiers. Phospholipids are normally occurring and have a phosphate and amine base substituted for one of the fatty acids. Mono- and di-glycerides are derived from triglycerides by the hydrolysis of the ester bond for one (mono-) or two (di) of the fatty acids diglyceride monoglyceride

Carbohydrates

The carbohydrates in foods are mixtures of carbon, hydrogen and oxygen and can be classified as: a) simple sugars and polysaccharides.

Simple Carbohydrates

Simple carbohydrates are water soluble and contribute to the sweetness of foods. There are two general types of carbohydrates : a) reducing and b) non-reducing. Examples of these are glucose (reducing) and sucrose (non-reducing). Reducing sugars contain a reactive aldehyde (CHO) group that is absence in non-reducing sugars. Thermal processing can cause reactions between reducing sugars and the amino-group of proteins, causing browning and altering flavors. This reaction is termed the Maillard reaction. Very high heat processing in a low water environment can cause carmelization (polymerization) of also results in a browning reaction.

Monosaccharides may have 6 carbons and are called hexoses or they may have 5 carbons and are called pentoses. Glucose (sometimes called dextrose), fructose and galactose are three common hexoses. Ribose and deoxyribose are two common pentoses. Two monosaccharides may be linked together to form a disaccharides. Sucrose is the most common disaccharide and is made of one molecule each of glucose and fructose. Sucrose is commonly referred to as sugar. Lactose is the major sugar in milk and is made up of one molecule of glucose and one of galactose. Maltose is a disaccharide made from two molecules of glucose. This linkage is formed by the removal of water(dehydration) and is broken by adding water back (hydrolysis)

Complex Carbohydrates

Cellulose is the most common polysaccharide and the major component of plant cell walls. Cellulose is a polymer of glucose molecules linked together by beta 1-4 linkages and cannot by digested by humans. Thus, cellulose is a major component of dietary fiber. Starch is also a polymer of glucose, but the glucose molecules are joined together by alpha 1-4 linkages that can be digested by humans. In plants, starch is an energy reserve. In animals, small amounts of energy are stored in liver and muscle as glycogen, a highly branched polymer of glucose. Pectin is a polymer of galcturonic acid and is not digested. In plants, pectin "cements" cells together. Polysaccharides may be added to foods for a variety of reasons.

Nutritionally, they are generally added to increase the dietary fiber content. Functionally, polysaccharides are added to thicken, form gels, bind water, and stabilize proteins. Starch is the most common polysaccharide added to food products. For some uses, starch may be chemically modified to improve stability or to alter its functional properties. Cellulose and cellulose derivatives are also added to a number of food products. The term, gum, is used describe some of the naturally occurring polysaccharides added to food.

Polysaccharides commonly added to foods include: Agar, Gum tragacanth , Algin, Locust bean (carob) gum , Carrageenan, Starch, Cellulose, Pectin, Guar gum, Xanthan gum , Gum arabic. These gums vary in the solubility in cold water and care must be taken to ensure that they are fully hydrated during food processing. Starches, commonly used as thickening agents in food, are plant storage polysaccharides the are either branched (amylopectin) or unbranched (amylose). The partial structure of amylopectin is shown below:

The proportion of the two starches varies from plant to plant and influences the processing of the foods in which starches are used, as well as the characteristics of the food. Starches with 100% amylopectin (waxy starch) create a pie filling like texture, are clear with a long texture and do not form films. Starches that have >20% amylose have a pudding like short texture, are cloudy and do form films. Regular starches require heating to replace the hydrogen bonds between starch molecules with starch-water bonds, which causes "gelatinization" and creates the thickening effect. Starches that are pre-gelatinized and dried are cold water soluble and are termed "instant" starches.

Proteins

Proteins are polymers of amino acids linked together through a peptide bond.. The shape and thus the function of a protein is determined by the sequence of its amino acids. Digestion of proteins produces amino acids, some of which are essential to the nutritional well being of the human.

Amino Acid - contain an amino group (-NH2) and an acid group (- COOH). There are twenty amino acids that are found in proteins.

Peptide Bond- A bond formed by the condensation of the amino group (-NH2) of one amino acid with the acid group (-COOH) of another amino acid resulting in the loss of water. Condensation Reactions - Removal of water (H2O) and formation of a bond. The reversal of this is hydrolysis which involves the addition of water. Peptide bonds are not easily broken. Mild thermal processing does not normally result in the breaking of peptide bonds to yield amino acids from proteins.

The Function of Protein in Foods Include:

Frequently the conditions used in processing are adjusted to optimize the effects of the processing on the proteins and subsequent characteristics of the food. In bread, for example, the brown crust is related to the Maillard reaction and the final structure of the bread is caused by the thermal gelation of the protein - gluten.

TRANSITIONARY DIET

To suit all men irrespective of age and sex food may be prepared by soaking wheat along with green or Bengal-gram in water for 24 hours and exposing it to air for 12 hours so as to make it sprout. During the process of sprouting water should be drained away through the meshes of a basket to which there should be no covering or lid. During sprouting and aeration the seeds should be placed under shade and not exposed to the action of sunlight. If summer heat is strong even while the seeds are under shade they must be often wetted by sprinkling water on them or the whole basket dipped in water and lifted up so that the whole quantity may be drenched and moistened. By "this process the sprouting seeds will be very soft and crispy for mastication. To make them softer still, they must be allowed to soak in 5 water for more than 24 hours. But if neglected long and left in water,, putrefaction begins and may emit bad odour.

In such a state they are not fit for eating. Bad smell is also given out if the seeds are covered during the process of sprouting. As sprouting seeds are very sweet, ants and other insects infest them and carry away the prepared food. Hence the whole basket containing these sprouting seeds should be protected by placing the basket on a stand in water. With these cautions the major portion of our uncooked food plate is ready.

Regarding measurements, wheat and grams should be mixed in the proportion of 3 to L The fist of every man is his own measure i. e., to say, three fistfuls of wheat and one fistful of either Bengal gram or Green gram will serve the purpose. The four fistfuls of the mixture when soaked and sprouted become two-fold in quantity, amounting almost to eight fistfuls. This quantity is sufficient for one individual for his morning and evening meals for two days, along with other fruits and curries. Out of the eight fistfuls of the soaked and sprouting seeds, if an individual takes two fistfuls out of them and mixes them 3 with half a cocoanut well scooped out and eats it along with three or four plantains and juicy fruit, one's hunger is quite satisfied.

Let us next explain the procedure in regard to the eating of this food. Put in your mouth a mouthful of the sprouting seeds mixed with cocoanut and bite a piece of plantain or any such soft pulpy fruit as papua, guava, sweet fresh sultanas, peaches etc., which are easily procurable in the place. At the close of tbe meal eat a juicy fruit such as an orange or a sweet lime, batavia or a mango.

For three or four days a few hours after a meal one may feel a sort of emptiness, hunger, or languor. To alleviate this feeling one may take a fruit or a tender and fresh vegetable and drink a little quantity of water as often as is required. If there is no hunger at the accustomed hour for food, one should postpone his meal till there is a keen demand for food.

Among vegetables, tomatoes, tender isnake gourds, ladies' fingers, cucumbers, etc., may be chosen. Pumpkins are equally good. After a week one gets accustomed to live on such diet and works as well as if he had taken his cooked meal.

Provided there is no mental uneasiness, nobody loses his weight or energy when this diet is taken. Any one can safely change his cooked diet for the above uncooked combination, all of a sudden, without any previous preparation.

As the whole creation is living on uncooked food, if man adopts also such similar food, nothing harmful or untoward will happen.

To begin anything new the start must generally begin from within. But to stimulate internal action, outward movements are necessary. In the case of starting a steam engine to move the machinery, steam is generated by filling the engine tank with water and placing burning coals under it. After this external action, steam is produced in the chambers of the engine which will move the piston attached to the fly-wheel of the engine. The internal and external actions are closely related. Similarly, in the living mechanism of man a similar correlative relation between his body and mind exists. In the commencement of a new thing a strong internal uplift in the shape of a determined resolution is necessary. To give strength to the mind, external means and environment must be created. After this co-operation of the mind and body, obstacles are easily overcome.

As there is such corresponding and close-relation between the body and the mind, the^ push must be given first with the stronger of the two. Then the other which is weaker of th& two gets strong and begins to co-operate harmoniously.

In the above uncooked food combinations^ cocoanut and wheat, Bengal and green grama only have been mentioned. But the reader need not be under the apprehension that these^ are the only food ingredients that should be used. In the place of cocoanuts any other nut variety which is available may be substituted. Similarly, grains may also be altered according to the convenience and facility of the-individual. The main thing to be remembered is that seeds, nuts, vegetables, or fruit should find a place in the menu.

As paddy which is extensively used as food cannot be consumed without its life being destroyed, it is not a fit article for natural food. When paddy is soaked and germinated it cannot be consumed wholesale together with the husk as in the case of wheat or other food grains. If an attempt is made to masticate the outer husk of the paddy-seedling, the tongue and the mucus membrane get ruptured and it will be impossible for the tongue to collect the masticated pulp into a ball and push it down the gullet of the alimentary canal through the narrow tonsils over the valve or lid (epiglottis) that forms a bridge over the bronchial tube. After such gulping if it is at all possible rough husk particles penetrate into and tear the tender mucus membrane causing haemorrhage either by vomit ting or by bowel evacuation. Paddy is only fit as a food article after it is husked and made into a powder for puddings or well washed for cooking purposes.

During the process of husking, the point that enables the seed to sprout is destroyed and hence rice is a dead body as opposed to the paddy seedlings with life. Paddy and other seedlings possess latent life-energy which can be converted into kinetic energy by soaking them and making them sprout into little plants. There are some religions which abhor taking things with life such as sprouting seeds* But the propounders of such religions entirely forget the laws of nature in which one with life is the prey of another. Even the eagle which appears to feast on carcasses and the decomposed flesh of animals does not always live on dead bodies. During the process of putrefaction of the carcass innumerable tiny worms generate before the raven gulps the flesh of the carcass. This is a clear proof of the raven's existence on live matter. The same analogy exists in the life of all animals in creation that subsist on foul food.

In the selection of food stuffs, every individual is at liberty to choose what he wants according to his circumstances, environments and facilities. Things that are cheap in one-place may be dear in another place and vice versa. Hence the poor need not be afraid of natural diet. It has already been pointed out that nutrition is available in each and every food ingredient For instance wheat is said to contain the required physiological substances, starch, proteid, carbohydrate, fat, salt etc. But the predominating substance in wheat is starch.

The other substances according to the tables of food experts vary in different gradations. To supply the excess and make up the deficiency of substances and to satisfy tastes, combinations of food ingredients are invented. In nature food stuffs are lodged one after another in the stomachs of animals. Till one food article is consumed, the second food stuff variety is not at hand. Before a second article is consumed the first article is almost digested and pushed out of the stomach bag of the animal. Hence in nature there is no combination system or the evils following such combinations. Nature always supports mono-diet and preaches its safety. This must be the ideal of a true health-seeker and health-preserver. Though all combinations whether cooked or uncooked are contrary to nature, cooked combinations are worse than uncooked ones as the former are already converted into dead matter by the action of fire.

We know that when a thing is gulped down the throat the discernment of taste vanishes. Taste is discernible only when the food pulp is pressed by the tongue against the palate above. It is quite undesirable that man should resort to unnatural methods merely for the sake of taste. After observing the methods of Nature, if man cannot exert his thought and common sense and alter his unnatural habits for the benefit and improvement of his health, his knowledge and civilization ate not worth while.

Except in the matter of physique and health man is advanced in every way. Physical culture experts recommend plain non-irritant and insipid articles of food though cooked. From this it is clear that all irritants and confectionery ore hindrances .to the progress and development of human health and athletic building.

The tongue and the nose which are natural gate-keepers do not allow hot, excessive, sour or bitter things to enter the system. It is only sweet and plain things that are liked most by the human tongue. It is only such things that are easy for digestion and assimilation. Among the food stuffs, oily substances as nuts and seeds are very valuable foods because they nourish the body and lubricate the system by appeasing the hunger of the individual. Oil-less food-stuffs, though bulky, cannot appease the hunger and enable the individual to work for a longer period. Oily substances remain long and hence enable the tissues to endure fatigue or a late meal.

A really healthy man never worries himself for a late meal like his fellow brother who-suffers from excessive bilious and acid secretions in his system and longs for the tinraly serving of dainty dishes. Though a poor man a healthy man enjoys it heartily whereas hisMte brother throws away most of his food, however good it might be. From this it can be learnt that stimulation and irritation of the slightest degree are bad for the natural healthy body. AH natural products such as grains, vegetables, fruits, nuts, and root-products (tubers) possess a good taste, refreshing and palatable, if they are chewed slowly. Even insipid vegetables and tubers form a delicious food when slowly chewed.

It is only in the process of cutting, drying, pounding, milling and cooking that most of the water and the natural salts are destroyed from the tender vegetables and other substances in which they exist in nature. To supply this deficiency and to give good taste, tamarind, ghee, coriander and other articles are added. Previously it has already been explained how cooked substances become dead matter and hinder normal digestion and deposit undigested matter in the bowels.

FOOD PROSPECTIVE OF INDIA

India is one of the world's major food producers but accounts for less than 1.5 per cent of international food trade. This indicates vast scope for both investors and exporters. Food exports in 1998 stood at US $5.8 billion whereas the world total was US $438 billion.

The Indian food industry's sales turnover is Rs 140,000 crore (1 crore = 10 million) annually as at the start of year 2000. The industry requires about Rs 29,000 crore in investment over the next five years to 2005 to create necessary infrastructure, expand production facilities and state-of-the-art-technology to match the international quality and standards.

The office of the Agricultural Affairs of the USDA / Foreign Agricultural Services in New Delhi says that one of India's proudest accomplishments has been achieving a tenuous self-sufficiency in food production and that the country produces a wide variety of agricultural products at prices that are at or below world values in most cases. The Indian palate is accustomed to traditional foods, mostly wheat and rice-based, rather than potato and corn-based western palate. In marketing perspective, this is considered an important factor for foreign marketers.

The USDA report says initially consumer-ready food products may have to be tailored to include Indian spices and traditional ingredients. In addition to traditional tastes, there are other social factors which affect consumption in India. Hindus account for approximately 80 per cent of India's population, and while only 25 or 30 per cent are strict vegetarians, beef slaughter is prohibited in all but two states (Kerala and West Bengal) and consumption of other meats is limited. Incidentally, India is the only country where the US-based MacDonalds sells its burgers without any beef content and even offers purely vegetarian burgers. India's middle class segment will hold the key to success or failure of the processed food market in India. Of the country's total population of one billion, the middle class segments account for about 350-370 million. Though a majority of families in this segment have non-working housewives or can afford hired domestic help and thus prepare foods of their taste in their own kitchens, the profile of the middle class is changing steadily and hired domestic help is becoming costlier. This is conducive to an expansion in demand for ready-to-eat Indian-style foods.

India's food processing sector covers fruit and vegetables; meat and poultry; milk and milk products, alcoholic beverages, fisheries, plantation, grain processing and other consumer product groups like confectionery, chocolates and cocoa products, Soya-based products, mineral water, high protein foods etc. According to latest official statistics, India exported processed fruits and vegetables worth Rs 5240 million in 1997-98. The horticulture production is around 102 million tonnes. Foreign investment since 1991, when economic liberalisation started, stood at Rs 8,800 crore. Products that have growing demand, especially in the Middle East countries include pickles, chutneys, fruit pulps, canned fruits, and vegetables, concentrated pulps and juices, dehydrated vegetables and frozen fruits and vegetables.

Another potential processed food product is meat and poultry products. India ranks first in world cattle population, 50 per cent of buffalo population and one-sixth of total goat population of the world. Buffalo meat is surplus in India. There is vast scope to set up modern slaughter facilities and cold store chains in meat and poultry processing sector. India's current level of meat and meat-based exports is around Rs 8,000 million. In last six years foreign investment in this segment stood at Rs 5,000 million which is more than 50 per cent of the total investment made in this sector.

Compared with meat, poultry industry has registered significant growth. India ranks fifth in the world with annual egg production of 1.61 million tones. Both poultry and egg processing units have come in a very big way in the country. India is exporting egg powder, frozen egg yolk and albumin powder to Europe, Japan and other countries. Poultry exports are mostly to Maldives and Oman. Indian poultry meat products have good markets in Japan, Malaysia, Indonesia and Singapore. While meat products registered a growth of 10 per cent, eggs and broilers registered 16-20 per cent growth. There are about 15 pure line and grand parent franchise projects in India. There are 115 layer and 280 broiler hatcheries producing 1.3 million layer parents and 280 million broiler parents. They in turn supply 95 million hybrid layer and 275 million broilers, day-old chick. Presently there are only five egg powder plants in India which is considered insufficient in view of growing export demand for different kind of powder - whole egg, yolk and albumen. The scope of foreign investment and state-of-the-art technology in this field is therefore tremendous.

Milk and milk products is rated as one of the most promising sectors which deserves foreign investment in a big way. When the world milk production registered a negative growth of 2 per cent , India performed much better with 4 per cent growth. The total milk production is around 72 million tonnes and the demand for milk is estimated at around 80 million tonnes. By 2005, the value of Indian dairy produce is expected to be Rs 1,000,000 million. In last six years foreign investment in this sector stood at Rs 3600 million which is about one-forth of total investment made in this sector. Manufacture of casein and lactose, largely being imported presently, has good scope. Exports of milk products have been decanalised.

Grains could emerge as a major export earner for India in coming years. India's food grains production is now at around 225-230 million tones. These include rice, jawar, bajra, maize, wheat, gram and pulses. Indian basmati rice enjoys command in the international market. Besides growing Middle east market for basmati rive, many other countries are showing interest for this food grain. In 1998-99 export of basmati and non-basmati rice stood at Rs62000 million. There is a total rice milling capacity of 186 million tones in the country. Among plantation, tea emerged as major foreign exchange earner. India is the largest producer and exporter of black tea. However, the most worrying factor for Indian tea industry is that from early next year with the implementation of tea imports into the country, India tea may face a stiff competition within the country as well, specially threat of Sri Lanka's presence in the Indian market is looming large.

The current year's tea export prospect is not that very good in terms of forex earnings because international prices has fallen significantly this year . India exports between 150-170 million kilogram's of tea per annum. Of course, the scope of foreign investment in this sector is good and the multinational tea companies would either be trying for marketing joint ventures with the Indian producers or acquire stakes in Indian tea companies. There is strong possibilities of third country exports through such joint venture as quality wise still Indian teas are ruling the international market. Alcoholic beverages is another are where India witnessed substantial foreign investment. Foreign investment in this sector stood at Rs 7000 million which about 70 percent of the total investment made so far. The IMFL (Indian Made Foreign Liquor) primarily comprises wine, vodka, gin, whisky, rum and brandy. Draught beer is a comparatively recent introduction in the Indian market. The Indian beer market is estimated at Rs7000 million a year. One of the major advantages for any investor eyeing the Indian liquor market is that India offers enough raw materials like molasses, barely, maize, potatoes, grapes, yeast and hops for the industry.

Yet another catchy investment sector is fisheries. There is growing canned and processed fishes from India. The marine fish include prawns, shrimps, tuna, cuttlefish, squids, octopus, red snappers, ribbon fish, mackerel, lobsters, cat fish etc. In last six years there was substantial investment in fisheries to the tune of Rs 30,000 million of which foreign investments were of the order of Rs 7000 million. The potential could be gauged by the fact that against fish production potential in the Exclusive Economic Zone of 3.9 million tones, actual catch is to the tune of 2.87 million tones. Harvesting from inland sources is around 2.7 million tones. The biggest bottleneck in expanding the food processing sector, in terms of both investment and exports, is lack of adequate infrastructure. Without a strong and dependable cold chain vital sector like food processing industry which is based mostly on perishable products cannot survive and grow. Even at current level of production, farm produce valued at Rs 70,000 million is being wasted every year only because there is no adequate storage, transportation, cold chain facilities and other infrastructure supports. Cold chain facilities are miserably inadequate to meet the increasing production of various perishable products like milk, fruits, vegetables, poultry, fisheries etc. Prevention of Food Adulteration laws is not only stringent one but time consuming also. It is considered as an archaic and no industry friendly food law. It substantial varies from Codex standard. Harmonization of multiple food laws is an urgent necessity.

Many of India's food-processing companies are known to be keen to import intermediate food products. As India's food-processing industry grows and becomes more sophisticated, there is no doubt that the market for intermediate food products and ingredients will grow. It is important that you, or your agents in India, ensure that intermediate food products are considered by customs officials as industrial intermediates and not as consumer products to minimise customs duty. Though law looks at intermediate food products as industrial intermediates, there have been reports that uninformed customs officials have treated them as consumer products.

Selection of Food

The concept of safe and wholesome food encompasses many diverse elements. From a nutritional aspect, it is food that contains the nutrients humans need and that helps prevent long-term chronic disease, promoting health into old age. From a food safety aspect, it is food that is free not only from toxins, pesticides, and chemical and physical contaminants, but also from microbiological pathogens such as bacteria and viruses that can cause illness.

While America's food supply is among the safest in the world, there are still numerous threats to the safety of the food supply. Some of these threats have been around since ancient times, while others are newer, the result of changing lifestyles, production practices, and even evolution of microorganisms themselves. Ensuring the safety of food is a shared responsibility among producers, industry, government, and consumers.

A major focus of this chapter is microbial food borne illness, a widespread, but often unrecognized, sickness that affects most people at one time or another. It is caused by eating food that is contaminated with pathogens such as bacteria, viruses, or parasites. At least four factors are necessary for food borne illness to occur: (1) a pathogen; (2) a food vehicle; (3) conditions that allow the pathogen to survive, reproduce, or produce a toxin; and (4) a susceptible person who ingests enough of the pathogen or its toxin to cause illness. The symptoms often are similar to those associated with the flu-nausea, vomiting, diarrhea, abdominal pain, fever, and headache.

Most people have experienced food borne illness, even though they might not recognize it as such, instead blaming it on the "stomach flu" or "24-hour bug." Symptoms usually disappear within a few days, but in some cases there can be more long-lasting effects such as joint inflammation or kidney failure. In the most severe cases people die from food borne illness. Every year more than 5,000 Americans die from eating contaminated food. It is difficult to trace a bout of food borne illness back to a particular food because illness can occur anywhere from an hour to several days, or even weeks, after eating the contaminated food. Epidemiologists faced with tracing a food borne illness outbreak may have to interview dozens of people, asking them to recall everything they ate for the past week. It is difficult for people to remember everything they ate yesterday, much less one week ago. Further complicating the picture is that one person may eat the contaminated food and not become ill, while someone else in a higher-risk group does. In 81 percent of food borne illnesses the cause remains unknown.

Additives

The use of food additives dates back to ancient times. Examples of these early additives are salt to preserve meats and fish, herbs and spices for seasoning foods, sugar to preserve fruits, and vinegar to preserve vegetables. Today manufacturers use more than 3,000 food additives. A commonly used definitition of a food additive is any substance added to a food either directly or indirectly through production, processing, storing, or packaging. Food additives serve a number of functions:

Preservatives to keep food fresh and to prevent spoilage. This is important, as in our modern lifestyle food is rarely eaten at the time or place it is produced. Calcium propionate inhibits molds and is often added to bread products for this purpose.

Nutrients to improve or maintain the nutritional quality of foods. Most salt contains iodine to prevent goiter, a condition resulting from iodine deficiency. Processing aids to maintain product texture such as retaining moisture, preventing lumping, or adding stability. Powdered foods such as cocoa contain silicon dioxide to prevent clumping when water is added.

Flavours to enhance or change the taste or aroma of a food. These include spices, herbs, flavor enhancers, natural and synthetic flavors, and sweeteners. Colours to give foods an appealing look. Many of the colours we associate with foods are from added colourings, such as caramel to make cola drinks brown and annatto to make margarine yellow.

Food additives are derived from naturally occurring and synthetic materials. Scientists can now synthesize in the labouratory many additives that used to be derived from natural substances, creating a larger and cheaper supply. Americans consume from 140 to 150 pounds of additives a year, mostly due to additives such as sugar, corn sweeteners, salt, pepper, vegetable colours, yeast, and baking soda. Food additives allow us to enjoy safe, wholesome, tasty foods year-round without the inconvenience of growing our own foods or shopping daily. Convenience foods are made possible by the use of food additives.

FDA approves all food additives before they can be added to foods. USDA authorizes additives used in meat and poultry products. Before manufacturers may use an additive, they must prove that the additive does what it was intended to do and that it will not be harmful to humans at the expected level of consumption. Two groups of additives are not subject to FDA's strict approval process—those that are prior sanctioned and those that are generally recognized as safe (GRAS). Prior sanctioned substances were already approved by FDA before the 1958 Food Additives Amendment to the Food, Drug and Cosmetic Act.

GRAS substances, including salt, sugar, spices, and vitamins, have been used extensively in the past with no known harmful effects, and therefore experts believe them to be safe. FDA may also label an additive as GRAS based on scientific evidence that it is safe. FDA and USDA continue to monitor prior sanctioned and GRAS substances to ensure that they really are safe as new evidence emerges. In addition, FDA operates the Adverse Reaction Monitoring System (ARMS) to investigate all complaints related to specific foods, food and colour additives, or vitamin and mineral supplements.

While the overwhelming majority of additives are safe for all people, small segments of the population are sensitive to some. Sulfites are an example of this; they cause hives, nausea, shortness of breath, or shock in some people. For this reason, in 1986 FDA banned the use of sulfites on fresh fruits and vegetables, such as in salad bars where they were used to keep lettuce and other produce looking fresh. Product labels must list sulfites if they are added. In the 1970s it was thought by some individuals that additives may contribute to childhood hyperactivity, but studies conducted since then have found no link.

Chapter 5

Food and Drugs

DRUGS, HORMONES AND ANTIBIOTICS

The use of drugs to control and treat animal disease, and of hormones to promote faster, more efficient growth of livestock is a common practice. An estimated 80 percent of U.S. livestock and poultry receive some animal drugs during their lifetime. This includes topical antiseptics, bactericides, and fungicides to treat skin or hoof infections and cuts; hormones and hormone-like substances to improve growth; antiparasite drugs; and antibiotics. Improper use of animal drugs may cause residues in the edible tissues of slaughtered animals that could be hazardous to consumers. Before a new animal drug can be marketed in the United States, the FDA Center for Veterinary Medicine (CVM) must approve it on the basis of quality, safety, and efficacy. When the drug is for use in food-producing animals, not only must animal drug manufacturers prove that the drug is safe for the animal, but also that the food products derived from the treated animals are safe for human consumption. FDA establishes tolerances to include a safety factor to assure that the drug will have no harmful effects on consumers of the food product. FDA and USDA work together to monitor the use of animal drugs, identify improper use, and take enforcement action if necessary.

There are two issues of concern related to the use of drugs in food animals. The first is the presence of drug residues in meat or milk obtained from an animal that has been given an animal drug. Some of these residues may be allergenic, toxic, or carcinogenic to humans in large enough doses. According to the National Research Council's (NRC) 1999 report, The Use of Drugs in Food Animals: Benefits and Risks, FDA programmes monitoring drug residues in animals are effective in protecting consumers from this danger. Because very few illegal drug residues are detected in meat, milk, or eggs, the health risk posed by drug residues is minimal.

Many food safety experts consider the second problem, antibiotic drug residues in farm animals, to be a problem of larger concern. Antibiotics for farm animals have two purposes. First, they are used to prevent and treat diseases, just as they are in humans. The second reason for administering antibiotics to farm animals is to improve growth and to promote feed efficiency—the production of more meat or milk with less input of feed. This is called a subtherapeutic dose, since it is given in doses lower than those required to treat an infection. Subtherapeutic use of antibiotics controls intestinal bacteria that interfere with an animal's ability to absorb nutrients. It also controls infections before they become noticeable, thus making animals healthier and allowing them to use nutrients for growth and production rather than to fight infections. Antibiotic use is one reason why the U.S. food supply is so abundant and affordable.

Bacteria will inevitably become resistant to the antibiotics used to kill them. This is because antibiotics do not generally kill 100 percent of their target bacteria. A few will always survive and pass that resistance on to successive generations of bacteria, and in some cases, to other unrelated bacteria. Eventually the genetic make-up of the bacterial strain changes enough so that the drug is no longer effective. This happens with human pathogens such as tuberculosis, as well as with pathogens that infect animals. The most common cause of antibiotic resistance is overuse of antibiotics. Most animal bacterial diseases cannot be passed on to humans, but there are notable exceptions—Campylobacter and Salmonella. Already these two bacteria have developed resistance to some drugs, particularly the fluoroquinolones, used to combat them.

There is some evidence of a relationship between the use of fluoroquinolone drugs in poultry and other food-producing animals and the emergence of fluoroquinolone-resistant Campylobacter and Salmonella in humans (WHO 1998).

The possibility exists that as pathogens in farm animals become resistant to antibiotics, if those same pathogens are passed on to humans, they will not respond to drug treatments. The NRC report states that there is a link between the use of antibiotics in food animals, the development of resistant microorganisms in those animals, and the spread of those resistant pathogens to humans. However, the report goes on to say that the incidence of this happening is very low, and that there are not enough data to determine whether the incidence is changing. The report concludes that alternatives to antibiotic use for maintaining animal health and productivity should be developed. The National Antimicrobial Resistance Monitoring System (NARMS), established in January 1996 as a collabourative effort among FDA, USDA, and the Centers for Disease Control and Prevention (CDC), seeks to gather more data on antimicrobial resistance to clarify the potential risks.

Food Allergens

Up to 6 percent of children and 2 percent of adults suffer from food allergy-the body's immune system reacting to certain substances in food, usually a protein. The immune system misinterprets a chemical component of a food as harmful and releases histamines and other chemicals to combat it, which results in hives, swelling, itching, vomiting, diarrhea, cramps, or difficulty breathing. Severe reactions may cause anaphylaxis, which can result in death. Eight foods—egg, wheat, peanuts, milk, soy, tree nuts (such as walnuts and almonds), fish, and shellfish—cause 90 percent of all food allergies. The only way to prevent an allergic reaction is to avoid that food entirely.

Food intolerance often is confused with food allergy since the symptoms are often the same. Food intolerance is an adverse reaction to a food that does not involve the immune system. Lactose intolerance is an example of food intolerance. A person with lactose intolerance lacks an enzyme needed to digest a form of sugar present in milk. Consuming milk products causes symptoms such as gas, bloating, and abdominal pain, but does not involve any immune system response. If a person has a true allergy to milk, the only way to avoid milk allergy symptoms is to avoid all milk products entirely. Special drops or tablets that help digest the sugar in milk are available for those suffering from lactose intolerance, allowing them to consume milk products.

To avoid substances to which they are allergic, consumers must know exactly what is in foods. The Food, Drug and Cosmetic Act requires a complete listing of food ingredients on food labels. Many food products are recalled due to improper food labeling, such as ice cream with a label omitting peanuts, or processed foods that do not declare soy products as an ingredient. Common food allergens can also show up in restaurant foods in unexpected places, for example, peanut butter in Asian noodles or egg products in meatballs.

Recent cases of students who suffered allergy attacks from peanuts have prompted school officials to ban peanut products from some school cafeterias. This is a difficult task, as not only would this outlaw the popular peanut butter and jelly sandwich, but also any snacks or candies that contain peanuts. While it may be possible to control which foods are sold in schools, it is almost impossible to regulate foods students bring from home. Educating students who have food allergies to read carefully food ingredient labels and not to accept foods if they do not know what the ingredients are is key to reducing food allergy attacks.

Toxins

In addition to synthetic chemicals such as pesticides, the food supply contains many naturally occurring toxins. In comparison to synthetic chemicals, scientists know very little about these natural toxins in terms of their toxicity and quantity in foods. They pose a greater risk than the synthetic chemicals because we eat at least 10,000 times more of them. Every food is a complex mixture of chemical compounds, some beneficial such as vitamins and minerals, but also some that are harmful. Even vitamins and minerals can be toxic if taken in great enough quantities. For example, vitamin A, a necessary vitamin, may be toxic in an amount only 15 times the recommended dietary allowance. Plants and animals developed toxic substances as protection against insects, microorganisms, grazing animals, and other potential dangers.

One of America's most loved foods, the potato, contains a very toxic substance called solanine. This naturally occurring toxin is present in larger amounts in the peel and in the eyes than in the potato. In the amounts normally eaten, solanine does not cause illness, but a diet of certain varieties of potato peels and eyes might contain enough solanine to cause illness and possibly even death. Solanine acts as a natural pesticide that protects the potato from the Colourado beetle, the leaf hopper, and other potato pests. In another instance, herbal teas are enjoying a renewed popularity in the United States. Consumers view these teas as a natural way of improving their health or treating diseases. However, chemicals in herbal teas can and have caused illness and death. Herbal teas are touted as the answer to many chronic ailments and as such are consumed at much higher levels than they were traditionally, which may lead to natural, but still harmful, side effects.

In societies where herbal use is steeped in tradition, knowledge about the benefits and dangers of herbal remedies passes from generation to generation. Very few of the herbs used in natural herbal teas have been studied or tested for safety. One of these is ephedra, commonly known as Ma Huang, an ingredient in many herbal teas marketed as weight loss products. Ephedra is an amphetamine-like compound with potentially powerful stimulant effects on the nervous system and heart. More than 800 adverse events associated with the use of ephedrine-containing products have been reported to the Food and Drug Administration. These range from episodes of high blood pressure, heart rate irregularities, insomnia, nervousness, tremors and headaches to seizures, heart attacks, strokes, and death. People who shun prescription drugs as unnatural or too strong with too many side effects may think nothing of drinking herbal teas, some of which can provoke very strong drug-like reactions and adverse effects in the body.

Seafood products contain some naturally occurring marine toxins that present unique food hazards. Molluscan shellfish, which includes oysters, clams, scallops, and mussels, can pick up toxins from algae that they feed on, and cause paralytic shellfish poisoning (PSP), neurotoxic shellfish poisoning (NSP), amnesic shellfish poisoning, and diarrhetic shellfish poisoning (DSP). The most serious is PSP, with symptoms ranging from tingling, burning, or numbness in the mouth or throat to paralysis, respiratory failure, and in severe cases, death. The algae that produce these toxins can be found during the warmer months anywhere. State authorities monitor harvest waters and close them to shellfish harvesting if algae is present. Since these toxins are not destroyed by heat, and can't be detected visually, the best control is for people to consume shellfish only from approved waters.

Tropical and subtropical reef fish such as grouper, barracuda, snappers, jacks, and king mackerel can accumulate ciguatera toxin by feeding on smaller fish that have ingested toxin-forming algae. Ciguatera can cause nausea, vomiting, diarrhea, and headaches in humans. Tuna, mahi mahi, bluefish, and mackerel have been the sources of scromboid poisoning, a type of foodborne illness caused by the consumption of scombroid and scombroid-like marine fish species that have begun to spoil.

This occurs when the amino acid histidine breaks down into histamine, usually as a result of inadequate refrigeration. Scromboid symptoms include a rash, burning or peppery taste sensations about the mouth and throat, dizziness, nausea, headache, itching, and swelling of the tongue. Puffer fish, known as fugu in Japan, is a great and dangerous delicacy in that country. An extremely toxic poison called tetrodotoxin accumulates in the internal organs of the fish. Only specially trained and licensed chefs are allowed to prepare fugu fish, as improperly prepared fugu causes paralysis, respiratory failure, convulsions, and cardiac arrhythmia within 20 minutes. Death is not uncommon.

Fungi, which include mushrooms and molds, also produce toxins that are harmful to humans. Molds produce toxins called mycotoxins, with the major mycotoxin-producing molds being Aspergillus, Fusarium, and Claviceps species. Molds usually grow on damp cereal grains such as rye, wheat, corn, rice, barley, and oats, or oilseeds (peanuts), and then excrete their mycotoxins during their life cycle. Most of these mycotoxins are very resistant to heat, so cooking does not reduce their harmfulness. The only way to prevent intoxication is by preventing the mold from contaminating the product during harvesting, drying, storage, and processing.

One mold in particular, Claviceps purpurea, has been implicated in a number of historical events. Eating rye and other cereal grains contaminated with Claviceps purpurea results in the disease ergotism. This disease was first recorded in 857 in the Rhine Valley and has been recorded numerous times since, sometimes affecting up to 40,000 individuals at once. Rye is particularly susceptible to ergot contamination. Cold and damp growing or storage conditions also promote the formation of ergot. Ergot is the source of lysergic acid diethylamide (LSD); it and many other ergot derivatives are hallucinogens. The symptoms of ergotism are varied, but include central nervous system disorders such as muscle spasms, confusions, delusions, convulsive fits, hallucinations, visions, sensations of flying through the air, and psychosis. Other common symptoms are a prickly sensation in the limbs, feelings of intense alternating heat and cold, and increased appetite between episodes of fits. Linnda Caporael and Mary K. Matossian propose that the witch trials of 1692 in Salem, Massachusetts, could very well have been the result of ergot poisoning.

They link the weather, crop, and economic conditions from the years 1691 and 1692 to an increased consumption of bread made from rye that could have been contaminated with ergot. The symptoms exhibited by those accused of being bewitched are suspiciously similar to the symptoms of ergotism. In another interesting footnote to history, Peter the Great had to cancel his plans to attack the Ottoman Empire in 1722 because his troops and their horses consumed rye contaminated with ergot, which caused hundreds either to die or go mad.

Fortunately the body has a very efficient mechanism to destroy many naturally and synthetic chemicals—the liver. The liver is capable of eliminating small quantities of many poisons, which allows humans to safely consume otherwise toxic chemicals. However, large quantities of toxins and chemicals can easily overwhelm the body's defenses. We often think of naturally occurring compounds as relatively safe, but in reality some are among the most toxic substances known.

Pesticides

Pesticides prevent, destroy, or control pests. Pests are any organism that causes damage to plants, animals, or foods, such as bacteria, viruses, rodents, worms, fungi, insects, or weeds. The term pesticide is very broad and includes herbicides (to control weeds), insecticides (to control insects), fungicides (to control mold, mildew, and fungi), rodenticides (to control rodents), and disinfectants (to control bacteria and viruses). Three-quarters of the pesticide use is for agriculture (mainly on crops in the field), but it is also used post-harvest during transportation and storage to prevent mold growth or insect infestation. While we may not think of household cleaners, pet flea collars, lawn and garden products, and insect repellants as pesticides, they are. About 350 pesticides are used on the foods we eat, and to protect our homes and pets.

Since the beginnings of agriculture humankind has used pesticides in an attempt to control nature to ensure good crop yield. Egyptian records from 1500 B.C.E. contain instructions for preparing insecticides to control lice, fleas, and wasps. The

Greeks were using sulfur by 1000 B.C.E. to control insects, as did European farmers in the eighteenth century. The Chinese controlled insects with a mixture of arsenic and water. In 1865 farmers discovered Paris green, a mixture of copper and arsenic, as a way to control the Colourado potato beetle. A similar substance called Bordeaux mixture saved the grape industry in France from a fungal disease in the 1880s. While we may think of pesticides as synthetic chemicals, the above examples show that many natural compounds also act as pesticides. The first synthetic insecticides and herbicides were produced in the early 1900s. Currently federal pesticide law registers 21,000 pesticide products and 860 active ingredients.

Pesticide use has both advantages and disadvantages. In comparison with other nations, the United States has an abundant and affordable food supply. American consumers spend only about 11 percent of their income on food, less than consumers in any other country. One reason for this abundance and low cost is improved crop yields, much of which is due to pesticide use.

1850 each farmer in the United States produced enough food and fiber for four people; by 1990 that number grew to 79. The American diet consists of more fruits and vegetables in part because of this increased harvest, which leads to an improvement in public health. Experts agree that the benefits from eating a diet rich in fruits and vegetables far outweigh the potential risks from pesticides. Even with modern methods of pest control, U.S. farmers still lose from 25 to 30 percent of their crop to pests. Globally pests destroy up to 45 percent of the world's crops. In addition to the benefit of increased yield, pesticide use in the United States satisfies the consumer's demand for uncontaminated and unblemished food.

But pesticides can be dangerous to human health and to the environment. Most pesticides break down quickly in the environment, but some may still be present years later, sometimes at a great distance from their original application. Pesticides sprayed on plants can move through the air and end up in the soil or water. Pesticides applied to the soil may end up in rivers and lakes or move down through the soil to contaminate ground water. As an example, DDT, which the United States banned from use more than 20 years ago, is still showing up in the Great Lakes ecosystem, presumably through rainfall and dust from countries that still use it.

In addition to being potentially risky, pesticides are expensive. Farmers today are reducing pesticide use in several ways. Many farmers are turning to integrated pest management (IPM) techniques to reduce the need for pesticides. Examples of IPM include using ladybugs or other "good bugs" to destroy unwanted insects, adjusting planting times to avoid pest infestations, disrupting insect reproduction cycles, and destroying areas where pests breed and live. Although pesticides are still used in conjunction with many IPM techniques, the amount used is less. In 1993 the federal government set a national goal that 75 percent of all farms in the United States use IPM techniques by the year 2000. Researchers are also using biotechnology to develop crops that are more resistant to insects and viruses, which reduces the need to apply insecticides.

Exotic Chemicals within Food

The work of Dr. Henry Delincee and Beatrice-Luise Pool Zobel is often cited regarding the unknown cancer risk of radiolytic byproducts such as 2-dodecylcyclobutanone or 2DCB as a source of concern. On several occasions has Dr. Delincee clarified that he does not agree with the interpretation of such citations. Furthermore it has been established by the World Health Organization that sufficient research has been conducted to conclude that "based on the current scientific evidence, including the long-term feeding studies, 2-DCB and 2-alkylcyclobutanones in general do not appear to pose a health risk to consumers." Lastly any specific findings are specific to foods that contain triglycerides (the main constituent of vegetable oil and animal fats) excluding many foods commonly irradiated from such concerns altogether. FDA has asked for repeated and conclusive testing of mutagenicity of 2DCBs in irradiated meat. An October 2005 study concluded that "No 2-DCB induced mutagenesis was observed in any of the test systems, both with and without exogenous metabolic activation" confirming previous findings.

CHEMICAL STERILIZATION

Sterilization is the elimination of all transmissible agents (such as bacteria, prions and viruses) from a surface, a piece of equipment, food or biological culture medium. This is different from disinfection, where only organisms that can cause disease are removed by a disinfectant. In general, any instrument that enters an already sterile part of the body (such as the blood, or beneath the skin) should be sterilized. This includes equipment like scalpels, hypodermic needles and artificial pacemakers. This is also essential in the manufacture of many sterile pharmaceuticals.

Heat sterilization is known to have been in used in Ancient Rome, but it mostly disappeared throughout the Middle Ages where sanitation was not usually a concern. The preferred principle for sterilization is through heat. There are also chemical methods of sterilization.

Autoclaves

A widely-used method for heat sterilization is the autoclave. Autoclaves commonly use steam heated to 121°C (250°F), at 103 kPa (15 psi) above atmospheric pressure, for 15 minutes. The steam and pressure transfer sufficient heat into organisms to kill them. Proper autoclave treatment will inactivate all fungi, bacteria, viruses and also bacterial spores, which can be quite resistant. It will not necessarily eliminate all prions (discussed later).

To ensure the autoclaving process was able to cause sterilization, most autoclaves have meters and charts that record or display pertinent information such as temperature and pressure as a function of times. Indicator tape is often taped onto packages of products to be autoclaved. The tape contains a chemical that will change colour when the appropriate conditions have been met. Some types of packaging have built-in indicators on them.

Biological indicators ("bioindicators") can also be used to independently confirm autoclave performance. Several simple bioindicator devices are commercially available based on microbial spores. Most contain pure strains of the heat resistant microbe Geobacillus stearothermophilus which are among the toughest organisms an autoclave will have to destroy (such as the Attests). Several of these devices have a self-contained growth medium (with or separate to the spores) and a growth indicator.

After a run in an autoclave, the internal glass in the Attest vial is shattered, allowing the spores into a differential liquid medium. If the autoclave destroyed the spores, the medium will remain a blue colour. If autoclaving was unsuccessful the G. sterothermophilus will metabolize, causing a yellow colour change after two days of incubation at 56°C (132°F). For effective autoclaving, the steam needs to be able to penetrate everywhere. For this reason, an autoclave must not be overcrowded, and the lids of bottles and containers must be ajar. Indicators should be placed in the most difficult place sterilization is wanted; for instance, if you are sterilizing the contents of universals (a type of small glass jar), the Attest vial should be placed in a universal, to ensure that steam actually penetrates these areas.

For autoclaving, as for all disinfection of sterilization methods, the cleaning off of any biological material is also critical. Biological matter or any grime may shield organisms from the property intended to kill them, whether it physical or chemical. Cleaning can also remove a large number of organisms at once. Proper cleaning can be achieved by physical scrubbing to remove dirt; this should be done with detergent and warm water to get the best results.

Manual cleaning works through agitation, where the organisms are literally brushed off using detergent. When manual cleaning instruments or utensils that have organic matter on them, cool water must be used because warm or hot water may cause organic debris to coagulate. Where it is not feasible, ultrasound or pulsed air can be used to remove debris. Ultrasound works by a process called cavitation, in which sound waves are pulsed through a water/detergent medium, causing tiny bubbles to form. When these bubbles become unstable, they implode, causing organic debis to be pulled off. Ultrasonic machines must be used with the lid in the closed position because of the creation of aerosols which can be harmful to the operator. Note that the common methods of cooking food do not sterilize food - they simply reduce the number of disease-causing micro-organisms to a level that is not dangerous for people with normal digestive and immune systems.

Chemical Sterilization

Chemicals are also used for sterilization. Although heating provides the most effective way to rid an object of all transmissible agents, it is not always appropriate, because it destroys objects such as most fiber optics, most electronics, and some plastics.

Ethylene oxide (EO) gas is commonly used to sterilize objects that cannot survive temperatures greater than 60°C such as plastics, optics and electrics. Ethylene oxide treatment is generally carried out between 30°C and 60°C with relative humidity above 30% and a gas concentration between 200mg/l and 800mg/l for at least 3 hours. Ethylene oxide penetrates very well, moving through paper, cloth, and some plastic films and is highly effective. Ethylene oxide however is highly flammable, and requires a longer time to sterilize than any heat treatment. The process also requires time for aeration post sterilization to remove toxic residues. Ethylene oxide is widely used and sterilizes around 50% of all disposable medical devices.

A rapid biological indicator is available for use in EO sterilizers. This indicator contains Bacillus subtilis, which is a very resistant organism. If sterilization fails, incubation at 37°C will cause a fluorescent change within four hours, which is read by an auto-reader. After 96 hours, a visible colour change will occur. The fluorescence is emitted when a particular (EO resistant) enzyme is present, which means that spores are still active. The colour change is brought on by a pH shift due to bacterial metabolism. The test is suitable for most types of ethylene oxide cycles. The rapid results mean that if a cycle was found to be ineffective, the objects treated can be quarantined and physicians quickly advised of possible contamination.

Ozone is used in industrial settings to sterilize water and air, as well as a disinfectant for surfaces. It has the benefit of being able to oxidize most organic matter. On the other hand, it is a toxic and unstable gas that must be produced on-site, so it is not practical to use in many settings. Bleach is another accepted liquid sterilizing agent. Household bleach, also used in hospitals and biological research labouratories, consists of 5.25% sodium hypochlorite. At this concentration it is most stable for storage, but not most active. According to the Beth Israel Deaconess Medical Center Biosafety Manual (2004 edition), in most cases, it should be diluted to 1/10 of its storage concentration immediately before use; however, it should be diluted only to 1/5 of the storage concentration to kill Mycobacterium tuberculosis. This dilution factor must take into account the volume of any liquid waste that it is being used to sterilize. Bleach will kill many organisms immediately, but should be allowed to incubate for 20 minutes for full sterilization. Bleach will kill many spores, but is ineffective against certain extremely resistant spores. It is highly corrosive, even causing rust of stainless steel surgical implements.

Glutaraldehyde and formaldehyde solutions (also used as fixatives) are additional accepted liquid sterilizing agents, provided that the immersion time is long enough – it can take up to 12 hours for glutaraldehyde to kill all spores, and even longer for formaldehyde. (This assumes that a liquid not containing large solid particles is being sterilized. Sterilization of large blocks of tissue can take much longer, due to the time required for the fixative to penetrate.) Glutaraldehyde and formaldehyde are volatile, and toxic by both skin contact and inhalation. Glutaraldehyde has quite a short shelf life (<2 weeks), and is expensive. Formaldehyde is less expensive and has a much longer shelf life if some methanol is added to inhibit polymerization to paraformaldehyde, but is much more volatile. Formaldehyde is also used as a gaseous sterilizing agent; in this case, it is prepared on-site by depolymerization of solid paraformaldehyde.

Ortho-phthalaldehyde (OPA) is a sterilizing chemical which received Food and Drug Administration (FDA) clearance in late 1999. Typically used in a 0.55% solution, OPA shows better myco-bactericidal activity than glutaraldehyde. It also is effective against glutaraldehyde-resistant spores. OPA has superior stability, is less volatile, and does not irritate skin or eyes, and it acts more quickly than glutaraldehyde. On the other hand, it is more expensive, and will stain proteins (including skin) gray in colour. Another chemical sterilizing agent is hydrogen peroxide. It is relatively non-toxic once diluted to low concentrations (although a dangerous oxidizer at high concentrations), and leaves no residue.

The Sterrad 50 and other Sterrad sterilization chambers use hydrogen peroxide vapour to sterilize heat-sensitive equipment such as rigid endoscopes. The Sterrad 50 sterilizes in 45 minutes and also penetrates some lumen devices. The most recent Sterrad model, Sterrad NX, can sterilize most hospital loads in as little as 20 minutes and has greatly expanded lumen claims compared to earlier models. The Sterrad has limitations with processing certain materials such as paper/linens and long thin lumens. Paper products cannot be sterilized in the Sterrad system because of a process called cellulostics, in which the hydrogen peroxide would be completely absorbed by the paper product.

Endoclens is another device used to sterilize endoscopes. It mixes two chemicals (hydrogen peroxide and formic acid) together to make its antiseptic as needed. The machine has two independent asynchronous bays, and cleans (in warm detergent with pulsed air), sterilizes and dries the endoscopes automatically. All air and water inlets are filtered, and the machine handles temperature, timing and chemical concentration. The total time for the whole process is 30 minutes, and a hard-copy report of the cycle is printed (as well as being stored electronically). Studies with synthetic soil containing bacterial spores showed this machine achieved sterilization effectively.

The Dry Sterilization Process, DSP, is a process originally designed for the sterilization of plastic bottles in the beverage industry. It uses hydrogen peroxide with a concentration of 30-35% and runs under vacuum conditions. Using the common reference germs for hydrogen peroxide sterilization processes, endospores of different strains of bacillus subtilis and bacillus stearothermophilus, the Dry Sterilization Process achieves a germ reduction of $10^6...10^8$. The complete cycle time of the process is 6 seconds. The surface temperature of the sterilized items is only slightly increased during the process by 10°-15°. Particularly due to the high germ reduction and the slight temperature increase the Dry Sterilization Process is also useful for medical and pharmaceutical applications.

A similar chemical used to sterilize instruments is peracetic acid (0.2%), which is used in the Steris system. Prions show a great deal of resistance to these sterilization chemicals. Hydrogen peroxide (3%) for one hour was shown to be ineffective in that it had a less than 3 log reduction. Iodine, formaldehyde, glutaraldehyde and peracetic acid also fail this test (one hour treatment). Only chlorine, a phenolic compound, guanidinium thiocyanate, and sodium hydroxide (NaOH) reduce the titre by more than 4 logs. Chlorine and NaOH are the most consistent of these. Chlorine is too corrosive to use on certain objects. Sodium hydroxide has had many studies showing its effectiveness. In all, the chemical antiseptics do not work well against prions. An interesting note is that treatment with aldehydes (e.g., formaldehyde) have been shown to increase prion resistance.

FOOD AND TECHNOLOGY

Food Technology, or Food Tech for short is the application of food science to the selection, preservation, processing, packaging, distribution, and use of safe, nutritious, and wholesome food. Food scientists and food technolgists study the physical, microbiological, and chemical makeup of food. Depending on their area of specialization, Food Scientists may develop ways to process, preserve, package, or store food, according to industry and government specifications and regulations. Consumers seldom think of the vast array of foods and the research and development that has resulted in the means to deliver tasty, nutritious, safe, and convenient foods. In some schools, food technology is part of the curriculum and teaches, alongside how to cook, nutrition and the food manufacturing process.

Early History

Research in the field now known as food technology has been conducted for decades. Nicolas Appert's development in 1810 of the canning process was a decisive event. The process wasn't called canning then and Appert did not really know the principle on which his process worked, but canning has had a major impact on food preservation techniques. Louis Pasteur's research on the spoilage of wine and his description of how to avoid spoilage in 1864 was an early attempt to put food technology on a scientific basis. Besides research into wine spoilage, Pasteur did research on the production of alcohol, vinegar, wines and beer, and the souring of milk. He developed pasteurization—the process of heating milk and milk products to destroy food spoilage and disease-producing organisms. In his research into food technology, Pasteur became the pioneer into bacteriology and of modern preventive medicine.

By 1945, the original four departments that had taught the subject under different names (including those at the University of Massachusetts and the University of California) had been retitled "food science", "food science and technology", or a similar variant. The founding of the Institute of Food Technologists in 1939 has led to the general use of the term "food technologist."

DEVELOPMENTS IN FOOD TECHNOLOGY

Several companies in the food industry have played a role in the development of food technology. These developments have contributed greatly to the food supply. Some of these developments are:

1. Instantized Milk Powder

D.D. Peebles (U.S. patent 2,835,586) developed the first instant milk powder, which has become the basis for a variety of new products that are rehydratable in cold water or milk. This process increases the surface area of the powdered product by partially rehydrating spray-dried milk powder.

2. Freeze Drying

The first application of freeze drying was most likely in the pharmaceutical industry; however, a successful large-scale industrial application of the process was the development of continuous freeze drying of coffee.

3. High-Temperature Short Time Processing

These processes for the most part are characterized by rapid heating and cooling, holding for a short time at a relatively high temperature and filling aseptically into sterile containers.

4. Decaffeination of Coffee and Tea

Decaffeinated coffee and tea was first developed on a commercial basis in Europe around 1900. The process is described in U.S. patent 897,763. Green coffee beans are treated with steam or water to around 20% moisture. The added water and heat separate the caffeine from the bean to its surface. Solvents are then used to remove the caffeine from the beans. In the 1980s, new non-organic solvent techniques have been developed for the decaffeination of coffee and tea. Carbon dioxide under supercritical conditions is one of these new techniques. U.S. patent 4,820,537 was issued to General Foods Corp. for a CO_2 decaffeination process.

Food Technology now allows production of foods to be more efficient, Oil saving technologies are now available on different forms. Production methods and methodology have also become increasingly sophiaticated.

FOOD AND DRUG ADMINISTRATION

The Food and Drug Administration (FDA) is an agency of the United States Department of Health and Human Services and is responsible for regulating food (humans and animal), dietary supplements, drugs (human and animal), cosmetics, medical devices (human and animal) and radiation emitting devices (including non-medical devices), biologics, and blood products in the United States.

Authorization and Mandate

As an administrative agency in the executive branch of the government of the United States of America, FDA derives all of its authority and jurisdiction from various acts of Congress. The main source of the FDA's authority is the Federal Food, Drug, and Cosmetic Act. This act give FDA various responsibilities including the responsibility of ensuring that no adulterated or misbranded food, drug or medical devices enters into interstate commerce. [1]

The FDA thus has the power to regulate a multitude of products in a manner that ensures the safety of the American public and the effectiveness of marketed food, medical, and cosmetic products. Regulations may take several forms, including but not limited to outright ban, controlled distribution, and controlled marketing. Additionally, the FDA sets the standards under which individuals may be licensed to prescribe drugs or other medical devices. Regulatory enforcement is carried out by Consumer Safety Officers within the Office of Regulatory Affairs and criminal matters are handled by special agents within the Office of Criminal Investigations (OCI).

Jurisdiction over Dietary Supplements

Because FDA is only given as much authority as Congress has granted the agency, the Agency cannot take certain actions outside of its mandate. One such area where this has caused confusion is with dietary supplements. Unlike drugs, the FDA does not pre-approve dietary supplement on their safety and efficacy. FDA can only take enforcement action against dietary supplements only after FDA discovers that a certain dietary supplment is unsafe.

Jurisdictional Over Food

FDA also has jurisdiction over content of health claims on food labels. However, because regulating the content of labels impacts First Amendment issues, FDA must balance concerns about the public health with the right to free speech.

Enabling Legislation

- 1902 – Biologics Control Act
- 1906 – Pure Food and Drug Act
- 1938 – Federal Food, Drug, and Cosmetic Act
- 1944 – Public Health Service Act
- 1951 – Food, Drug, and Cosmetics Act Amendments PL 82-215
- 1953 – Flammable Fabrics Act PL 83-88
- 1960 – Federal Hazardous Substances Labeling Act PL 86-613
- 1962 – Food, Drug, and Cosmetics Act Amendments PL 87-781
- 1965 – Federal Cigarette Labeling and Advertising Act PL 89-92
- 1966 – Fair Packaging and Labeling Act PL 89-755
- 1966 – Child Protection Act PL 89-756
- 1970 – Federal Cigarette Labeling and Advertising Act Amendments PL 91-222
- 1972 – Consumer Products Safety Act PL 92-573
- 1976 – Medical Device Regulation Act PL 94-295
- 1986 – Comprehensive Smokeless Tobacco Health Education Act PL 99-252
- 1988 – Anti-drug Abuse Act PL 100-690
- 1990 – Nutrition Labeling and Education Act PL 101-535

- 1992 – Prescription Drug User Fee Act PL 102–571
- 1997 – Food and Drug Modernization Act

Selected history establishing public need:

- 1862 – President Lincoln appoints chemist, Charles M. Wetherill to the Department of Agriculture. This appointment led to the Bureau of Chemistry.
- 1906 – Upton Sinclair's The Jungle is published: this contributes to the creation of the FDA which received power through the 1906 Pure Food and Drug Act.
- 1927 – The "Bureau of Chemistry" is reorganized into two separate entities. Regulatory functions are located in the "Food, Drug, and Insecticide Administration", and non-regulatory research is located in the "Bureau of Chemistry and Soils".
- 1930 – The name of the "Food, Drug, and Insecticide Administration" is shortened to "Food and Drug Administration" (FDA) under an agricultural appropriations act.
- 1937 – Over 100 people died after consuming a raspberry-flavored sulfa elixir which had been rushed to market by the S.E. Massengill Company without any testing. About 70 percent of the elixir was diethylene glycol, which is now known to be poisonous (related to antifreeze). However, the FDA was able to remove the sulfa elixir from the market because elixirs at the time were to contain alcohol as a solvent (not diethylene glycol).
- 1938 – The resulting sulfa elixir scandal and public outcry led to the passage of the Federal Food, Drug, and Cosmetic Act of 1938, which gave the FDA the power to preapprove all new drugs introduced into interstate commerce.
- 1959 – During a 10-week period leading up to Thanksgiving, the FDA recalled cranberry crops that may have been exposed to a weed killer, aminotriazole, which was known to cause cancer. The

FDA sampled 3653 batches amounting to over 33,000,000 pounds of cranberries and cranberry products. Samples that were deemed safe and did not contain the weed killer were stamped with FDA approval.

- 1960 – Frances Oldham Kelsey, who was in charge of reviewing new drug applications, refused to allow Thalidomide in the United States market. Already being manufactured and sold throughout Europe, Kelsey insisted there was not enough evidence of the drug's safety. Receiving pressure from thalidomide manufacturers, Kelsey would not budge.
- 1961 – November, Germany takes thalidomide, known as kevadon, off the market after several thousand newborns suffered the teratogenic effects – they were born with grave congenital abnormalities.
- 1982 – Cyanide poisoning in Tylenol (a brand of the over-the-counter drug acetaminophen) capsules results in many deaths, leading the FDA to begin tamper-resistant packaging.
- 1990 – The FDA promulgates regulations banning "gifts of substantial value" from drug companies to doctors. Minor gifts (like meals, tickets, and travel) are not banned.
- 1992 – Congress passes a new law creating a faster approvals process to legalize new drugs. The FDA must hire more reviewers and speed up reviews without sacrificing proper study and testing. The drug industry must pay "user fees" with every new drug application. A drug is given "fast-track" status if it meets a medical need not currently being met by any medication. Approval times drop from 30 to 12 months on average. 60% of new drugs come on the market in the U.S. first, before other countries. Before this law, when the approval process was slower, more new drugs came out in other countries first.

- 1997 – The FDA loosens restrictions on consumer advertising. Drug companies are allowed to spend less time describing risks and side effects on TV commercials. A large increase in TV drug ads caused a large increase in drug sales within months.

Organization

Currently, the FDA is divided into five major Centers, each with its own orgins and history:

- The Center for Drug Evaluation and Research (CDER)
- The Center for Biologics Evaluation and Research (CBER)
- The Center for Devices and Radiological Health (CDRH)
- The Center for Food Safety and Applied Nutrition (CFSAN)
- The Center for Veterinary Medicine (CVM)

Leadership

The FDA is headed by acting Commissioner, Dr. Andrew von Eschenbach, who succeeds Dr. Lester Crawford who resigned on September 23, 2005 only two months after his final Senate confirmation and a stormy tenure as deputy commissioner and acting commissioner, prior to his confirmation.

Criticisms

The FDA has come under much criticism from many groups, including the Government Accountability Office. FDA regulations are blamed for causing high drug prices, keeping life-saving drugs off the market, prohibiting access to emergency contraceptives, allowing unsafe drugs on the market because of pressure from pharmaceutical companies, and censoring health information about nutritional supplements and foods.

It has been proposed that the FDA be relegated to a voluntary inspection agency in order to remedy these problems. Others disagree with the proposition to leave the agency with only authority to do voluntary inspections because that could create new problems. They believe that consumers would not demand food and pharmaceutical products to be tested and that therefore they would not be evaluated for health and safety risks. And, they believe advertising claims of drugs would be uncontested in a court of law. They fear that the industry would essentially be left to regulation by corporations with a heavily invested future in the production and sale of these untried and untested pharmaceuticals.

The Drug Approval Process

The FDA is charged with the task of approving or rejecting drugs that pharmaceutical companies want to market. Critics of the FDA's handling of this task generally fall into two groups. The first group claims that the approval process is too extensive, and keeps vital drugs off the market longer than is necessary. The second group argues that the process fails to properly screen for drugs with dangerous side-effects.

Dexfenfluramine, troglitazone and rofecoxib (trade name Vioxx) are a few recent, high-profile examples of drugs approved by the FDA which later caused harm to patients. Dexfenfluramine was a diet drug which had been available outside the United States for several years. Critics charge that the FDA failed to pay attention to safety concerns raised by post-marketing data from abroad, which indicated an increased risk of pulmonary hypertension. Troglitazone is a diabetes drug that was also available abroad at the time the FDA approved it. Like dexfenfluramine, post-marketing safety data indicated that the drug had dangerous side-effects (in this case, liver failure). The drug was approved over the objections of several FDA reviewers, and was later pulled from the market.

In the case of Vioxx, a study indicated that a group taking the drug had four times the risk of heart attacks when compared to another group of patients taking another anti-inflammatory, naproxen. The FDA was aware of this study, but the manufacturer (Merck) argued that naproxene had aspirin-like protective effects. The FDA accepted this reasoning. After numerous lawsuits against Merck, the manufacturer voluntarily withdrew it from the market in 2004.

To avoid such mistakes, the FDA ensures that newly approved drugs have passed vigorous testing, which includes animal testing, clinical trials of healthy individuals, and clinical trials of individuals suffering from the disease the drug is meant to treat. The FDA also verifies safety, quality, efficacy, along with drug interactions, and how various drugs may work depending on age, race, and sex. Critics argue that this process is long, tedious, and costly, and dramatically lengthens the time it takes effective drugs to hit the market.

The FDA does fast-track new treatments for serious diseases where no treatment currently exists. This rule attempts to address situations where the risks of keeping lifesaving drugs off the market outweigh the risks the drugs might pose to consumers. Almost one-fifth of FDA scientists surveyed said they had been pressured to recommend approval of a new drug, regardless of their own opinion of its safety, effectiveness or quality.

US Drug Packaging

In most countries, medications are prepackaged in sealed foilpacks and sold in marked packages with the name of the drug and the dose clearly stated. This method prevents the degradation of drugs due to exposure to humidity, oxygen and light. The United States is the only country where prescription medications are bought in bulk packages by retail pharmacies (non-hospital) and are provided to consumers in plastic pill containers. This practice is criticized because it shortens the useful life of many drugs. This practice has also allowed fraudulent pharmacies to mix expired medications with new medications. There are no controls in place at retail pharmacies to ensure that the drugs being sold have not expired.

HIGH DRUG PRICES

The Cost of Drug Development

Many maintain that FDA regulations and policy contribute to what they view as unnecessarily high drug prices in America. One concern is that the cost of the approval process may provide a disincentive for firms to develop new drugs and require high prices to recoup their investment and bring in a profit. For instance, Nobel economist Gary S. Becker says that regulations make drug development so costly that "drug companies must charge high prices during the limited period when they enjoy patent protection against generic competitors" to recover their outlays. He says that a major step to reduce drug prices would be to eliminate the regulations introduced in 1972 which raised the cost of bringing drugs to market and artifically slowed the process.

According to a study by research scientist Mary J. Ruwart, Ph.D, regulations passed in 1962, namely the Kefauver-Harris Amendments, are responsible for more than 80 percent of the cost of today's drugs. 1995 and 2002 studies by Joseph A. Dimasi claim that it costs, on the average, approximiately 800 million dollars to bring a drug to market. This includes the high cost of failed research programmes (which it is presumed must be pursued in order that some may succeed), and the drug company's opportunity cost of capital, which is very high because it is compounded over long (15-20 year) development cycles.

Dimasi's critics question whether this is a fair allocation of costs, and have alleged that conflicts of interest exist because the data was obtained from drug manufactures, and the center which employs Dimasi is partially funded by pharmaceutical companies. More specifically, they point out that he failed to consider government research grants and tax rebates, and claim that the scope of the research was too narrow because it only included new chemical entities (NCEs). Such critics suggest a revised cost that is under 200 million dollars, about 29% of which is spent on FDA-required clinical trials. However, the objective of the DiMasi paper was not to determine "out of pocket costs" for individual projects, but to ascertain the "price of innovation" in terms that reflect a firm's incentive to perform research and development of novel pharmaceuticals. Furthermore, under no circumstance would it be reasonable to forgo clinical trials entirely, and a marginal decrease in their cost would have a correspondingly small effect on total drug development costs.

Competition

A second way in which the FDA is seen to be responsible for high drug prices is by opposing the importation of cheaper drugs from foreign sources, which is held to be an anti-competitive policy that keeps drug prices artificially high in the United States. Prices of almost all pharmaceutical drugs in Europe are significantly lower than in the United States.

With regard to patented drugs, this argument fails to suggest any beneficial policy changes. If there is a single supplier of a drug, then the difference in prices is simply a variable pricing strategy which benefits both the drug manufacturers and consumers in less-affluent markets. If unhindered re-importation were allowed, either shortages would occur in cheaper markets (likely without satisfying U.S. demand), or companies would have to set the same price in all markets. Because a large proportion of the industry's revenue comes from the U.S., Europe, and Japan, a universal price would likely be close to the current prices in those markets (excluding countries with price caps). Not only would the industry's ability to conduct research be crippled by reduced profitability, but also consumers in many markets would be unable to afford the drugs.

Where price differences do exist for patented drugs, the lower prices are often due to government imposed price caps, not because of "competition" from the manufacturer's other markets. These price controls result in artificially low margins in these markets, which in turn lead to less available capital for research and development. Because of this, many contend that through higher prices, U.S. consumers pay a disproportionate amount of the cost of developing new medicines.

It is common for generic manufacturers to enter the market very soon after a drug's patent protection is lost, and for both companies to begin selling at dramatically lower prices. Importation is not banned by the FDA, so long as the imported drug complies with FDA regulations regarding importation. They observe that the FDA requires imported drugs to meet the same safety, efficacy, and manufacturing standards as those manufactured in the United States. These standards are similar in the United States, the European Union, Japan, and most of the world (represented by the WHO), all of which observe guidelines set forth by the International Conference on Harmonisation (ICH). Although some drugs that are approved by European regulatory agencies are not approved in the U.S., this would not be expected to affect the prices of approved drugs.

Some offer the observation that prices of nutritional supplements in Europe are much more expensive than in the U.S. They note that nutritional supplements are regulated in Europe, but not in the U.S. (as a result of the passage of the Dietary Supplement Health and Education Act, which severely limits the ability of the FDA to regulate them). Many nutritional supplements require a prescription in Europe, but not in the U.S. Hence, they reason that a cause of high pharmaceutical costs in the U.S. is regulation. Consequently, they reason that if the FDA discontinued regulating pharmaceuticals that they would be much more affordable. Requiring individuals to pay to visit a doctor to obtain a prescription for a drug further increases costs to the consumer. Many countries have much less strict regulations on what drugs may be dispensed without a prescription. These drugs are available for importation without a prescription in the underground economy through the internet, but few take advantage of this due to legal fears.

Protecting U.S. Pharmaceuticals from Foreign Competition

The FDA has been criticized regarding its delayed approval of foreign drugs to protect the US pharmaceutical companies from foreign competition. Eli Lilly's Fluoxetine was the first SSRI to be approved by the FDA. Kali-Duphar, the Dutch manufacturer of another antidepressant fluvoxamine, had first attempted to apply for FDA review in the early 1980's (much earlier than Eli Lilly) but fluvoxamine was not approved until the rights were bought by the US pharmaceutical company Reid Rowell. Critics have suggested that the FDA was attempting to protect Eli-Lilly's fluoxetine so it could gain a foothold in the US market before approving fluvoxamine.

Similarly, the FDA has blocked the approval of the French sunblock Meroxyl and critics have suggested that the reason behind this was an attempt to protect US sunscreen manufacturers. Helioplex is a sunscreen additive manufactured by the Neutrogena division of the US pharmaceutical giant Johnson and Johnson. Helioplex will soon hit the US market and is the only US competition to Meroxyl. Even though helioplex is not a sunscreen itself, it prevents the breakdown of avobenzone and oxybenzone, which are two US approved sunscreens. Meroxyl, which helps prevent skin-cancer by blocking UVA rays from the sun, has been available in Canada and Europe since 1993 but the FDA did not allow it to be sold in the U.S. until 2006.

Drug Approval

One of the key issues of drug safety dealt with by the FDA, and responsible for much recent controversy, is related to the concept of patents. When a patent is awarded, the drug's creator is given exclusive manufacturing rights. If the drug is extremely popular, this motivates other companies to invent their own (different) drugs which accomplish the same effect. For example, Cialis was created because of the popularity of Viagra. However, the question is, when new, competing substances come out should they be approved, not because of their absolute safety, but because of their relative safety compared to an approved drug. For example, say "drug b" was created to compete with "drug a". Now if "drug b" was the first one out, and it had a 5 percent chance of heart attack, the FDA might find this acceptable. However, if "drug a" was already out, and it had a 2.5 percent chance of heart attack, then the FDA would be reluctant to approve "b". Only people who were ignorant of that higher risk would take drug b — unless it were significantly cheaper, and the purchaser preferred the price savings of "b" to the relative safety of "a".

This phenomenon is at the center of a present controversy over the recall of Vioxx, which is causing more attention to be brought to the FDA. David Graham, a scientist with the FDA, says he was pressured by his supervisors not to warn the public about dangers of drugs like Vioxx, and so recommended to congress that a separate agency be created which is dedicated to continuously monitoring drug safety.

Under the Prescription Drug User Fees Act, the FDA charges fees to pharmaceutical companies in order to shorten the average length of the drug approval process. These fees are meant to offset FDA staff costs and related expenses. This can be considered to be a conflict of interest, as the companies who are supposed to be regulated by the FDA are those who are paying them to conduct the approval process. Some critics further allege that this "pay-off" may sacrifice the quality of studies. However, these concerns are often based on an inadequate understanding of the process. These fees are charged to all companies (except for orphan drug submissions and first-time small business applicants), regardless of the priority or expedited status of the review. Several options do exist to speed the review of a proposed drug, but the criteria for priority status are designed in the interest of public health and are not tied in any way to monetary payments.

Incentive to Delay Approval of New Drugs

Many economists who study the FDA are critical. Their views, however, are controversial. Economists Milton Friedman, Daniel B. Klein and Alexander Tabarrok are three economists who argue that the FDA causes a net harm. Friedman (1979) notes that the FDA can make two types of errors. Type 1 is to approve a drug that has deadly or harmful side effects in a large number of people. If you make this error, like approving a thalidomide, you will be blasted by the news media, and your reputation will be ruined.

Type 2 is refusing approval of a drug that is capable of saving many lives or relieving great distress and that has no untoward side effects. If you make a type 2 error, few will know it, as the people whose lives might have been saved will not be around to protest, and their families will have no way of knowing that their loved ones lost their lives because of the caution of an unknown FDA official.

This dichotomy was brought to the fore in the early days of AIDS. Noted AIDS author Randy Shilts published a future timeline analysis in the *San Francisco Chronicle* showing a minimum delay of 20 years to approve the new AIDS drugs and get them to patients. Standard industrial project expediting techniques of identifying critical paths and starting tasks in parallel were foreign to the medical bureaucracy. A massive demonstration by ACT UP and other groups occupied FDA headquarters, hanging a "Silence = Death" banner over the entrance. Afterwards, the "Pert chart" for approval of protease inhibitors and other drugs was given a major rework and procedures introduced for expediting timelines for both normal and compassionate/experimental drug introduction.

Friedman theorizes that the harm the FDA causes results from the nature of the bureaucracy and would happen even with the best intentioned and benevolent individuals in charge: "With the best will in the world, you or I, if we were in that position, would be led to reject or postpone approval of many a good drug in order to avoid even a remote possibility of approving a drug that will have newsworthy side effects." At the time, Friedman recommended that the FDA be abolished to remedy the problem. Much of the basis of his original criticisms has been eliminated as FDA now approves drugs on a far more rapid basis (e.g., fast track) and in fact is now sometimes accused of being anxious to approve drugs. One thing is for sure: there will always be people with strong opinions on both sides of the issue because of the societal need for safe drugs and the often enormous economic benefits to manufacturers.

Drug Purchases Require a Prescription

According to Kerry Howley in Reason Magazine, the requirement to obtain prescriptions to purchase drugs places unnecessary burdens on individuals, not only by directly increasing the price of the drugs but by requiring that individuals pay to see a doctor in order to obtain a prescription. A 1997 Study by Kline & Company found American consumers saved almost $13 billion a year by using over-the-counter medicines switched from prescription-only status. And, a study by MIT economist Peter Temin found that visits to the doctor for the common cold fell by 110,000 a year between 1976 and 1989 as the FDA switched cough and cold medicines to over-the-counter status.

Regarding Blood Donation

In the past, it was the practice in America and other countries to separate blood donations on the basis of race, ethnicity, or religion, or to exclude certain groups from the donor pool on those bases. Currently, in the U.S., these practices have been eliminated, although American Red Cross and FDA policies prohibit accepting blood donations from homo- and bisexual men, specifically from any "male who has had sex with another male since 1977, even once", or from intravenous drug users or recent immigrants from certain countries with high rates of HIV infection. While the inclusion of homo- and bisexual men on the prohibited list has created some controversy, the FDA and Red Cross cite the public policy need to protect the blood supply from HIV & similar diseases as justification for the continued ban, issued in 1985.

Censorship

The Federal Food, Drug, and Cosmetic Act ("FDCA") defines a drug, in part, as any article intended to prevent, cure, or mitigate a disease or condition. Any claim that a product could prevent, cure, or mitigate a disease or condition are referred to as "drug claims." Any seller that makes a drug claim about their product would be, by definition under the FDCA, claiming that their product is a drug. Once defined as a new drug under the FDCA, the seller would have to ensure that their product adhere to all the standards of a new drug including obtaining a new drug application from FDA through the use of clinical trials to prove safety and efficacy. Thus, the FDA is often criticized for restricting the ability of certain products (e.g., nutritional supplements, foods, cosmetics, etc.) from making certain claims related to the products impact on overall health of the consumer. The FDA defends its ability to restrict these claims based on the definition of a drug under the FDCA and its ability to regulate new drugs. Dietary supplements and certain foods are allowed to make structure/ function claims and health claims that resemble drug claims, but are regulated differently.

Regarding Nutritional Supplements

The FDA has been criticized for engaging in censorship because it prohibits dietary supplement manufacturers from making drug claims. Supplements manufacturers are only allowed to make limited claims regarding how the supplement affects the structure or function of the body, i.e., structure/ function claims and are prohibited by law from making drug claims that the supplement could prevent, cure, or mitigate a disease or condition, which are drug claims.

A bill was introduced in the US House of Representatives on May 12, 2005 by Congressman Ron Paul to prevent the FDA from censoring this information. It is currently pending. Julian Walker, M.D. of the Health Freedom Action Network says: "This rogue agency illegally prohibits manufacturers of food and dietary supplements from giving accurate information about their products' health benefits." Life Extension Foundation claims that the prohibitions are a violation of the Constitutional Right to Free Speech. On November 10, 2005, Ron Paul introduce a bill for the Health Freedom Protection act (H.R. 4284) to stop "the FDA from censoring truthful claims about the curative, mitigative, or preventative effects of dietary supplements, and adopts the federal court's suggested use of disclaimers as an alternative to censorship.

The FDA was also criticized for banning the essential amino acid Tryptophan after a manufacturing incident in Japan contaminated one batch. Regardless of the origin of the toxicity, Trp was banned from sale in the US, and other countries followed suit. Critics claim that such bureaucratic action neglects that Trp is an essential amino acid found in most foods, and have led some to renewed questioning as to whether the FDA was a science based or political agency.

The FDA prohibits information on health benefits for substances for which there is ample scientific evidence. For example, those who sell calcium are prohibited from mentioning that it reduces the risk of bone fractures. The FDA has also been criticized for intervening in the controversial nutritional supplement business. A raid against one supplement company, the "Life Extension Foundation," garnered criticism from critics for their entrance into a store by smashing through a glass doors with a battering ram. After a costly and lengthy legal battle, the Life Extension Foundation was cleared of all charges.

Drugs in Food and Food Safety

The FDA prevents providers of foods from making certain drug claims. For example, the FDA has threatened the cherry industry with legal measures unless it stops mentioning certain health benefits. The FDA has sent letters to cherry distributors saying that when health benefits are mentioned, the cherries then become "drugs" that are subject to seizure. Food safety advocates have criticized the FDA for allowing meat manufacturers to use carbon monoxide gas mixtures during the packaging process to prevent discolouration of meat. This discolouration is an important indicator that the meat is spoiling due to bacterial growth. The United States is the only country that allows this technology. Such technology has been banned in Europe. Food safety critics have suggested that the powerful agricultural lobby has used its political power to influence the FDA's approval of this process.

A second criticism that food safety advocates have made against the FDA has involved their approval of certain coal tar derived food dyes such as FDC yellow 5 and 6 which are banned in most European countries. There are concerns about carcinogenicity of these food colours. A third criticism of FDA food safety regulations has involved the lax pesticide regulations in the United States agricultural products.

A fourth important criticism of FDA food safety regulations has involved the FDA approval of the use of bovine growth hormone in dairy cows. This hormone increases milk production in cows but critics have pointed out that there was a surplus of milk production even before the use of bovine growth hormone. There is some evidence that BGH increases levels of IGF-1 in cow milk which can promote the growth of cancers in humans. A fifth important criticism of FDA food safety regulations has involved the use of growth enhancing agents in cows which includes the use of antibiotics. The use of antibiotics are believed to be the primary cause for the development of antibiotic resistant strains of bacteria which pose a real threat to mankind.

Medicines

The FDA approves the labeling information to appear on the labeling of both over-the-counter (OTC) products as well as prescription products. Some have criticized the FDA's restriction of certain information on OTC products as being counterproductive. For instance, the FDA prohibits aspirin packages from containing the research-backed information that taking an aspirin every day reduces the risk of heart attack. Some argue that the restrictions save consumers from having bad information, but the counter argument is that they are also prohibited from having good information. Some medicine manufactures have proposed a compromise, where the FDA could say what they want on the label of a medicine while the manufacturer could say what they want as well. However, this proposal has been rejected by the FDA.

Preemption and Prescription Drug Labeling

In the preamble to the new prescription drug regulations, which go into effect on June 30, the FDA has stated that it believes that the warnings it approves for prescription drugs represents both the minimum and maximum that a pharmaceutical company is allowed to state on its labeling. If courts adopted this theory of preemption, lawsuits against a pharmaceutical companies for failure to warn consumers on the possible dangers of a drug could not prevail if the FDA was fully aware of the information and did not require the warning. Essentially, the FDA is arguing that as a part of the federal government its decisions on what warnings should appear on labeling of a prescription drug product cannot be second-guessed by states or state courts because its federal action "preempts" states from regulating this arena. It should be noted that the FDA's pronouncements in the preambles to final rules are merely the FDA's interpretation of the law and have no binding effect on state or federal courts.

Food Irradiation

The irradiation of food for purposes of safety and longer self life is regulated by the FDA. The FDA has concluded that such irradiation is safe; though controversy continues, including the extent to which irradiation removes nutritional elements from meats and produce. The FDA is responsible for logo that must be placed on irradiated products to inform the consumer.

Chapter 6

Food Waste Management

FOOD SCRAP MANAGEMENT

The intensification of agriculture and food production in recent years has led to an increase in the production of food co-products and wastes. Their disposal by incineration or landfill is often expensive as well as environmentally sensitive. Methods to valorise unused co-products and improve the management of wastes that cannot be reused, as well as techniques to reduce the quantity of waste produced in the first place, are increasingly important to the food industry. With its distinguished editor and array of international contributors, Waste management and co-product recovery in food processing reviews the latest developments in this area and describes how they can be used to reduce waste.

Californians throw away more than 5 million tons of food scraps each year. That's 16 percent of all disposed materials going into landfills from businesses, residents, and institutions such as schools and prisons. Although green material collection programmes have been implemented in many cities and counties, management of food scraps provides additional opportunities to help meet the State's diversion goals as well as provide greater uses for this resource. A suggested order for food scrap management is to (1) prevent food waste, (2) feed people, (3) convert to animal feed and/or rendering, and (4) compost.

Restaurants, fast food establishments, and cafeterias can do a lot to minimize or reduce potential cost increases by incorporating simple waste prevention and recycling programmes and procedures that will eliminate much of the waste that is thrown away. With proper purchasing and handling, and careful preparation and storage, food service establishments can help reduce waste and save money! Your restaurant may already be using many of these ideas to reduce costs as well as waste. Try a few new suggestions, see how they work, and then continue to expand your waste reduction programme.

FOOD DIVERSION THROUGH ANIMAL FEED

Does your business or institution dispose of bakery or food preparation wastes, or post-consumer food scraps that might be used as animal feed? Diverting food scraps to animal feed can help food generators by:

- Decreasing disposal costs.
- Assisting local governments in meeting mandated waste reduction goals.
- Earning payment for food residuals.
- Enhancing food generators' public image.
- Supporting local farmers, dairies, or livestock producers.

The two main ways to divert food to animal feed are (1) direct feed to animals, and (2) converting residuals to a grain supplement, which is then fed to animals. Food scraps include anything from plate scrapings (postconsumer) to produce culls to food processing waste (preconsumer). Key factors in deciding whether this diversion option works for you are the quality of the food residuals, rate of generation, and existence of animal feed operations in your area appropriate for the type of food scraps generated.

Animal feed can be a viable option if a significant quantity of food residuals is generated on a regular basis and storage space is available to keep the material fresh until it can be transported.

Direct Feed to Animals

While care must be taken to prevent the spread of diseases such as swine fever, Exotic Newcastle disease, and Bovine Spongiform Encephalitis (BSE), also known as "Mad Cow Disease" (BSE update), farmers and ranchers can supplement their livestock's diet with the right type of food scraps, given a consistent supply. Food material generators and farmers or ranchers often have an informal arrangement. The generator must find a farmer willing to take the food scraps.

Pigs Are Swine

Some hog farmers participate in the "Garbage Feeding Programme" administered jointly by the U.S. Department of Agriculture (USDA) and the California Department of Food and Agriculture (CDFA). This programme requires a license and regular inspections. The collector must heat-treat all post consumer food scraps and food scraps that have been in any contact with meat scraps. At a minimum, the materials must be heated to 212 degrees Fahrenheit for 30 minutes prior to feeding it to swine. Some counties have further requirements. This heat treatment prevents potential transmission of diseases such as Trichonella, enteric coliform bacteria, swine fever, and foot and mouth disease. Food scrap generators should verify licensing prior to making arrangements with any pig farmer. Licensing is obtained through the CDFA for $20 per year and includes a booklet that describes how to set up a heating or steaming system.

Four Stomachs Are Better Than One

Cattle, sheep, and other ruminants are more restricted in what they can eat, but many dairy farmers or ranchers will accept certain types of food residuals as a feed supplement. If you have pre-consumer vegetable material, such as produce culls or a fruit or vegetable processing byproduct, it may be suitable for a local farm or ranch. Many types of food scraps can be fed directly to ruminants; however, some are not acceptable to cattle. To prevent the transmission of disease, ruminants should not be fed anything containing mammalian flesh. Also, certain vegetables such as onions or garlic are known to taint the flavor of milk from dairy cows. Contact a local dairy farmer, sheep ranch, or cattle rancher (or their animal nutritionist) to determine if your food scraps are appropriate for ruminants.

Poultry and Other Flying Objects

Chickens, turkeys, ducks, and geese love most fresh foods and have a broad diet. They can eat spaghetti with tomato sauce, steamed brown rice, grapes, fresh greens and lettuce, chopped cooked potatoes, corncobs, apple cores, whole grain bread, raw tomatoes, and their own eggs hard-boiled, including the ground shells. Kelp or blood meal are good sources of needed minerals. Any egg, meat, blood, or feather meal must be cooked to prevent the spread of disease. It is also important to note that chickens should be fed fresh, preconsumer foods, not plate scrapings or foods that have spoiled.

Exotic Animals

Exotic or less common animals at zoos and specialty farms may be potential consumers of unwanted food residuals. Some exotic animals have diets that allow them to eat foods unsuitable for traditional farm animals, such as citrus fruits. Check with local farms and zoos to see if the material you have is suited for these animals.

Feed Manufacturers

Ever wonder what animal feed is made of? While most feed is made from agricultural crops such as alfalfa, corn, wheat, soy, and rice, some also contains food residuals from large bakeries, food processing plants, rendering plants, and sometimes even candy factories. Animal feed manufacturers that use food residuals combine foods to make a "recipe" that is appropriate for specific animals. If the supplier has a surplus that is high in proteins and/or carbohydrates, there is a chance they may receive payment for the material. Bakery wastes in particular are of interest to many animal feed manufacturers, as well as other dry, high-protein and/or carbohydrate materials.

Prevent Spread of Diseases

Not all food residuals are suitable for animals. For example, no vessel or aircraft waste, whether it is foreign or domestic in origin, should ever be fed to livestock. Serious animal diseases are spread by this illegal practice. As mentioned above, ruminants should not be fed anything containing mammalian protein due to the risk of BSE, or "Mad Cow Disease." Also, all animal products should be cooked to prevent the spread of other diseases such as Salmonella, Trichonella, and Exotic Newcastle Disease.

Rendering

If you have excess grease or uncooked meat, bone or animal blood, contact a local renderer for collection. These companies collect and process these materials into feedstock for a variety of products, usually for a small fee. Improper disposal of grease can cause many environmental problems and is a leading cause of beach closures. Rendering companies are listed in the yellow pages under "rendering" or "grease collection."

Half of US Food Goes to Waste

The new study, from the University of Arizona (UA) in Tucson, indicates that a shocking forty to fifty per cent of all food ready for harvest never gets eaten. Timothy Jones, an anthropologist at the UA Bureau of Applied Research in Anthropology, has spent the last 10 years measuring food loss, including the last eight under a grant from the US department of agriculture (USDA). Jones started examining practices in farms and orchards, before going onto food production, retail, consumption and waste disposal.

What he found was that not only is edible food discarded that could feed people who need it, but the rate of loss, even partially corrected, could save US consumers and manufacturers tens of billions of dollars each year. Jones says these losses also can be framed in terms of environmental degradation and national security. Jones' research evolved from and builds on earlier work done at the University of Arizona. Archaeologists there began measuring garbage in the 1970s to see what was being thrown away and discovered that people were not fully aware of what they were using and discarding.

Those earlier studies evolved into more sophisticated research using contemporary archaeology and ethnography to understand not only the path food travels from farms and orchards to landfills, but also the culture and psychology behind the process. The fact that the US is a wasteful nation is not necessarily news, of course. The country has long has been chastised for its wilful consumption of the world's resources, and many aspects of the country's culture encapsulate what environmentalists disparagingly refer to as today's "throw-away society."

Similarly, researchers have known for years about the volumes of food Americans toss into the trash. But only recently, though, has that been quantified as a percentage of what is produced, and the UA statistics are the first tangible proof that Us food production is frighteningly wasteful. A certain amount of waste in the food stream cannot be helped of course. Little can be done, for instance, about weather and crop deterioration. The apple industry, for instance, loses on average about 12 per cent of its crop on the way to market.

Apples in the US are harvested over a two-month period and then stored and sold year-round. People in the apple business use aggressive methods to maintain their crop, with fresh apples hitting the supermarkets on a regular basis and marginal ones sent to be made into applesauce and other products. The goal of apple growers is to provide a nutritious product, all year long, at fairly constant prices. Jones says they've adopted a conservative business plan that forgoes the boom-and-bust cycles that other fruit and vegetable growers aim for and opts instead for a steady income stream.

But Jones argues that fresh fruit and vegetable growers, in contrast, often behave like riverboat gamblers. They will take a risk on the commodity markets if they think it will help them make a financial killing. A bad bet often means an entire crop is left in the field to be ploughed under. Jones' research also shows that by measuring how much food is actually being brought into households.

On average, households waste 14 per cent of their food purchases. Fifteen per cent of that includes products still within their expiration date but never opened. Jones estimates an average family of four currently tosses out $590 per year, just in meat, fruits, vegetables and grain products. Jones says that consumers better need to understand that many kinds of food can be refrigerated or frozen and eaten later. Nationwide, he says, household food waste alone adds up to $43 billion, making it a serious economic problem.

Cutting food waste would also go a long way toward reducing serious environmental problems. Jones estimates that reducing food waste by half could reduce adverse environmental impacts by 25 per cent through reduced landfill use, soil depletion and applications of fertilisers, pesticides and herbicides. Consumers and retailers are also of course responsible for minimising food waste, but it is manufacturers, who are being squeezed by high raw material prices and low retail costs, that stand to gain most by establishing greater operational efficiencies to cut out unnecessary waste. By demonstrating how wasteful food production in the US currently is, the UA study suggests not only where savings could be made, but also how far many companies are from making them.

MANAGING FOOD MATERIALS

Proper control of final products, and the waste streams associated with food preparation is an important source reduction technique. Improved ordering and inventory control significantly affect the three major sources of waste resulting from improper inventory control: excess, out-of-date, and obsolete raw goods. Below are options for reduction at the start.

- Order bulk supplies.
- Terminate useless packaging from the vendor.
- Refuse samples that will become waste.
- Work with suppliers to return shipping materials and packaging.
- Purchase reusable items.
- Purchase durable items such as air hand dryers that are designed to reduce waste.
- Purchase only the amount of raw goods needed for a set period of time. This practice will help eliminate out-of-date and excess goods and products.
- Develop a review and approval procedure for all raw goods and products purchased. The primary purchaser can regulate the quantity of materials purchased by other personnel to reduce excess and outof-date inventory.
- Clearly label all materials. Labels can indicate contents, storage and handling, and expiration dates.

Donations, Sales, and Composting of Food Material

Food preparation businesses seeking to reduce food waste should look for opportunities to work closely with potential reusers such as food donor programmes. After donating edible food to reusers, food businesses may work with facilities such as grease renderers, animal food manufacturers, local farmers, or composters who can collect food materials and use them in their operations. Composting is also an option for managing solid food waste.

Segregate Food Wastes for Beneficial Uses

To increase their recyclable potential, food materials should be clean and free of trash such as paper, glass, and plastic. Also, depending upon the requirements of recyclers, solid food wastes should be separated from liquid food wastes to enhance their recyclability.

Excess edible food should be kept separate from waste food and routed to a local food bank or food donor programme. North Carolina.s model .Good Samaritan Law. was enacted in 1989 and revised in 1991. This law protects any good faith donor from civil or criminal liability unless injury is caused by gross negligence, recklessness, or intentional misconduct of the donor. The local health department can provide handling and storage procedures applicable to your area. Currently, more than four million pounds of food materials are donated each year to North Carolina food rescue programmes alone.

Solid food waste should be segregated from waste oils and greases. Hog, cattle, and poultry producers are interested in collecting food waste to use as animal feed. Dairy and bread waste may be fed to hogs without further handling, but other food waste or mixed food waste must be cooked before being fed to hogs. Farmers who use other or mixed food materials must be licensed garbage feeders. Zylphia Smith of the U.S. Department of Agriculture, Animal Plant Health Inspection Services (APHIS) at (919) 856-4170 can provide information about state regulations and a list of licensed garbage feeders. Local cooperative extension agents also may assist with locating markets for waste food.

Waste Oils and Grease

Free grease is that used for or generated by cooking and has not been mixed with water. It is generated from pots, pans, grills, and deep fat fryers and comes from butter, lard, vegetable fats and oils, meats, nuts, and cereals. Free grease should be kept out of the drains and handled separately. Rendering facilities mays purchase free grease and meat wastes and provide storage and collection. The market price depends upon factors such as volume, quality, and hauling distances. The rendering services will process free grease by sampling it for pesticides and other chemicals and filtering and volatizing impurities before reselling it, where prices may range from one to three cents per pound. If the volume of the wastes generated from one restaurant or cafeteria is too small for the rendering facility, businesses should explore the feasibility of setting up a cooperative collection among similar businesses.

Trap Grease is that Collected in a Grease Trap

Because fats coat, congeal, and accumulate on pipes and pumps and sometimes obstruct sewer lines, some food service establishments may be required by their local government to maintain grease traps. Specific information about trap maintenance is presented below. Some rendering services and local septage haulers will service or pump out these traps for a fee, and some services may reduce the pumping fee if the restaurant is a free grease customer.

Dry Cleanup to Keep Wastes out of the Drain

Food preparation facilities should develop dry cleanup procedures to the greatest possible extent. Some municipalities will charge (surcharge) for any discharge of BOD, COD, TSS, and O/G above a certain level. For a restaurant that uses 3,000 gallons of water per day, serves seven days a week, and has an average BOD of 1,250 milligrams per liter (mg/L), an annual surcharge could be as much as $1,173.1 Dry cleanup procedures will reduce the amount of food waste that enters the drains and, thus, help reduce the possible surcharges.

The "first pass" in equipment and utensil cleaning should be made with scrapers, squeegees, or absorbents to prevent the bulk of food materials from going down the drain. Studies have shown that for a fast food restaurant, 93 percent of the oil and grease discharged to the wastewater treatment plant is generated from ware washing. For a full service restaurant, 75 percent of the oil and grease discharged to the wastewater treatment plant is generated from the pot sink. Waste collected on this first pass. could be set aside for rendering or, possibly, composting.

Spills

Dry cleanup can be applied also to spills in the kitchen. Spills of dry ingredients should be swept up or vacuumed to prevent them from being washed down the drain.

Garbage Disposals

Businesses that use garbage disposals to dispose of food waste are simply transferring disposal from a landfill to a wastewater treatment plant. Disposal of food waste via the sewer system is more costly than landfill disposal and acts as a disincentive to reduce generation of food waste or to separate food for donations, rendering, animal feed, or composting.

Maintaining Grease Traps

Food preparation facilities that discharge to a municipal sewer should contact the local wastewater treatment plant (WWTP) for any requirements concerning the need for interceptors and grease trap management. The most important management procedure for grease traps is that a company representative be present during any cleaning, pumping, or skimming performed by a contractor. This safeguard permits management to respond appropriately to any questions about the services performed.

Pump out schedules should be properly established and strictly followed to prevent overflows, downstream blockage, excessive oil and grease, and BOD loading to wastewater. It is important that these pump outs are complete, i.e., the grease caps removed, the sides scraped or hosed down, and the trap refilled with water. The contractor should indicate whether the trap is refilled with clean water or water from the trap. P
A food preparation facility should never "hot flush"(continuously run hot water) the grease trap as the heated, liquefied grease will be flushed down the sewer. While hot flushing may divert the need for pumping, the facility is liable for any costs associated with clogs caused by the flushing.

Skimming services are available to skim grease traps on a regular basis. These facilities will reprocess the grease collected and notify owners when complete grease trap pump outs are necessary.

Bioaugmentation, the addition of selected microorganisms (primarily bacteria) to the trap for improved operation, should be evaluated for each case. The bioaugmentation process is basically a passive treatment system to facilitate grease digestion and control buildup of the grease cap. The effectiveness of bioaugmentation is determined by a variety of factors including retention time in the trap, temperature of the wastewater, strength of the wastewater, and contact surface area. Some information indicates that for completely effective bioaugmentation, a retention time of one to five days is needed; however, a typical grease trap is designed for only one day of hydraulic retention. Since these parameters vary with location, an evaluation of each case should be made. The local WWTP should be contacted before any additives are used.

Alternative Grease Trap Designs

Some grease trap systems are designed to periodically heat the trap to de-solidify grease so that it can be automatically skimmed and collected. The high-quality grease collected from these systems may have high reuse potential. These grease traps, which may also be smaller than standard traps, can be located under a specific device above ground (i.e., the pot sink).

Management Commitment

The most critical step to successful waste reduction is commitment by the owner(s)/managers of a facility to a waste management plan. A detailed waste reduction programme should be developed that outlines policies and procedures for dealing with waste and assigns individual responsibilities for all waste related activities. Employees will be aware of the degree of commitment by management and will rise or fall to the level that is expected or allowed. It is, therefore, important to have realistic goals that can be achieved, recognized, and rewarded.

Employee training is a significant component of a waste reduction programme, and all employees from managers to the clean-up crew should be included. The training sessions, which should be repeated on a regular basis, should teach waste awareness, the impact of various food wastes on the wastewater stream, proper waste handling methods, and the importance of keeping non-food garbage out of food waste containers.

An Employee Suggestion/Awards Programme should be established to maintain employee motivation. Employees can be rewarded for proper waste handling practices.

Current incentive programmes (.employee of the month.) can also incorporate employee waste handling practices as evaluation criteria. An employee awareness programme should be highly visible, and managers and supervisors must strongly support these programmes.

Also, employees should be solicited for ideas/suggestions for conducting efficient dry cleanups, segregating food wastes, or recycling other solid waste products. Employees also may have ideas about methods to generate less food waste or more effectively manage inventory. The most effective waste reduction programmes make use of a team concept in which employees at all levels make contributions.

FACILITY WASTE REDUCTION PROGRAMME

Composting Food Wastes

Businesses interested in diverting wastes to composting could open their own compost facility or investigate the possibility of using local government or private compost facilities already in operation. North Carolina has a compost demonstration programme for individuals interested in composting. For regulatory information or a The Grease Goblin is the mascot for DPPEA.s Oil and Grease Management Programme. He serves as a reminder to keep grease out of sinks and drains before it becomes a nuisance.

RESTAURANT AND HOTEL WASTE REDUCTION

Ideas for protecting the environment and realizing the cost benefits of waste reduction should be responsibilities of all employees in all job functions. Once waste reduction opportunities are identified, employees should be trained so they are comfortable with implementing the changes. Training should be repeated periodically to ensure that new employees are included. An employee suggestion and awards programme can be established to maintain enthusiasm for the programme. The remainder of this fact sheet lists specific activities that restaurants can undertake to reduce waste.

Reduction and Reuse

Avoid over packaging for take-out orders. Place rubber mats around bus and dish washing stations to reduce china and glass breakage. Work with suppliers to take back and reuse corrugated cardboard boxes, five-gallon buckets, and other packaging. Use refillable condiment bottles instead of single use packages. Refill them from bulk containers. Use cloth rags instead of paper towels. Encourage use of reusable dishes instead of styrofoam or other disposable ware. Use reusable take-home trays for regular customers.

Recycling

Establish glass, plastic, and cardboard recycling with a local collector. Place a recycling bin in the dining area in which customers can place empty beverage containers.

Food Waste Management

The National Restaurant Association estimates that 20 percent of all food prepared commercially in the United States goes to waste. Donate excess edible food to a local food bank or food rescue programme. North Carolina has a strong. Good Samaritan.law that protects restaurants from liability associated with food donations. Rotate perishable stocks at every delivery to minimize waste from spoilage, i.e., first-in, first-out.

Contract with a rendering service for recycling used cooking oil, meat, and/or trap grease. Ensure that grease traps are properly maintained; clean fryers and filter the oil daily to extend the life of both the fryer and the oil. Never .hot flush.(continuously run hot water)

through a grease trap. Check with your local government solid waste programme for local composting facilities or animal farms that will accept non-edible food waste. Scrape leftovers into a food waste container prior to washing. Avoid sending food waste down the garbage disposal as this waste is only transferred from the landfill to the wastewater treatment plant.

Purchasing

Choose environmentally friendly cleaning products, and try to purchase cleaning agents in concentrate. Ask for and purchase products such as paper towels, toilet tissue, menus, order pads, cash register tapes, plastic bags, dish trays, rubber mats, brooms, and benches made from recycled materials.

FOOD PROBLEM

Agricultural research and development (R&D),which has generated astounding increases in food production in the twentieth century, is vital to assuring food security for the burgeoning global population in the coming decades. But changes in the financing, management, and organization of agricultural R&D are occurring rapidly. After decades of sustained growth, the rate of growth of spending on agricultural research has slowed in most countries since the early 1980s, and in some countries spending has even shrunk. The private sector is paying for and conducting an ever larger share of agricultural research, while governments are reducing their agricultural R&D spending. These and other changes have tended to push the agricultural research agenda in new directions, raising questions about whether agricultural R&D will be able to help meet the food needs of the poor and hungry beyond 2000.

World food security beyond 2000 depends on continued global investments in agricultural research and development. The basic facts are well known. World population is expected to increase by about 2.3 billion people by 2020, the amount of new land that can be brought under cultivation is limited, and other natural renewable resources used in agriculture, like water, are becoming increasingly scarce. Ensuring the future security of adequate food supplies is not a question of simply maintaining agricultural productivity; it has to be one of continuing to improve global agricultural productivity, particularly through research and innovation. Moreover, developments in agricultural R&D in wealthier nations are increasingly intertwined with those in developing countries. An accounting, review, and assessment of what has happened is therefore timely.

Investment Patterns

Worldwide, agricultural research spending grew rapidly for most of the post-World War II era, generating extraordinary growth in agricultural productivity around the globe. New high-yielding rice and wheat varieties developed with this funding, together with new farming practices, triggered Asia's Green Revolution of the 1960s and 1970s, in which large yield increases averted the famines widely predicted for that region.

During the past 15 years, however, a sea change has taken place in agricultural R&D policy and spending patterns. New data in an IFPRI volume to be published by Johns Hopkins University Press shows that in inflation-adjusted terms, public investment in agricultural R&D around the globe rose from US$7.2 billion in 1971 (expressed in 1985 prices) to US$15 billion in 1993, putting the overall average annual growth rate at 3.6 percent. But the rate of growth in public investment slowed sharply over this period. In developed countries, the annual growth rate of real public investment in agricultural R&D fell from 2.7 percent during the period 1971-81 to 1.7 percent in 1981-91. Similarly, in developing countries, the growth rate of public investment in agricultural research fell by just under half, from 6.4 percent in the 1970s to 3.9 percent in the 1980s. More dramatically, real funding for international agricultural research centers, which played a key role in bringing about the Green Revolution, increased by more than 14 percent per year in the 1970s but by less than 1 percent per year between 1985 and 1996. Developing countries now account for more than half of all global public R&D investments, and how those funds are used will significantly affect future global food security.

Development Policies of Food

In recent years, priorities for public agricultural research have changed dramatically. The public research agenda has broadened. Public funding has shifted toward research on postharvest handling, food processing and food safety, and environmental issues such as soil erosion and groundwater pollution, and away from research dealing with production agriculture. These adjustments reflect the increasing influence of nontraditional interest groups—environmentalists, food processors, and consumer groups—in the formulation of agricultural science policy, as well as the expanded research role of the private sector. In addition, some governments have pushed public funds toward more basic research, the benefits from which are more difficult for the private sector to appropriate, and away from applied research of more immediate consequence for industry.

Donor funds directed toward both international and national-level agricultural R&D agencies (especially those in Africa) have reflected first-world concerns with the environment and agricultural aspects beyond the farm. In addition, donors increasingly seem to view agricultural R&D as a means of directly and rapidly tackling poverty problems rather than as an activity best suited to stimulating productivity and growth over the longer term, with poverty reduction brought about as a consequence of that growth.

Recent IFPRI-led research shows how the organization and management of public agricultural R&D have also been changing. In the developed countries (for which the most comprehensive and up-to-date data are available), many previously public roles have become privatized, and the line between private and public research is becoming increasingly blurred. Private R&D firms have increasingly been able to bid for publicly funded projects, some public research and technology transfer institutions have been explicitly privatized (for example, plant breeding and horticultural facilities in the United Kingdom and extension services in New Zealand), and others have received a mandate to sell their research services to private firms (for example, universities in most developed countries and extension agencies in New Zealand and the United Kingdom).

In addition, public agricultural research facilities are being phased out in many countries—in the Netherlands and the United Kingdom about 50 percent of the facilities were merged or closed between 1980 and 1995—and management and employment structures have been altered. Changes include the introduction and expansion of contestable funding arrangements among alternative, often public, research agencies (as in New Zealand) or competitive grant processes (such as the U.S. Department of Agriculture's National Research Initiative), a shift away from long-term contracts toward shorter fixed-term contracts for researchers (especially in the United Kingdom), and expanded accountability and oversight procedures (as in the research and development corporations that now play a significant part in funding rural research in Australia).

Similar changes have taken place in some developing countries as well, although the timing and specifics of the changes are different and the private sector has generally played a smaller role as both a funder and performer of R&D. Some countries (especially in Africa but also in Asia and Latin America) have seen a contraction in real public support for agricultural R&D. During the late 1980s and early 1990s, some of this shrinkage in domestic support was partly supplanted by an increase in donor funding for research, but in more recent years overall donor funding has declined and spending priorities have shifted away from agricultural R&D.

The pace and focus of biological innovation in agriculture and related industries, who pays for R&D and how much, and the costs and benefits of the research all depend on the form of property protection afforded the results of specific R&D projects. Many countries are enacting or revising laws to protect biological material and the innovations and research processes surrounding that material. These national efforts are increasingly being shaped and circumscribed by international laws and conventions. These changes in property protection appear to be changing the roles of the public and private sectors with regard to the funding, performance, and dissemination of agricultural R&D, but much else is changing too, so the specific effects of changing property rights are not clear. Moreover, many of the details of these property-rights policies remain unresolved, which makes it difficult to be definitive about their ultimate impact on the nature and rate of technical progress in agriculture.

THE PRIVATE SECTOR'S ROLE

In many developed countries, the private sector has become a much more substantial provider of agricultural research. Spending on private agricultural research has risen by just over 5 percent per year since 1981 and now amounts to almost half of total agricultural R&D expenditures in developed countries. This rapid increase has been partly a result of expanded property rights over biological innovations and, in some countries, a movement away from public funding for near-market research that previously may have "crowded out" private research. The emerging modern biotechnologies are an important element in this expansion as well.

The private sector has a very different agricultural research focus from that found in the public sector. For example, in five countries that collectively account for more than 40 percent of developed-country agricultural R&D investments (Australia, the Netherlands, New Zealand, the United Kingdom, and the United States), over 80 percent of public research, but only 12 percent of private research, is devoted to farm-level technologies such as improved crop and livestock production practices. Moreover, in different countries, private agricultural R&D tends to be specialized in different areas and then exported elsewhere, reflecting the increasing international flow of R&D goods and services. For example, post harvest research accounts for between 30 and 90 percent of private agricultural research—in countries such as Australia, Japan, and New Zealand, it is the dominant concern of privately funded agricultural R&D. In contrast, while agricultural chemical research on fertilizer, herbicides, and pesticides is of minor importance in some countries, it accounts for more than 40 percent of private agricultural research in the United Kingdom and the United States and more than 75 percent of private research in Germany.

Interestingly, however, the composition of private R&D has been changing over time. In the United States, for example, agricultural machinery and postharvest research accounted for over 80 percent of private agricultural R&D in 1960, but by 1992 it amounted to only 42 percent of private agricultural R&D. Private investments in plant breeding, veterinary, and pharmaceutical research, which are more directly related to agricultural productivity, increased substantially during the same period.

The crucial issue for global food security is whether or not the recent changes in public and private agricultural R&D have made global agricultural R&D more effective in increasing agricultural productivity and contributing to food security. Have the changes led to efficiencies in the total quantity and quality of research being undertaken? Are lower-cost sources of funds being used? Are resources being more effectively allocated among competing programmes, projects, and institutions? Is research emphasis being divided more appropriately among commodities, natural resource management, and other areas of research? Are research resources being allocated more effectively between basic and applied research and extension and between farming and food processing and safety research?

It is too soon to provide clear answers to many of these questions. It is possible, however, to determine some potential costs and benefits of the changes that have taken place. A particular concern is the slowdown in the growth rates of public agricultural R&D funding, especially since a broad array of empirical evidence shows that in the past such investments have generated annual rates of return well in excess of 30 percent.

The expanded role of the private sector in agricultural R&D also raises important questions. When research boards and committees are dominated by industry representatives, public funds may be directed to projects that benefit only limited sectoral interests rather than those projects that will have the largest effects on overall agricultural productivity. For example, extensive industry representation may lead to R&D that focuses on larger, perhaps more capital-intensive agricultural operations or on issues of concern only to particular agroecological areas. In addition, more directed public-private ventures may crowd out industry research funds, thereby exacerbating the tendency for private investments in R&D to be underfunded. On the other hand, increased industry input may result in more effective applied research programmes.

In principle, increasing competition for research funds can improve research productivity and reduce research costs by helping funders choose the best research opportunities and the most appropriate scientists. However, competitive processes can also cost more to manage. The challenge is to devise institutions that minimize all the costs of research decision making, including the costs of misallocating resources and the costs of competing for funds.

The shift away from very long-term contracts (or tenure) for researchers to shorter-term contracts also has its potential pluses and minuses. On the plus side, it is easier to remove "dead wood" from the research system, provide short-term incentives for greater research productivity among all researchers, and give research administrators greater flexibility in managing resources. However, the removal of long-term guarantees of employment reduces incentives for gifted individuals to pursue research careers that require large personal investments in human capital.

The consequences of rationalizing public research facilities may be less ambiguous. Where rationalization has taken place to respond to recent changes in scientific methods and to take advantage of new economies of size and scope, there have been clear gains in economic efficiency. Where "rationalization" has simply been a pseudonym for budget cuts, the results depend on whether the expected rates of return on investing in R&D were higher than returns from using the funds for other purposes.

Broadening the research agenda may have led to some benefits. Environmental and food safety issues are often public good issues, and from society's perspective private markets fail to provide the right amount and mix of R&D. Accordingly, many believe that reallocating public research funds to these issues and away from near-market research programmes must enhance people's economic welfare and may improve global food security by making agricultural production practices more sustainable and food more nutritious. The answer to even these questions remains unclear, however, since no formal evidence is available on the payoff to public R&D on environmental or food safety issues, or their effects on food security.

To the extent that public resources have been diverted toward agribusiness and food processing research (as in the United Kingdom and New Zealand, and possibly in Australia), projects funded in these areas may have displaced projects in the area of farm productivity that are more likely to enable the world to feed its poor more effectively. The shift in public funding from developed to developing countries raises other questions. It is not clear whether developing countries can recruit and retain adequate numbers of talented scientists, given that salaries are often low and lag behind inflation. Some research systems in developing countries spend too much on labour and too little on other operational requirements, leaving scientists without the tools they need to work effectively.

There is, then, both cause for concern and cause for hope with respect to the changes taking place in global agricultural R&D investments. Many of the changes discussed here have been relatively recent, however, and the effects of research on economic output are visible only after long lags. Thus, it may be years before the effects of these changes become clear. In the meantime, policy choices and change will occur, and researchers can produce much useful data and analysis to help inform these policy decisions, specifically information on the nature and likely consequences of the changing pattern of funding and performing R&D, the local and spillover effects of agricultural research, and the effects of the changing intellectual property regimes on research. It is decisions on these issues that in turn will have potentially profound, long-run consequences for the world's future food security.

FOOD HAZARDS

Experts describe food safety problems in terms of hazards, with those hazards categorized as chemical, microbiological, or physical. They have long considered the most dangerous hazards to be those of microbiological origin, followed by those of naturally occurring toxins. However, pesticides and additives have been prominent subjects for the media, which may lead some people to focus on those hazards more than others. But as more stories emerge of people becoming ill from bacterial contamination, the public is increasingly aware of the importance of microbiological hazards. People do die from microbial hazards, but deaths due to consuming pesticide residues or food additives are rare. Water is a food, and also is subject to microbial contamination. Some pathogens, such as Cryptosporidium parvum, are more waterborne than foodborne. While this chapter does discuss microbial contamination of water, it is beyond the scope of this book to consider waterborne hazards primarily caused by pollution, such as heavy metals, or pathogens that follow pathways other than the digestive tract.

Chemical Hazards

Chemical hazards include agricultural chemicals such as pesticides, herbicides, rodenticides, insecticides, fertilizers, antibiotics and other animal drugs, cleaning residues, naturally occurring toxins, food additives, allergens, and toxic chemicals from industrial processes that can enter the food chain directly during processing or indirectly through plants and animals.

The Environmental Protection Agency (EPA) controls chemicals applied at the farm; the United States Department of Agriculture (USDA) controls antibiotics and animal drugs; and the Food and Drug Administration (FDA) controls additives and residual chemicals on processed foods.

Microbiological Hazards

Microbiological hazards include disease-causing bacteria, viruses, and parasites. Many of these microorganisms occur naturally in the environment and can be foodborne, waterborne, or transmitted from a person or an animal. Cooking kills or inactivates most pathogens, while proper cooling and storage can control them before or after cooking.

Bacteria

Bacteria are single-celled organisms so small they can only be seen with a microscope. Bacteria are everywhere and most are not pathogenic (disease-causing). The human gastrointestinal tract is home to more than 300 species of bacteria (Doyle 2000). Fortunately, only a few of these cause illness. Some bacteria are beneficial and are used in making foods such as yogurt, cheese, and beer. Others cause food to spoil, but do not cause human sickness. This difference between spoilage bacteria and pathogenic bacteria is important in the prevention of foodborne illness. Since pathogenic bacteria generally cannot be detected by looks, smell, or taste, we rely on spoilage bacteria to indicate that a food should not be eaten. Not many people will eat food that has become slimy or that smells bad. Pathogenic bacteria cause foodborne illness in three different ways.

Viruses

Several viruses also cause foodborne illness. Viruses differ from bacteria in that they are smaller, require a living animal or human host to grow and reproduce, do not multiply in foods, and are not complete cells. Ingestion of only a few viral particles is enough to produce an infection.

Humans are host to a number of viruses that reproduce in the intestines and then are excreted in the feces. Thus, transmission of viruses comes from contact with sewage or water contaminated by fecal matter or direct contact with human fecal material. Raw or undercooked molluscan shellfish (oysters, clams, mussels, and scallops) are the food most often associated with foodborne viral diseases. Human pathogenic viruses are often discharged into marine waters through treated and untreated sewage. As shellfish filter contaminants from these polluted waters, they store them within their edible tissues. Shellfish grown and harvested from polluted waters have been implicated in outbreaks of viral diseases. In spite of this, surveys done in Virginia and Florida estimated that 850,000 and three million people respectively, consume raw oysters (Wittman 1995). The other main source of transmission is from infected food workers who have poor personal hygiene. An infected worker can transfer viral particles to any food. Therefore, proper handwashing and using a clean water supply are vital to controlling the spread of foodborne viruses.

Scientists do not know as much about viruses as they do about bacterial pathogens. One problem has been a lack of good labouratory methods to detect viruses. Without rapid, easy, inexpensive testing methods it has not been possible to study how viruses are transmitted, the number of people who become ill from foodborne viral infections, or the best methods to control viruses. Because of these problems, health care providers often do not order tests to detect viral infections, which causes foodborne illness from viruses to be even more underreported than for bacteria. Epidemiologists estimate that 67 percent of foodborne illnesses can be attributed to viruses, although only a small percentage of total foodborne illness deaths are due to viruses.

Hepatitis A is a virus commonly associated with foodborne infections. The incubation period for hepatitis A, before a person develops any symptoms, is anywhere from 10 to 50 days. It is during this period before symptoms appear that a carrier is most infectious and most likely to spread the disease. Hepatitis A, and many other viral and bacterial pathogens, is most often transmitted via a fecal-oral route. The fact that a person is infectious even before they know they have the disease makes it difficult to control. An outbreak of hepatitis A associated with eating clams in China in 1988 sickened 292,000 people. Since 1996 a vaccine offering lifetime immunity to hepatitis A has been available, but rarely used in the United States.

Parasites

Some parasites also cause foodborne illness. Parasites must live on or inside a living host to survive. The most common foodborne parasites are Anisakis simplex, Cryptosporidium parvum, Toxoplasma gondii, Giardia lamblia, and Cyclospora cayetanensis. Giardia, Cryptosporidium, and Toxoplasma are all protozoa, or single-celled organisms. Cyclospora was not known to cause human sickness until 1979, when the first cases were reported. Since then fresh produce has been associated with several outbreaks of foodborne illness from Cyclospora. Giardia has been identified more than any other pathogen in waterborne disease outbreaks, but there also have been foodborne Giardia outbreaks. Cryptosporidium is also primarily a waterborne pathogen. An estimated 21 percent of waterborne outbreaks from drinking water are due to parasitic agents, mainly Giardia and Cryptosporidium. These two parasites are the most common cause of human parasitic infections in the United States. Toxoplasma gondii is common in warm-blooded animals, including cats, rats, pigs, cows, sheep, deer, chickens, and birds. It can be found in feces and raw meat from these animals. While not a problem for healthy adults, it can cause a very severe infection in unborn babies and in people with immune system disorders. Anisakis simplex and related worms are found in raw or undercooked seafood. Although currently rarely diagnosed in the United States, it is expected that with the increase in consumption of raw fish in the country, anisakiasis will increase. As with viruses, parasitic infections are underreported due to poor testing and diagnostic methods.

Trichinosis, caused by the parasitic worm Trichinella spiralis and associated with eating undercooked pork, is now relatively rare in the United States. The reported incidence of trichinosis has declined from an average of 400 cases per year in the late 1940s to 13 cases in 1997. This decline is due to laws that prohibit feeding garbage to hogs, the increased freezing of pork (freezing kills the parasite), and the practice of thoroughly cooking pork. The largest outbreak recently, in which 90 persons were infected, occurred in 1990 and was caused by the ingestion of a Southeast Asian dish that is made from raw pork sausage. Other recent cases have been associated with eating undercooked horse meat and undercooked wild game such as cougar, boar, bear, and walrus.

BOVINE SPONGIFORM ENCEPHALOPATHY

Bovine spongiform encephalopathy, or mad cow disease, is a fatal brain disease of cattle. The brain of affected animals appears sponge-like under a microscope. BSE first appeared in the United Kingdom in 1986. Since then more than 173,000 cattle in the United Kingdom have become infected. All these cattle and the herds to which they belonged were destroyed. New cases have dropped significantly since the U.K. government enacted measures to stop its spread. Scientists believe the disease may have first been transmitted through feeding cattle protein made from sheep carcasses infected with scrapie, the sheep form of the disease.

Meat-and-bone meal made from infected animals and used as a protein source for cattle feed may also have been a causative factor and was a common practice for several decades. In the early 1980s a change in the manufacturing process that eliminated steam heat treatment may have played a role in the appearance of the disease. Although BSE has not been found in cattle in the U.S., spongiform encephalopathies affect other animals too, and have been found in the United States in sheep (called scrapie), mink, elk, deer, cats, and humans.

The human form is Creutzfeldt-Jakob disease (CJD). It is a rare disease that occurs in approximately one person per million. A new type of CJD, new variant or nvCJD, has been linked to BSE exposure. This new variant of CJD differs from the traditional type mainly in that it affects younger people. To date, approximately 100 cases of nvCJD have been diagnosed, all in Europe. Although scientists know little about the origin, transmission, and nature of spongiform encephalopathies, the most accepted theory is that the causative agent is a prion, a type of pathogenic protein. In 1997 Stanley B. Prusiner from the University of California, San Francisco, won the Nobel Prize for his work on prions. Infective prions are thought to be found only in the brain tissue, spinal cord, and retina of infected animals, not in meat or milk products. Gelatin and beef tallow both undergo a manufacturing process thought to produce a product free of the BSE causative agent. In Papua New Guinea CJD is known as kuru and is believed to have been transmitted through cannibalism. Scientists were puzzled as to why kuru affected mostly women, until they discovered that during funeral ceremonies women traditionally ate the dead person's brain, while men ate the muscle. This tradition has recently been curtailed.

So far there have been no cases of BSE or nvCJD in the United States. The USDA Animal and Plant Health Inspection Service has monitored American cattle for BSE for the past 10 years, with all tests for the disease negative. No beef has been imported from Britain since 1985, and since 1989 there has been a ban on imported cattle from any country where BSE exists. FDA prohibits the use of most mammalian protein in the manufacture of animal feed given to cattle and other ruminants. Much research still needs to be done to better understand this relatively new disease.

PHYSICAL HAZARDS

Physical hazards are foreign objects such as insects, dirt, jewelry, and pieces of metal, wood, plastic, glass, etc. that inadvertently get into a food and could cause harm to someone eating that food. FDA has established maximum levels of natural or unavoidable defects in foods for substances that present no major human health hazard. These are called Food Defect Action Levels. This is the maximum amount of unavoidable defects that might be expected to be in food when handled under good manufacturing and sanitation practices. They are allowed because it is economically impractical, and sometimes impossible, to grow, harvest, or process raw products that are totally free of natural defects. Unavoidable defects include insect fragments, larvae, and eggs; animal hair and excreta; mold, mildew, and rot; shells, stems, and pits; sand and grit. The allowable levels of these substances are set at very specific levels deemed not to be a threat to human health. If a food contains more than these allowable levels, it is considered adulterated. While it may be unpleasant to find such substances in food, eating them at such low levels is not a health hazard and will not lead to illness.

Chapter 7

Food Planning

IMPROVEMENT OF FOOD CROPS

Within the limits dictated by regional agricultural practices and food habits there is a great scope in India for improvement both in food crops and in diet. (1) The preponderance of rice in Eastern and South-Indian diet should be reduced. (2) A mixed diet composed of wheat, rice, barley, maize or ragi is bound to be better balanced than a diet based on only one staple, e.g., rice or ragi. The consumption of atta in rice-eating regions is also to be favoured on account of its higher content in certain minerals such as calcium. Amongst the poorer peasantry of Northern India bajra and jowar are consumed instead of wheat, and, since the former are much poorer in nutritive value than wheat, the diet is deficient. "But good ragi or bajra," observes McCarrison, "either alone or with rice, when eaten with a sufficiency of milk or milk products or fish and green leafy vegetables and fruits, is one of the best diets used by the Indian races." Jowar, like barley, yields a large percentage of malt. Malted jowar produced by fermentation, pounded and mixed with other grains for the preparation of rotis, or used with milkand butter, is a valuable food. (3) The preponderance of carbohydrates in the form of wheat and sugar should be reduced, and the digestibility of protein elements of the diets improved. It is often found that the vegetable protein, dal, is not easily assimilable and causes fermentation. The best Indian dais are arhar and mung. Soya beans represent an important additional source of vegetable protein if taken in relatively small quantities with the cereals.

A decided improvement in the use of dais would consist in grounding the pulse as far as possible into flour and then consuming it by itself or in mixture with grains or cereals. This would aid both preparation and assimilation. (4) The addition of milk and milk products in various forms is a much-needed improvement, since animal foods are taboo for a large of the population. The consumption of butter should be preferred to that of ghee, which is less easily digestible. Besides, the long standing and heating involved in ghee-m&kmg lead to the loss of Vitamin A, sadly wanted in the villages, as the occurrence of eye sores and ulcers abundantly indicates. If the use of butter leads to a shortage of ghee, oil should be more freely used in cooking. (5) The conservation of fisheries and greater use of fish as a principal article of diet are also indispensable. The use of larger vessels and of power and mechanical appliances in the fishing industry, and of cold storage will greatly increase the supply of fish and lower costs in India.

In Japan there has been an increase of 182 per cent in the consumption of fish since 1900; for anxious attention has been drawn there to the relative excess of carbohydrates and the positive lack of protein in that diet by the discovery that the value of the soya bean is greatly modified by an excess of rice.1 This is also true of Bengal and Madras, where the nutritive value of the dais is similarly lost. Throughout India there has been little attempt to conserve and develop fisheries or to regulate fishing in the breeding season. Fishing urgently needs to be regulated by laws that will prevent the use of unsportsmanlike traps and nets, the capture of female fish ready to lay their eggs and the dumping of sewage, oils and wastes into rivers. (6) A greater dependence on vegetables and on fruits would diminish the demand for rice, or of wheat. (7) The quantity of fat is often very inadequate, although the conditions of hard field labour make this element of diet of paramount importance. It is noteworthy that throughout Northern India the consumption of ghee and raw sugar is increased generally in the summer months when agricultural work becomes harder than in the rest of the year.

The extension of the white potato or sweet potato would give a greater yield of starch per acre than is secured from rice. It is estimated in Europe that potatoes will feed 420 persons per 100 acres, while grass, turned into beef, will feed only 15.2 Simon reckons that after the introduction of intensive horticulture, France could easily feed from two to four times her present population. A great deal remains to be done in the directions of scientific storage of grain, of refrigeration offish, meat, dairy products, etc.

The Expansion of Beans, Pulses and Oil-Seeds

With the loss of India's cereal market abroad and with the increase of population pressure, there is no doubt that the production of wheat and barley will become more and more unremunerative. As a matter of fact intensive investigations in the United Provinces have shown that the percentages of losses are the largest in these crops. Any diminution of the wheat acreage, if continued, would imply a decline of the food and living standards inthe wheat-eating regions. Such diminution should accompany the expansion of oilseeds, beans, potatoes and fibre crops, which can be promoted in many wheat areas. For instance, it should be possible to encourage the cultivation of malting barley, potato, soya, linseed and hemp in the Punjab, the U.P. and the C.P. Another possibility is the cultivation of more vegetable fodder to feed the cattle. In the rice areas, the problem of future food supply will be, first, to find out a better staple which will supplement rice, as China has found in the soya, and, secondly, to encourage the cultivation of quick-growing pulses in semi-wet areas, and of cane, beans, and oil-seeds outside the zone of natural rice lands.

While in small quantities pulses form a valuable supplement to the diet mainly composed of rice, the greater use of potato in place of rice is desirable. A diet based on a combination of rice with another cereal is also to be preferred to a diet based exclusively on rice. The present under-nourishment of the poorer sections of the rice zones of India is to be attributed to the high percentage of starch in rice, which so dilutes the protein, e.g., of the dal, that the digestion cannot absorb, or even tolerate the quantity which ought to be taken to neutralise the starch. In Japan the chief cause of under-nourishment of the cultivators, according to Grey, is the same preponderance of starch in a rice diet, which sodilutes the protein consumed that extremely large quantities must be taken, thus placing severe strain on the digestive system.

The problem in India would be for the physiologist to find out which peas, grams and beans would be more nutritive and more easily assimilated with wheat or with rice. The dais contain about twice as much protein as wheat and four times as much as polished rice. Arhar, mung and gram are the richest in proteins and these should also be kneaded into flour and made into chapattis with wheat, barley or other appropriate cereal. Rice, however, cannot be made into chapattis. Thus rice-eating peoples exhibit a tendency to take dal in large quantities, this leading to indigestion. As India's population pressure increases, the production and consumption of peas, grams and pulses will, indeed, expand in substitution of grains.

Such legumes will contribute to replenish soil fertility, add valuable proteins to the dietaries of a vegetarian population and also provide part of the concentrated food for cattle. The total yield of gram in India from 15,822,000acres was 3,671,000 tons in 1934-1935. The Kabuligram is one of the best types in India, and its introduction and increase of yield may be found useful in different Provinces. Even here the poverty of the cultivators stands in the way of adequate use of dais, which is reduced throughout Northern India, where vegetables such as radishes, carrots, onions, brinjals, etc. are available.

In the Review of Agricultural Operations in India(1930-1931), we read: "If falling prices for cereals and fibre crops, coupled with the use of higher-yielding varieties of beans and pulses (thus maintaining the same standard of production on a smaller area), leads to an increase in the area under pulses, the eventual gain to the agriculture of the country might be considerable." In Europe the dry farinaceous vegetables, peas of all kinds, beans and lentils, are cultivated especially on the shores of the Mediterranean and in the regions adjacent to the central zone. In France, Italy, Portugal and Spain, where these are used on a large scale, they replace certain amounts of cereals without noticeable disadvantage. The cultivation of these vegetables is combined advantageously with that of wheat and corn both to increase and vary the food resources of the southern zone.

With a higher population density in India not only beans and pulses but also oil-seeds yielding vegetable oils and fats will increase in acreage and consumption. Vegetable oils play an important and varied role in foods throughout the world. These serve as equivalents for rather different substances but chiefly as replacements for animal fats in the crowded Oriental countries. In the region contiguous to the Mediterranean olive oil is considered a food of the first order; in Central Europe oils extracted from coniferous plants or from the fruits of the beech and nut trees, and in Eastern Europe oils of sesame, flax, hemp and poppy supplement animal fats. Generally speaking, north of the Alps in Europe lard and oleomargarine are now gradually superseding butter, while south of the Alps liquid oils, obtained chiefly from olives and cotton seeds, are preferred to lard, margarine and butter. In India the production of oil-seeds has shown no increase and even diminished in some Provinces, and thus the increasing population cannot avail itself of an important substitute for animal fat, milk and milk-products, the consumption of which has definitely been reduced among the lower income groups.

Every effort should also be made to introduce into India the soya, which is rich in both fats and proteins, and make rice supplementary to it. The soya flour contains over 41 per cent of protein, while wheat has less than 11; and it contains over 20 per cent of fat while wheat has just over1 per cent. Taylor observes: "Under usual circumstances more protein can be secured from the unit of land in the form of legumes than in the form of grain, and much more than in the form of meat. He illustrates that the position of soya bean products in the Chinese diet is an illustration of skilful adaptation in covering with available domestic food- stuffs the minimal requirements for the congested population. With a very meagre amount of meal and practically no use of products, the Chinese have lived on what appears to have been a well-balanced diet by the use of the soyabean and other legumes, supplemented with salted or pickled vegetables, pea-nut oil and occasionally fish. Soyabean is used in the preparation of cooking oil, bean curd and other foods. According to a Chinese expert rice polishing and soyabean cakes, which have never been used as human food except in time of famine, are desirable addition to the diet since these are valuable cheap food for human beings.

The Nutritional Importance of Root Vegetables

Finally, protein wastage in the dietary due to the formation of ammonia for neutralising acid radicals could be effectively reduced by the addition of adequate quantities of tubers and root vegetables such as potatoes, radishes, beet-roots, onions, kachusand ols (collocacia) many of which are not only rich in carbohydrate but also in alkali, Vitamin C andiron, and are also cheap in price. Onion and garlic, apart from their food values, are useful as antiseptic materials. An increased consumption of root vegetables will be useful in yet another way. Some of these, especially potatoes, not only yield more peracre but also require less water for cultivation. Thus the greater cultivation and consumption of root vegetables will be appropriate adjustments to drought conditions in zones of heavy population. It may be noted that some of the pulses popular in the Indian dietary are rich in alkali. Hung dal contains the largest quantity of alkali radical, and next in order come kalai, arhar and masur. As a cheap dietary, a judicious mixture of rice and wheat with pulses, potatoes and roots and green leafy vegetables which makes the acid and base balance each other, will be much more appropriate for rice-eating peoples as population pressure increases. The fat which is deficient in wheat and rice may be contributed by milk and milk products and vegetable or fish oils.

In the wheat zones, instead of the cheaper millets like bajra such cereals as barley and maize, as well as potato, both sweet and white, gram and soya could be profitably introduced and more largely adopted in the dietary. Bajra bread and sweet potato, barley and jowar, are already indicative of the pressure of population on subsistence in Northern India as the preponderance of rice with an inadequate quantity of dal shows the hand-to-mouth existence in parts of Bengal and Southern India. Land might be made to yield more starch in the form of the white potato or sweet potato, which may cut down the production and consumption of rice in India. White potato grows on land too steep and too dry for rice.

In the Punjab the various Scotch varieties of potatoes have yielded about 40 maunds more tubers per acre than the local varieties and are of better quality and size. Germany in recent years, with much less intensive methods than are practised in Japan, has been able to secure more starch per acre from potatoes than Japan, for instance, has secured from rice. The possibilities of solving the population and food problem through changes in diet should be intensively explored and widely advertised in India.

Planned crop production must also take into account the relation between the nutritive quality of food grains to soil and agricultural practice. Recent investigations have shown that the wet varieties of rice are not merely heavier in yield but are richer in protein, fat, and potash contents than the dry crop variety. Food grains, root vegetables and fodder crops treated with organic manures are found to be richer in regard to vitamins and other growth-promoting factors than those grown on synthetic manures. Irrigation also has its effects both upon the yield and quality of food grains. Studies in the nutritive quality of crops are, however, just beginning in India, but these should ultimately guide agricultural practice, ensuring at once the combination of high yield with improved nutritive value of food-crops.

A systematic crop and food planning, taking into consideration the dual need of producing heavy-yielding and energy-producing crops, supplemented, as these should be, by the accessory food products necessary for health and efficiency, must be undertaken in India especially in the areas of population pressure. It is in these areas that food tends to be inadequate or unbalanced; and planned crop production may offset food deficiency and contribute to improve diet and health conditions and distribute the labour of the peasant families to better advantage throughout the year.

FRUIT FARMING AND INDUSTRY

A successful crop-planning would anticipate an economical use of land in India by increasing the yield of food-crops and reducing of the cost of their production. This, in turn, would economise man- power and at the same time release millions of acres of land for the expansion of industrial crops like fruits and vegetables of all kinds, cane, oil-bearing seeds, tobacco and fibres. The cultivation of such crops would react favourably upon the standards of farming and living directly and in- directly, if large indigenous manufactures for the disposal of their products could be established; this might draw off the surplus labour from the land.

Fruit farming is already an important industry in many areas of India, carried on in connection with subsistence farming in uneconomic holdings by specialised castes of vegetable gardeners. Near Benares and Allahabad, for instance, fruit growing has been an indispensable support for the agriculturists, who find ready markets for lemons and guavasin the cities and even for wider distribution. Inparts of the Doab, Oudh, North Bihar and North Bengal plantations of mangoes are numerous. The export of mangoes from Durbhanga, Bhagalpur and Malda is considerable. Similarly, a thriving mango industry has developed in the Bombay Presidency and an orange industry in the Central Provinces and Assam. Even a common fruit like the banana is cultivated systematically in parts of Western Bengal and the Konkan, and a prosperous export trade exists in the neighbourhood of Calcutta. Fruit growing in the plains of India, however, awaits the development of cheap, rapid and reliable transport, of cold storage facilities at the markets and of methods of preserving the surplus crop, such as jam-making, bottling, tinning and sun-drying or evapouration. India annually imports fruits and vegetables valued at about one crore of rupees. The development of the fruit industry on modern scientific lines will not only add valuable foods to the Indian vegetarian population but will also contribute towards diversification of employment and support of small farming.

Sugar-Cane Farming and Industry

Apart from Cuba, India with her 3,478,000 acres (1934-1935) under sugar-cane is the largest producer of sugar in the world. The area has increased from2£ millions in 1929-1930 to about a million acres at the present time; the area under improved canes has increased five-fold. The number of factories has increased, since the grant of protection, from29 to 145. India now produces 6,200,000 tons of sugar, which is more than twice as much as Java, her competitor in the home market. With 145factories employing 200,000 workmen India saves about Rs. 1,250 lakhs, the value of sugar manufactured in 1934-1935. Out of this sum, it is estimated, Rs. 600 lakhs go to the cultivators as price for cane; Rs. 120 lakhs are paid for transportation by rail, road and river; Rs. 300 lakhs go to the labourers in the form of wages and Rs.50 lakhs are paid as salaries. The imports of sugar have decreased from about a million tons in 1930-1931 to only 223,000 tons in 1934-1935.India's yield of sugar-cane per acre, however, still remains low, only about one-third of her total acreage un cier cane producing improved varieties.

It should be mentioned that in tropical India, where canes suitable for the factory could be grown,cane cultivation is at present unimportant. Outside the tropics India's cane area is concentrated, 75per cent of the cane area being found in the Indo-Gangetic plain, to the north of the tropic of Cancer; here cane has a very long dry season, so that the indigenous variety is very different from the cane of Cuba, Java or Hawaii from which the refined sugar, i.e., 1 -4 tons, of modern commerce is obtained. The yields also are much larger in Madras (6,380 Ibs.) and Bombay (6,950 Ibs.) than in the United Provinces (2,700 Ibs.), where there has been the most considerable development of cane cultivation and sugar manufacture. It may be mentioned in this connection that recently a thick cane grown at Coimbatore, Co 419, has proved most satisfactory among the canes for tropical India. It has exhibited better growth and yield than even the wonder cane of Java, POJ 2878, in certain parts of tropical India.In the whole of India the average yield, however, is only 2,956 Ibs. This has recently increased to3,307 Ibs. to the acre as compared with 2 tons in Cuba, over 4 tons in Java and more than 4£ tons in Hawaii.

Greater average yield of cane per acre, which can only be secured by better tillage, irrigation, manuring and supersession of the indigenous type of cane, and better average recovery of sugar, which can only result from improved technique and organisation, will firmly establish the Indian sugar industry on sound lines. This would assure remunerative prices to the farmers, provide seasonal employment fora large number of workers, and aid towards a better population adjustment and planning.

Impobtance of Oil-Seeds

The development of agricultural industries like the production of vegetable oils and fats, and of cotton mills, sugar, soap, tobacco and hemp factories will divert the floating agricultural labourers and small cultivators; and thus a judicious balance of agriculture and rural industrialisation would be the chief remedy for the excessive population pressure. In the whole of India oil-seeds represent a valuable crop in the dry season and an important item in rural economy. Linseed, rape-seed, sesame and ground-nuts could be greatly expanded in output and thus help to meet the increased food demands of the growing population and establish the manufacture of oils and fats, which have important industrial uses, on a sound footing.

For many years over 20 per cent of India's total exports, in weight and in value, consisted of oil- seeds, after all the home demands were met; andin quality or quantity, or both, India is supreme with half the world's supply of sesame and ground- nuts (Madras), a third of its cotton (Bombay),two-thirds of its rape and mustard (United Provinces), and one-eighth of its linseed (Central Provinces), the best of its coco-nut (Malabar),and 100 per cent of its castor (Deccan). In some cases, the cotton-seed for instance, improved varieties would greatly increase the yield of seeds, though the peasant's need for oil already makes him prefer a variety that yields more seed than fibre.

Owing to the population pressure there has, however, been no increase in production of the four principal oil-producing seeds during the last thirty years. In fact the tendency is towards decrease. Similarly, the exports have fallen. In the case of linseed, exports have tended upwards in recent years, assisted as they have been by the Ottawa Preference granted to India by the United Kingdom. The exports of rape-seed and sesame, which have always been relatively less important than the exports of linseed, have contracted very consider- ably in volume, and now hold a minor position in India's export trade. When we come to ground-nuts, however, the position is entirely different, both in respect of production and export. From the pre-war period the production has expanded by five and a half times, in fact, this expansion has taken place since the end of the war. Similarly, the exports have increased during the same period by two and a halfto three times their pre-war and also their immediate post-war volume. Further, this is not a ca_e of a large percentage increase from a small figure of production and export in the pre-war base period, but from a production of some 600,000 tons and an export of over 200,000 tons valued at 3| crores of rupees.

Development of Oil-Crushing Industry

With heavier population in India it will be un- economical to grow more oil-seeds for exporting them either raw or in 'the form of cakes, as this would mean a serious drain of nitrogen. On the other hand, with formidable rivals like the Argentine in the supply of linseed, China in the production of sesame, and Roumania in the supply of rape-seed, with the difficulty of supplying uniform and reliable products for the European industries and with applied chemistry constantly discovering new substitutes for old products, it would be on the whole advantageous to develop a large indigenous oil-crushing industry in the country. The cake would mostly be used up in the fields and consumed by the cattle, while the vegetable oils and fats would support the growing soap manufacture and other industries in the country.

With increase of industrialisation the Chinese—whose export of soya beans has risen to the first place, amounting to about one-fourth of China's total export trade—press a third to a fourth of the beans before shipment. The oil goes to Europe and America, while the residue is made into cakes and used as a fertilizer or as cattle food. A considerable portion of the cake is also shipped to Japan for use as a fertiliser for mulberry. The local manufacture of oil and oil-cake is a far more economical utilization of oil-bearing seeds and beans than that which India has adopted. There will be obvious agricultural advantages from utilisation of oil cakes as valuable manures, now lost to the country, which would be available for such crops as sugar-cane, cotton, tobacco and tea, and in the diversification of industry. Oil mills, which now number 205 and give employment to 10,348 hands in India, have greatly increased during the last three decades. In Madras alone the number rose from six in 1921 to 34 in 1931, the number of hands employed being 276 and 900respectively. Besides these factories there are a number of mills working at a smaller scale through- out India, while in addition the primitive bullock-driven oil-crushing industry is established in large villages of India. The total trade, however, is small and admits of considerable expansion.

Among the Indian essential oils sandal-wood is the most valuable and is a monopoly of Southern India, especially Mysore, but it is now facing fierce competition from Australia. The Indian essential oil industry is not yet set on a firm footing. Vetivertajoqa, cardamom, coriander, ginger, cloves, etc. and several varieties of fragrant gums and resins are still being exported largely instead of being marketed in India. There is scope for extending the production of such crops by systematic cultivation as is done in some other countries, while the recovery of the essential oils in situ is likely, with proper organisation, to prove remunerative.

Uses of Vegetable Oils in India and Foreign Countries

There is a considerable consumption of vegetable oils in India, and the internal demand will increase with increase of population and the scarcity of ghee and butter. A still more important outlet for vegetable oils lies in industrial development. There is a great scope in India for the manufacture of soaps and of vegetable fats. The quantity of soapsimported into India rose from about 250,000 cwts .in 1909-1910 to about 450,000 cwts in 1929-1930.With the establishment of a few soap-factories on modern scientific lines in the country the total imports of soap were reduced to 296,000 cwts in1932-1933 and 303,000 in 1933-1934. There is also a considerable number of establishments where soap is made by crude methods in India. Since a large section of the Indian consumers object to the use of animal fats; there is great scope for the production of vegetable oils and fats for use in soap manufacture. India also imports annually over one crore of rupees' worth of vegetable ghee, vegetable fat, etc., most of which is consumed as edible fats or substitutes for ghee. America has applied extensively the hydrogenation process to the lard compound industry, while Europe has applied it in the margarine industry to a large number of vegetable and animal, chiefly marine oils. Factories in India which may render vegetable oils and fats edible by hardening, refining and deodorising, will meet the steady and growing demand for hardened fats both for soap manufacture and as a cheap ghee substitute.

Vegetable oils have also other uses in industries the establishment of which will lead to the expansion of oil-bearing seeds and the development of remunerative agricultural industries.

Most of our oil-bearing seeds have to face the increasing competition of other agricultural countries and from similar products, the supply of which has also been increasing rapidly. The recent world depression in agriculture has also resulted in the falling off in the demand for cattle-feeding stuff, which has distinctly lowered the price of and demand for oil-seed, cake and compounds made there from. The establishment of a large oil-crushing industry is so important in India for prevention of the annual economic drain in the form of loss of oil-cakes possessing inestimable value as fertilisers and cattle food and oils, which might, if properly manipulated, prove of use for soap, colour, paint, varnish and the linoleum industries, that it is necessary to shepherd the new and growing industries by the imposition of an export duty on oil-seeds and oil- cakes. The manufacture of cheap ghee substitutes would also be important from the standpoint of the Indian dietary, the price of ghee at present being too high to be used normally in the peasant's household.

Fibre Production and Manufacture

Among the fibre crops jute, cotton, hemp and silk are important. As regards jute it appears that both production and export have reached saturation points for the present at least, and until new uses of jute are forthcoming any expansion in the world market in jute cannot be hoped for. The Jute Enquiry Committee recently recommended the ex- tension of voluntary restriction of jute cultivation and suggested that the land set free by restricting jute cultivation could be most profitably utilised in the cultivation of rice, sugar-cane and finer varieties of tobacco. The Committee have found jute meeting with competition which is developed along two mainlines: (a) progressive elimination of jute sacks as containers for grain in transit owing to increased adoption of bulk handling; (6) substitution of jute by paper, and to a less extent by cotton, for the making of bags. The danger is real and the remedy lies in putting forth every effort to retain trade which the industry now holds; and in initiating and vigorously pursuing a policy of research with the object of discovering fresh markets and new uses for jute. Agricultural research should continue with the object of obtaining new strains of jute which may give better results either in the matter of yield, or quality, or both.

The trend of cotton production has been a definite increase, especially in the six or seven year's ending1929. The highest figure reached was 121 lakhs of bales (of 400 Ibs. each). Since then there has been a decrease. From a quinquennial average of 25million acres, the area under cotton has now dropped to 22-5 in 1932-1933. Such decrease of cotton cultivation has been due to unfavourable seasons, increase of cane cultivation, cheaper cotton prices and the damage from the pink boll worm. India now imports certain grades of longer staple cotton which she cannot produce in sufficient quantity to meet her requirements. Both the pre-war and post- war averages of raw cotton imports were 12,000 tons, but in 1932-1933 the figure reached was 85,000tons. There is thus large scope, with the extension of irrigation, for the improvement both of the quality and yield of cotton. Only about one-seventh of the total cotton area in India is under improved varieties. Longer stapled varieties can be grown successfully in the irrigated areas of the Punjab and Madras.

Sann hemp occupies in India some 6 lakhs acres annually. Though a considerable proportion of the production is consumed locally, the export trade is of considerable value, representing 281,000 cwt. in 1932-1933. Method of retting and preparing the hemp fibre have to be improved if Indian hemp can maintain its position in foreign markets in com- petition with the Naples and the Russian supply. Manilla hemp is also a powerful competitor of India, especially in the British market.

The production of silk was formerly of great importance in Indian agriculture. Some of the finest silks in the world were formerly obtained in the villages of Murshidabad and Maldah, where mulberry cultivation and cocoon rearing reached high standards. Sericulture and silk-weaving ought to be revived wherever conditions are favourable, and this would add an important subsidiary cultivation and industry for the Indian peasants. It is well known that both China and Japan produce silk of great importance in their export trade and cocoon production, and silk reeling and weaving are important bye-occupations for the small farmers in those countries.

Industries, large, medium-sized or small, are the most important means of relieving the present heavy pressure of population on the soil. India' space of industrialisation is exceedingly tardy. In any system of industrial planning in India it is essential to stress the important role of those industries in particular which are distributed nearer the sources of the raw materials and offer facilities to the peasants to obtain remunerative prices for the cultivation of raw materials and industrial crops, which may supplement their subsistence cropping.

The Preference of Vegetable Foodstuffs

The man-land ratio has contributed to the exclusion of foods of animal origin in India. For the last few decades milk and milk-products yielded by the cow, the mother of the ubiquitous and irreplaceable bullock, have strikingly diminished in consumption; and this has resulted in a serious impoverishment of the diet of the peasantry. Yet the value of the present milk output of 700-800 million maunds in India is estimated as much nearer Rs. 400 than Rs. 300 crores a year, and is larger than the estimated value of cattle labour from Rs. 300 to Rs. 500 crores and of cattle manure worth about Rs. 270 crores.

Of all parts of India the Punjab and the North-Western Frontier Province show the largest consumption of animal products in the dietary. But even in the Punjab the bulk of the food constituents and energy values is drawn from the vegetable products. Kartar Singh, who collected a number of family budgets from Lyallpur in the Punjab presented the relative importance of animal and vegetable products in the Punjab diets.

The lower percentages of both calories and proteins derived from animal products than those obtained from vegetable products are due to the fact that a large consumption of the former is incompatible with the economical use of small-holdings. That vegetable products give more of food values is giving the amount of various constituents in each class of food purchased for one rupee in Lyallpur. To produce 1,000 calories in the form of milk requires two and a half to four times as much land as to produce 1,000 calories in the form of wheat, rice and other cereals. Similarly, fruits and vegetables and particularly meat and beef, give in general a much lower caloric return per acre than cereals and root vegetables such as potatoes.

Owing to excessive agricultural protection, several European countries, despite increasing population, have shown a considerable reduction in the calorimetric value of food and the preference of bread and potatoes to meat, fruit, vegetables and dairyproduce. Thus the clearly marked evolution of consumption of food-stuffs and better nutriment in the direction of variety, marked for the last half century, has been checked.

The difference in caloric yield of various foods per unit of land is also reflected in their prices, as for instance in the Punjab. The reason, there- fore, why the Eastern countries ordinarily do not and cannot favour animal products cannot be exclusively religious. Vegetarianism is ultimately a result of a heavy population pressure.

What Buck has observed about the Chinese dietaries accordingly holds good also of the Indian dietaries: "Greater amounts of such animal foods as dairy products and eggs introduced as a new industry would diversify farming, but might be less economical of the land, except in a very limited way. While it remains to be proved that all the necessary essentials of a good diet can be obtained from the vegetable kingdom, still the evidence points to such a probability. If so, then the advantages to be had from the raising of animals depend largely upon their economical utilisation of bye-products and on their place in soil fertility maintenance."

As a matter of fact McCollum and Simmonds have found that diets made up of a mixture of maize, alfalfa leaf and cooked peas, subsequently dried, have led to considerable growth and reproduction and must be regarded as satisfactory.

Leafy vegetables (saks), which are largely consumed in India, contain iron compounds which help towards an adequate oxidation of food-stuffs in the system. Observation shows that in the West meat is absent entirely from the menus of certain categories of workmen who are endowed with vigour and energy, whereas none have been found who abstain permanently from the use of fats or milk. In many agricultural districts of France, Italy and Spain the populations eat meat once a year, on the day of the patron saint. In the crowded countries of the Eastman can afford but small additions of meat, fish, poultry or egg to his diet, consisting in great measure of vegetable food, including the leafy vegetables whose nutritive values the West has never learnt to appreciate.

Maximum Land Utilisation

As population pressure increases there is a tendency everywhere not merely to use more carbohydrates than proteins, since the former are cheaper, but also to supersede all dairy products, animal foods and fruits; and this often causes an unbalance which is particularly characteristic of the poorer sections and communities. It must be conceded that the Indian dietary involves a minimum land requirement, about 97 per cent of the food energy consumed by the peasant family being derived from seeds, roots and vegetables. while the superiority of German to British agriculture is due to much higher proportion of arable to grass- land and a dietary in which the energy is obtained more economically, i.e., from potatoes compared with meat, and in meat from pork than that from beef as in Great Britain. In India the advantage is due to double-cropping which is made possible here as well as in China by the long growing season under conditions of summer rainfall, as well as to the complete omission of animal raising and dependence on a vegetarian diet based on seeds, roots and leafy vegetables.

Where hand-cultivation is seen at its best, as in the case of rice, India's yields are high, though much lower than in

China and Japan, but these are otherwise low as compared with crop yields in other countries. The gradual expansion of cultivated area and the almost complete conversion of pastures into tilled lands in the congested areas of India have resulted in the impoverishment of cattle. The heavier the population, the smaller is the holding in India. The inability to devote any but a mere fraction of the tiny holding to fodder crops aggravates the fodder shortage, which becomes a serious fodder famine two or three months before the monsoon in consider- able parts of India. The triangular problem of food supply is illustrated in the United Provinces, for instance, by the fact that about a million animals graze over only 5,000 square miles in the forests of the United Provinces. The forest area represents only 5 per cent of the total area of the province and aids very little in meeting fodder requirements since less than one million of the 32 millions of cattle ever go near the forests. Of the total net cultivated area of 295 million acres in India, 251million acres grow food-grains. Only 10 million acres represent special fodder crops. The majority of the Indian cattle obtain their requirements from what- ever grazing is available, from straw and stalk and other residues from the human foodstuffs, and are starved seasonally in the dry months when grasses whither.

Inverse Correspondence between Cattle Density and Crop Area

It is needless to state that in the United Provinces, Bihar and Orissa, and Bengal, the cattle cannot obtain their minimum feeding requirement at all. The competition of both the human and bovine population for maintenance on small-holdings which must yield both food and fodder crops has resulted in the steady deterioration of animals' food supply and of their breed and efficiency. One might expect that heavy population density thins out bovine population. But it is one of the striking economic paradoxes in India that the Provinces which have the smallest crop area per capita maintain the largest numbers of cattle. In fact the density of bovine population per crop area varies directly with human population density and inversely with the crop area per person.

In China, and particularly in Japan, the struggle for human subsistence has, as we have seen, crowded out all but draught animals and types such as pigs and chickens which forage for themselves. In Japan, where about 5J million farming families cultivate roughly 15 million acres, a little under 3 acres per family, the number of cattle is exceedingly small, only 1,512,000; pigs, goat and sheep forming another million. In India the animal population is excessive and the uneconomical maintenance and multiplication of useless superfluous cattle, due to religious and humanitarian considerations, represent a problem which baffles the efforts of all social and economic reformers.

India's Superfluous Cattle

Agriculture in India, as elsewhere, is economically impossible if the fodder of the working animals must be bought; and the farm must provide it, either in the shape of fodder crops, or of the bye-products of other crops, the straw and stalks (principally those of the jowar, bajra, maize and now of sugar- cane and the straw of wheat and gram) which form the bulk of the fodder supply. The result is a close interrelation between the size of a holding, the classof crops grown, and the number and quality of the cattle employed; and it is this which accounts for the violent contrasts between the cattle in different tracts, from the costly and powerful animals of large holdings in the Punjab canal colonies, the upper Ganges Doab or North Gujarat, to the miser- able half-starved beasts in the rice tracts of Bihar, Bengal and Orissa. In the latter areas the cattle are much smaller, the holdings are smaller and the number of plough bullocks kept is larger. In wheat, cotton and millet zones of India the total number of cattle lie between 20 and 30 per hundred acres of net area sown with from 8 to 10 plough cattle, whereas where the rice is the predominant crop between three or four times the number is expected.

Multiplication of Cattle to Counteract Inefficiency

The increase of the cattle population in India decade by decade in the present fodder situation suggests a vicious circle.

This was observed by Royal Commission of Agriculture: "The number of cattle within a district depends upon, and is regulated by, the demand for bullocks. The worse the conditions for rearing efficient cattle are, the greater the numbers kept tend to be. Cows become less fertile and their calves become undersized and do not satisfy cultivators, who, in the attempt to secure useful bullocks, breed more and more cattle. "This may be vividly illustrated by contrasting the conditions of fodder cultivation and cow-keeping in Meerut and Bulandshahr on the one hand and Gorakhpur and Basti districts on the other.

In the Doab climate and social tradition have evolved an efficient mixed farming, a moderate number of live-stock being maintained by fodder cropping. Fewer but more efficient cattle in the Doab provide nutrition for the people help materially to maintain soil fertility and increase its total output for the cultivators. In the eastern districts of the United Provinces, on the other hand, the more considerable proportion of cattle is useless and their multiplication implies a progressive deterioration of breed of cattle and economic position of the cultivators. In the United Provinces only about 6-8 percent of cows yield 3 seers of milk per day and 26-5 percent of the buffaloes yield more than 4 seers of milk. Out of such cows and buffaloes 75 per cent belong to Meerut and Agra divisions. As regards bulls, there is only one bull to 263 cows in the Province, while the Report of the Royal Commission on Agriculture mentions one bull to 56 cows as the conservative demand. Bulls are decreasing owing to scarcity of fodder, disease and decline of the practice of dedication. In the Sub-Himalaya East, which includes Gorakhpur and Basti districts the number of bulls declined by 23 and 30 per cent between 1920-1925 and 1925-1930 on the figures of the 1920 Census, while in the West Indo-Gangetic Plain, these increased by 22 and 16 per cent.

An intensive investigation of the cattle population in the district of Sitapur, in Oudh, has shown certain striking results which are typical of the zones of heavy concentration in India.

Since 1891 the total cattle population increased in the village surveyed from 338 to 357; cows and bullocks increased from101 to 196 and plough bullocks and buffaloes from120 to 330. On an average 209 bullocks are employed in cultivating 100 acres of land.

The economic minima have been estimated to be 1 acre in the case of light soil and three-fourths of an acre in hard soil in Bengal, which a pair of bullocks working eight hours a day should cultivate. Not merely are the majority of the bullocks superfluous but out of a total number of 142 cows114 are found unproductive. Twenty-one of these yield half a seer, 5 yield up to 1 seer and only 2over 1 seer of milk per day. Out of 54 cow-buffaloes, however, only 3 are found unproductive, 4 yield milk up to 1 seer, 30 between 1 and 2 seers; 9 between 2 and 3 seers and only 1 over 3 seers of milk per day. There is chronic starvation on the part of the cattle, which accounts for on an average of one-third of the total cattle mortality. Many plough bullocks are sold off in winter, or their rations are ruthlessly decreased whenever they are not worked in full, while the milch cattle are kept on after lactation, solely on poor and inadequate grazing.

On the other hand, scrub bulls are allowed every- where to cover heifers, which are generally immature, so that the herd multiplies although many of the animals do not get a chance to live. In considerable parts of India which are hot and dry the dry weather leads to such diminution of supply of fodder grass that except in tracts adjacent to grazing areas or where migration to distant pastures at certain seasons is possible there is virtual starvation of cattle. Even in the wet parts of India the grass is so coarse and becomes so deficient in nutriment in the hot weather that the beasts have seriously deteriorated. These hardly produce sufficient return from milk or from the production of work animals and rightly fetch but little for slaughter. Particularly in the zones of heavy human concentration do these represent a serious chronic drain on the very limited resources of small farmers.

Better Breeds in Regions of Inadequate Rainfall

It is one of the striking paradoxes with which we are familiar in economic life in India that while she has a total cattle population of 2142 millions, her working cattle, numbering about 60 million, fall far short of her demand for draught power. India's total cultivated area is about 300 million acres. A pair of bullocks to 10 acres of arable land is hardly sufficient for careful tillage in considerable parts of the country. In most Provinces it is the useless and uneconomical stock which forms a large and increasing proportion of the animal population. Another curious paradox is that most of India's superior live-stock come from those parts where rainfall is low, water supply scarce and grass- land resources deficient. With the development of irrigation and expansion of the cultivated area, grazing areas are reduced everywhere and animals coming from the irrigated zones are much inferior in condition, sc far as their performance is concerned, while they are more susceptible to parasitic infections and disease in general. In the tracts of heavy rainfall the phenomenal concentration of human population has also led to the invasion of all grass-lands and pastures by the plough and has made fodder scarcer and scarcer, and probably both climatic and nutritional causes account for the deterioration of the local breeds. In the Ganges Valley as we proceed eastward the rainfall becomes heavier, population increases and the cattle become punier and lighter in weight.

Both a chronic fodder shortage and moist hot climate result in a rapid deterioration of the stocks, which leads the peasants to multiply more and more of the superfluous, under-developed beasts. Thus while in the dry areas where natural grasses are deficient the stock-owners maintain a moderate bovine population, supplement fodder by valuable foodstuffs and carryon a remunerative business by selling the animals and their products, in the moist areas both human and bovine population multiply indefinitely, jeopardizing the health and welfare of both and gradually narrowing their economic base. Due to the excessive burden of the animal population and the intensive grazing, browsing and lopping, the vegetation over large tracts of Northern India has reverted to the bush and scrub jungle and coarse grass type from which the live-stock cannot derive an adequate sustenance.

Effects of Malnutrition among Cattle

Investigations clearly indicate that the existence of goitre, osteomalacia and other bone troubles, emaciation, birth of weak calves and pica are due to malnutrition. At Coonoor, animals living on imperfect diets have shown a greater tendency to infections of the respiratory and gastro-intestinal tract, and of stone-formation in the bladder. A great loss of body calcium is a predisposing factor in the greater incidence of certain diseases in heavy milking cows such as milk fever, tuberculosis and Johne's disease. The latter is now rapidly spreading in India. Other types of losses, such as those resulting from irregular breeding and abortion of non-infectious origin, which are quite common in India, are also probably due to faulty dieting on a calcium and Vitamin A deficient ration.

Vitamin A deficiency in the diet of cows is also found to produce blindness among calves. Prolonged malnutrition or famine leads to the suppression of oestrus. Thus in India in the drought years village cows do not bear calves, or bear them only in alternate years or even only once in three years when the body reserves for minerals and other essentials are re-established. As numbers of cattle increase or as the increase of tillage encroaches on the better grazing land, the pressure on the available supply of food leads to further poverty in the local breeds, and a stage is reached when oxen from other Provinces or male buffaloes are bought in to assist cultivation as inBengal. Weight for weight, a small animal consumes a much larger quantity of food than a bigger animal. Thus an animal weighing 500 Ibs. is estimated to consume not half but about two-thirds of what an animal weighing 1,000 Ibs. would consume. Thus real improvement can come only from raising the quality and limiting the quantity.

Increase and Deterioration of Cattle

In many districts in Bengal the land is never ploughed until a good shower of rain has softened it. This explains also why cows are sometimes yoked to the plough and the miserable animals of the delta appear to do as much work as the finer beasts of the United Provinces. Every available inch in Bengal, it might be said, of the land that is fit for cultivation and not required for human occupation is brought under the plough or planted with fruit-bearing trees. Public grazing grounds have almost disappeared. The absence of grazing facilities in some of the over- stocked districts is deduced from the Cattle Census Report of Bengal of1915. Over and above this there are the shortage of £grazing nutriment and deterioration of the grasses; due to the uncontrolled and excessive use for decades. Of a total cropped area of about 31 million acres in 1915 only 01 million acres were under fodder crops. The staple fodder in Bengal was paddy straw | from about 23 million acres. In a Government Report we read: "Even if the whole of this straw were made available as cattle food (it is well known it is not) the supply would be insufficient for the barest requirements. It works out at about 2 seers per day, whereas the normal consumption should be about5 seers.

Taking three districts in the order of their agricultural decline, viz., Hooghly, Burdwan and Jessore, we find that between 1920-1930 the live-stock have yet increased phenomenally. Every pathway or cattle track is narrowed down by the cultivator whose field is on either side, until barely room is left for two persons to pass each other on foot. The banks of tanks and the slopes of the embankments of public roads are the only grazing-grounds and the cattle subsist mainly on paddy straw, paddy-husks and the coarse grass which grows in tanks almost silted up. Just after the rice crop has been cut they get enough to eat, but at other times of the year they are half-starved. The lack of sufficient pasture, the absence of good fodder and the inability of the peasants to stall-feed their beasts have led in Bengal to a deterioration of cattle unparalleled in the rest of India. As cattle become smaller the cultivator increases their numbers to offset their inefficiency. On the other hand, as the cattle become smaller the amount of food needed in proportion to their size increases. For it must not be supposed that the food required by 100small cattle is the same as that needed by 50 double the size. All this accelerates the rate at which the conditions become worse for both the breeding and maintenance of good live-stock.

Economic Folly in Increasing Scrub Cattle

The live-stock is thus fast and progressively in- creasing and deteriorating not only in many districts in Bengal but also in the densely populated parts of Orissa and Madras, in the eastern districts of the United Provinces and in north and south Bihar. Economic folly cannot go further. But the folly is being repeated by small-holders who have the largest proportion of useless cattle that drain on their meagre resources. The small-holder has his own way of meeting the fodder shortage; he sells his cattle in the beginning of summer, as soon as he can spare them, and buys new ones as the agricultural operations begin, thus avoiding the expense of feeding them at the time when fodder and grazing is shortest. But this sometimes involves great loss for him and profits for the peripatetic cattle-dealers who swarm about in the countryside when the monsoon begins. In India, as a whole, the bovine population increased from 152-8 to 214-2 millions between 1912-1913 and 1934-1935—an increase of45 per cent in two decades. The major portion of his increase comes from small cultivators in the zones of human concentration where the majority of the holdings are uneconomic.

With a chronic fodder shortage, the offspring from the under-fed and under-bred animals become progressively poorer in each generation. The only redeemable feature recently found by the Punjab Government—if it can be considered so—is that these scrub cattle are almost immune to the ordinary live-stock diseases and to the periods of particular shortage of grass in drought years—traits which would decimate the better-bred stock. Thus no improvement of the breed of cattle is possible unless the chronic fodder difficulty is solved, and its solution is rendered more and more difficult by the multiplication of scrub cattle. In the Punjab Report we read, "If the scrub cattle are 'bred up'(improved) by the introduction of good bulls of foreign breed, and the half-bred progeny have to compete for the present inadequate ration of fodder, they will fall an easy prey to disease and drought, because they will have lost some of their mothers' hardiness and immunity." Thus does the vicious circle extend, including in its expanding ambit cattle, crops and men.

Since fodder and pasturage are deficient large numbers of inefficient cattle which are preserved in a state of semi-starvation consume fodder that is sadly required for the better cattle. Overgrazing leads to the deterioration of the grass-lands, erosion of their surface soil and the loss of nutriment value of the fodder, which often acquires harmful quality on account of deficiency of certain mineral contents such as phosphorus and auximones. On the other hand, surface tillage due to the lower strength of the cattle and inadequate manuring lead to deterioration of arable land.

Malnutrition thus 'pursues its harmful course in an ever-widening vicious circle; the cultivator is too often ill-nourished and ravaged by disease which is commonly the result of his ill-nourishment. Obviously, the poorer the beast is fed, the poorer in food-value must be its produce. In most districts of the Punjab the physicians generally agree that at least half the prevalent illnesses are due to malnutrition, cause l by the dairy produce being poorer in essential body- building chemicals than it ought to be. It must be remembered that the dairy animals are better fed in the Punjab than in most Provinces of India. Throughout India the cultivator and his animals are in competition for the sustenance which can be grown on the available land and are alike ill-nourished, both toiling wearily in a heartless effort to extract from the ill-nourished earth enough to keep them from starvation.

Religious Sentiment

The numbers of cattle have become so large and their efficiency has fallen so low in India as results of the process having advanced so far that the task of reducing the number of useless animals and of reversing the process of deterioration is now extremely difficult. In several ways social and religious sentiments which belong to more spacious times in the past, and have now become obvious economic misfits, have conspired to aggravate the difficulty. To kill a bullock or a cow is a deadly sin in Hinduism. The orthodox Hindu often objects to sell, even in extreme circumstances, because sale is usually to a butcher and leads to the slaughterhouse. Rather than selling the cattle to the cattle-dealer he sends them to a gowshala or lets them loose to die. There is a remarkable difference in this respect as between Hindu and Muslim communities, with its reactions upon agriculture and animal husbandry.

North of the Jhelum in the Punjab, Darling observes, cattle-breeding should be as easy as everywhere else it is difficult; for, except among the few Hindus, there is not the least prejudice against the sale to the butcher of infirm or aged stock, and it is even rare for a bullock or cow to be kept from affection after it is past work. Nor does anyone object either to castration or to inoculation on religious grounds. Further, north of the Jhelum bulls are nearly always tied up and to the south, according to Hindu custom, they are allowed to roam wherever they like. In the one case breeding can be controlled and in the other bulls wander about the fields consuming or damaging at least three times as much fodder as they need, and covering as they please. The difference is of great importance in a country where cows are of all sorts and good bulls far too few.

Unless the Hindu sentiment is abjured altogether the Indian cultivators cannot take a practical view of animal keeping and will continue to preserve animals many of which are quite useless from birth to death, the number of these being the greatest among the small cultivators who can afford it least. Secondly, the ancient right of dedicating a bull as an act of piety was once a public service, the animals in old times being carefully selected and of a good class. Now the animal dedicated is generally selected for its worthlessness and the sire has often become a vagrant pest. The open field system of the vast majority of the Indian villages makes it difficult to control the promiscuous mating of animals. Miserable, half-starved males roam about in the countryside, perpetuating their species and further reducing their quality in the country.

The Dual Purpose Cattle

An important remedy lies in the direction of evolving suitable types of dual purpose animals, the males being efficient as field workers and the females as milch animals. Such cattle are obtainable in India, many of the best breeds posing these dual qualities. Such dual breeds will include buffaloes, the high butter content of whose milk makes them specially valuable for ghee production and the basis of prosperity of mixed farming in the Punjab, Gujarat and the United Provinces. Buffaloes, how- ever, can compete on the whole favourably with ordinary cows, as they are heavier milk-yielders, and possibly even with improved cows in areas where coarse forage is abundant. Another advantage for the peasant in buffalo keeping is that buffaloes can be more easily disposed of even for slaughter than the cattle.

High-grade cows of Indian milch breeds are, however, already after only a comparatively few years of selective breeding, able to hold their own, under suitable conditions of management, in regard to the over-all cost of milk and butter-fat production. The male cattle also is more useful as a draught-animal than the male buffalo in the greater part of India. Thus the evolution of the dual purpose cattle will render buffaloes largely superfluous as sources of milk and reduce their numbers in the country. The development of mechanical transport, which will enable milk to be brought rapidly to the cities from the distant villages where cows can be kept economically, may greatly aid dairy farming. Refrigerating apparatus and pasteurisation may also contribute towards the economical maintenance of milch cows and buffaloes in the country-side and towards the solution of the chronic scarcity of milk in all Indian towns.

OBSTACLES TO MIXED FARMING

With such facilities, a type of simple dairying on the basis of two or three better class milch cows in each holding and growing fodder crops, may increase the output and maintain the fertility of the land, provided that the number of both human and animal dependents on the farm does not overstep proper limits. A balanced combination of dairy and cereal farming may thus have the obvious advantages of providing for the proper nutrition of the cultivator's family, increasing the income from the land and at the same time minimising the risks of over-production of money-crops, and of soil depletion, both of which hare difficult to avoid. Belgium, Netherlands and Germany provide excellent examples of countries which are densely populated and highly industrialised and in which cattle form a part of a system of intensive cultivation based on dairy farming. The proportion of dairy cows in the herds was as high as 52-7 in Belgium and 50-5 in the Netherlands in 1933. In Germany the large proportion of cows (56'8) in the herds is especially noteworthy and indicates the importance of the dairy industry.

Milch cows predominate on the smaller holdings in Germany, where they are also frequently used for work, and as the size of the holding increases the relative number of dairy cows tends to diminish. In South Germany the custom of working the cows in the fields is common, but the practice does not obtain in the plains of the northern and eastern Provinces, where attention is concentrated on dairying and the production of beef. The existing grass- land is insufficient to provide adequate feed for the stock and recourse is had to import of fodder, development in the supplies of hay, clover, Lucerne and sweet lupine and to the utilisation of cattle cake consisting largely of the residual product of Germany's important oil-seed and nut-crushing industry. In India the indigenous manufacture of vegetable oils might also increase the production of concentrated feed, which could be an important factor in the rationalisation of dairy farming.

Such a high proportion of milk cows in the total cattle population in Central Europe are ample evidence of the success of animal husbandry. Similar figures about dairy farming are not available in India. The percentage of milk cows in the total bovine population is only 22 and 20. The yield of milk is only 1 maund, 1 seer. Mulch-cows yielding less than two seers of milk per diem are regarded as uneconomical. The preponderance of useless cows and bulls is evident from the above investigations. On the other hand, in those areas in India, where mixed farming is in vogue, only a moderate but efficient bovine population is maintained on the holdings, which grow more fodder crops and yield much larger quantities of milk and milk products for both consumption and sale. A recent survey of seven of the most typical breeding tracts of India has revealed that while in India as a whole Wright has estimated that only 7 to 8 ozs. of liquid milk per head per day are consumed, these areas show aper Capita consumption of milk and milk products of about 10 ozs. per day. A balance of 13 ozs. Is mostly sold off the holdings as milk or ghee though a small proportion is stored as ghee for future use. In addition, the skimmed milk is also consumed, the average consumption per head being8-75 ozs. per day.

In the zones of heavy human population pressure, however, where the cultivator cannot obtain adequate subsistence for his family from the holding it is impossible to expect the development of mixed farming, based as it is on the production of fodder crops. Where neither suitable grazing is available nor fodder crops can be grown, the working bullocks can be kept in proper condition only by the practice of controlled breeding, and elimination of the unfit. It will be enough gain for the small cultivator if his bullocks can improve their draught power and their supply of humus to the soil. Even the cow ordinarily does not at present produce enough milk for her calf in these tracts, and the introduction of the milch type cattle, which requires more food, would be futile. Here and there, where the holdings are larger, the well-to-do cultivator may take advantage of the expansion of the market for milk and ghee by maintaining a few good type milk animals and growing fodder crops for them. But on the whole in the areas of human concentration in India where the majority of holdings are undersized, the slender resources of the farmer, and the necessity of devoting every section of his holding to food or to crops which yield him a direct cash return, prevent the adoption of systematic dairying.

Overcoming the Cattle Crisis

In a country of dense population, as India is, the combination of dairy industry with farming can only be attempted in tracts where there are large, actual, or potential grazing areas. For the rest of India, the adoption of dairy farming, the expansion of fodder crops, stall feeding, and the improvement of breed, all hang together, and these ultimately rest on a planned programme of reduction of superfluous and useless cattle. Definitely the first step towards mitigating the present cattle crisis should be the compulsory castration of all unfit and useless male stock and legislative restriction, wherever practicable, of the number of calves in each herd. Not only scrub bulls but also uncastrated bullocks used for carts should be castrated to prevent damage to the breed. Greater increase of the inferior cattle aggravates the fodder situation and makes dairying impossible.

That a notable victory has been won over popular prejudice is shown by the fact that in the Punjab alone in 1932-1933, 482,000 animals were castrated. Ringing of the bad cows so as to make covering impossible should also be introduced and popularised. This is done in the south-west of the Punjab. The Netherlands Government has recently embarked upon a policy of restricting cattle numbers and to this end a Cattle Crisis Act was passed in 1933.It was planned to reduce the number of cows by200,000 by the end of 1934. The Agricultural Bureau under the jurisdiction of the State, purchases and slaughters cows, and the beef is used for export or canned for special sale to the unemployed. The State has provided a grant, which is augmented by a slaughter tax on all cattle slaughtered for home consumption. At the same time production is controlled by specifying the number of calves to be retained in the herds.

India must adopt a definite programme of reduction of cattle numbers and of controlled breeding. With decreased but more efficient cattle, the expansion and improvement of fodder cropping and pasturage, introduction of silos, stall feeding and controlled grazing in favour of superior stocks will be easier. Outside the zones of human concentration the development of dairy farming in association with intensive agriculture will supply milk, butter or ghee to the dietary, add to the cultivator's income and prompt him to look after the female animals better. The improvement of fodder will react favourably on agricultural practice by increasing the productivity of land, without which the introduction of new varieties of crops can do little more. In India the tendency to view the improvement of crop production as involving two separate problems according as the crops are intended as food for manor for beast is apt to be exaggerated.

There is a vital link between animal husbandry and crop production, and much improvement of Indian agriculture may accrue from the peasant devoting himself more to fodder crops and peas and beans which, or the production of which, may be used for food-stuffs, animal feed and fertiliser, and pay less attention to other kinds that are nearer the stage of over-production. Above all, it will relieve agricultural idleness, and lead to a better distribution of human and cattle power in the fields. In large parts of India, from the Punjab, Sind and Rajputana in the north, to Mysore and parts of Madras in the south, there are no doubt extensive grazing grounds where excellent work-cattle are produced under the ranch system at small cost. The production of these would be concentrated upon both for local use and for export as long as the best grazing areas are not taken up for more intensive cultivation, which will inevitably lead to the deterioration of the size and quality of the stock. But in the rest of India population pressure will on the whole exclude the development of an intensive system of mixed farming combined with dairying. Redistribution of the animal population among the thinly populated Provinces, and migration to the Western or Eastern Indies and other tropical regions where the Indian cattle show themselves to be hardier and more immune to tick-borne diseases than the local breeds, are some remedies. But the real remedy lies in a practical view of animal keeping and working on the part of the Indian peasant. China and Japan do not raise animals because they seek to economise the land and human food resources as far as possible. In India the reverence for the mother cow defeats itself because it is responsible for raising millions of half-starved worthless beasts, which have now become a serious burden on her small holdings.

Such multiplication not only leads to the waste of her scanty grassland resources and makes it more and more difficult for the upkeep and breeding of superior live-stock, but it also contributes to soil deterioration and deprivation of the masses of dairy products in their vegetable dietary, which is poorer and less varied than in China or Japan. The excessive burden of uneconomical stock in India, indeed, aggravates human poverty and mal- nutrition, as men and beasts are engaged in a cruel and vain triangular struggle to wrest from the ill-nourished, over-burdened soil more and more crops, fodder and grasses to keep them from starvation. India, with her human burden of 377millions, and her 48 millions of "average men" estimated without food, can ill afford to add in- definitely to her enormous bovine population of 214millions at the rate of 20 per cent per decade and permit the cult of ahimsa to get the better of the improvement of human food resources.

Malnutritionoptimum

The question of finding out an optimum nutrition for the people of India is cognate to, and as important as, that of finding out an optimum density for the Indian population. Deficiency diseases are on the whole not widespread in India, at least in years of normal rainfall and abundant harvests, but them ere absence of typical deficiency diseases is not enough. Every civilised government must aim at optimum health and efficiency of the people. In India the study of the incidence of malnutrition has not even begun, although the most considerable section of the population may be regarded as living on a sub nutritional level, which gravely affects their powers of resistance and efficiency.

That typical deficiency diseases become prevalent in regions affected by scarcity, has been abundantly shown by a survey undertaken by the author in several scarcity areas in Western Bengal in the summer of1935. A food survey was also taken up which indicated that a considerable section of the population depended upon rice refuse and polishings, edible or inedible leafy vegetables, containing largely cellulose and water.

Food Values of Drought Diets

India's drought and famine foods need careful physiological scrutiny. These show a unique adaptability to unfavourable conditions of food supply brought about through centuries of trial and error in food selection. Examination of men, women and children in famine camps and relief works should be made also with the object of establishing standard famine diets. Side by side the incidence of food-deficiency diseases should be carefully investigated.

An analysis of the food values of diets, carefully collected by me in Western Bengal among labourers in Test works at Chhatra and Sonamukhi in the district of Bankura, and Bud bud and Ausgram in the district of Burdwan, has shown serious under feeding. Sample diets have been taken not only from among the labourers in the Test works but also from among the peasants in villages in their hinterland who are engaged elsewhere. Aswatha, tamarind and other fresh or dried leaves, fruits of babla, aswatha and bat, kuro of rice and refuse of jack fruit and scales of fish have been foundamong the materials consumed in conditions of need.

Deficiency Diseases

Ulceration of the tongue and raw surface in the lips and corners of the mouth and eyes have been found ordinarily among the hospital cases in Bankura. Cases of extreme emaciation were, however, not to be found in the works because of the toil involved, which shut out the debilitated, but enquiries indicated that not a small percentage of the workers earned below the maximum 2 As. Wages because of the strain. Extreme fatigue was indicated by their repeated disengagement at intervals. A dozen nutritional oedema cases were discovered in Thana Ausgram from village Kelity; these persons came for receiving doles in Guskara relief centre in Burdwan.

Where the people have been eating between one-third and one-half of their normal food, deficiency diseases, such as painless diarrhoea, dropsy, ulceration and general waste and loss of muscles and weight and retardation of puberty in females, may be found prevalent here and there; and a group of medical men from Calcutta with an itinerary in the famine-stricken areas may collect valuable data in this connection.

A serious menace in the district of Bankura is the spread of leprosy, which has increased at least two-fold during the last twenty years. It has been estimated that there are now about 45,000 lepers in the district and that in some parts about three-fourths of the villagers are affected. Leprosy may have something to do with soil exhaustion and depletion of certain mineral elements or other food values in cereals. It is probable that the fight against leprosy, in order that it may succeed, has to be carried out both on economic as well as hygienic fronts, and that along with careful treatment and segregation, very difficult to secure among the aboriginals and semi-Hinduised lower castes, a programme of enriching the soil with adequate organic and chemical manures will prove helpful in combating this fell disease, now spreading like wildfire in the habitations of Bankura and Birbhum.

Inelasticity of Indian Food Habits

The masses of India are not only on a sub-nutritional level but also suffer from the inelasticity of dietaries due to religious prejudice, social custom and inertia. Economic and religious considerations blend together and determine whether fish, flesh, milk and eggs, which contain a high percentage of protein of good quality, will enter into the dietary or not. Many deficiency diseases, as, for instance, dysentery and diabetes, arise among a population of rice-eaters, due to an inadequate intake of proteins; thus faulty and unbalanced diets are as much responsible for disease and mortality in India as deficient or inadequate diets.

The city ward drift has caused changes in the dietetic habits of the people, reducing the amount of various protective foods in their dietaries and making them more susceptible to infections. In the cities and towns animal fats such as butter, cream and ghee, which are much superior to vegetable fats and oils, are beyond the reach of the majority of the population. Fish, meat, beef, and eggs, which are all dearer in the cities, are given up by castes and communities, habituated to these, when they migrate from the villages. Workers who have migrated from Eastern Bengal, where fish is cheapest and most abundant in India, cannot obtain these in adequate quantities; while milk and milk products as well as fruits are too dear in Calcutta city.

Among the Bombay working class the Konkanis, who come from the coastal district, and are accustomed to eating fish in their villages, similarly have often to discard it in Bombay city where it is a costly diet and its dietary value is not at all commensurate with the money spent. In all Indian towns the percentage of the total food eaten by urban dwellers derived from cereals is too high, and the animal and total protein, and the milk products, much below what is recommended by Western standards. A recent survey, undertaken by Professor H. Wilson, of three children's institutions of Calcutta, a Mohammedan, a Hindu and an Anglo-Indian respectively, showed that the diets were poor in total animal protein, animal fat, and, above all, in calcium. The consumption of milk and milk products was either nil or negligible in relation to the total food consumed. The institutions appear to show the best return for money spent, in spite of the fact that, qualitatively, the diets fell below those of the families. Dietetic experiments with skimmed milk among South Indian children have indicated that stomatitis, a common deficiency disease, disappears when skim milk is fed. School girls (ages 5to 17 years) studied by Wilson in Lahore showed 40 percent incidence of rickets.

Convulsions, malnutrition and septic skin conditions account for a considerable proportion of infantile deaths throughout India. Adulteration and artificial substitution also deprive many foods of much of their real food value in India. These evils are more serious and wide spread in this country than in the West, and in the cities than in the villages. Further, as industrialization develops, the food grains are less frequently brought to the homes and ground in hand-mills in the towns. The milling and polishing both of wheat and rice deprive them of important food materials.

Inappropriate Food Preparation

Inappropriate food preparation thus leads to a good deal of waste. Rice, for instance, is deficient in Vitamin A, and this deficiency may be extreme if the rice is used parboiled, the process of parboiling and subsequent drying in the sun depriving the rice grains of such small amounts of this essential as they originally contained. It may or may not be deficient in Vitamin B, according as the rice used is milled and polished, home-pounded, or parboiled. If the first, it does not contain enough Vitamin Bfor its own metabolism, nor does that provided by the legumes used with it suffice to make good the deficiency. It is in such circumstances that beriberi is prone to arise. It may be mentioned that beriberi is a cause of widespread sickness in Japan and accounts for a considerable number of deaths. Penrose estimates that probably over 50 per cent of Japanese students suffer from beriberi at sometime in their school and college careers. Different varieties of rice, unpolished as well as polished, differ in degrees of digestibility of starch. It has been found that the rate of enzymic hydrolysis increases with increased polishing until, with a very high degree of polishing, there is no change indigestibility. The viscosity of the cooked rice flour, however, increases with polishing. The difference in digestibility of unpolished and polished rice is greater in red rice and in coarser varieties in general than in white or fine rices.

The red portions of the ordinary rice are now usually discarded by all classes. We read in the Bihar and Orissa Census Report: "Except the sweepers, Haris, Sahars, etc., almost all classes have recourse to polished rice, which has resulted in serious losses of vitamin, as a result of which beriberi is noticed in places"; while in Bengal, although the new comers among the immigrant labourers still adhere to cheap red rice generally, those who are living long in Bengal prefer white milled rice. Similarly, white wheaten flour (maida)consumed by the middle classes in Bengal is as deficient in Vitamin B as polished rice, and researches show that animals fed on maida develop polyneuritis. It is necessary to find out the best method of husking paddy without polishing and removing the outer covering of the grain.

The All-India Village Industries Association have found, after a survey of various methods of pounding rice in different parts of the country, that Dheki husking and husking by pestle and mortar polishes the rice to some extent while husking on earth, stone, cement and wooden chakkis gives better results. Since the consumption of food other than rice is exceedingly small among the poorer classes, the nutritive value of rice, influenced as it is by the degree of milling, becomes of great significance. Recently the Inter governmental Conference of Far-Eastern Countries on Rural Hygiene have drawn attention to the possibility of checking the spread of mechanical rice mills in rural areas, with a view to conserving the healthy habit of consuming home-pounded rice and to means of making under-milled rice easily available to those who wish to purchase it.

The need of consuming under-milled rice and wheat which contain Vitamin B that counteracts beriberi. There are some diseases, such as diarrhoea, dysentery, beriberi, malnutritional oedema, epidemic dropsy and xerophthalmia which are found especially in Bengal and Madras and are caused by faulty unbalanced diets. Bengali children who are fed on polished rice and are provided with other foods in small quantities show a high incidence of rickets. Wilson's measurements of the A.C.H. (arm-chest-hip) index of nutrition indicate that children in anorphanage in Calcutta, from which foods were investigated, are 50 per cent, while those in a better class school are 12 per cent, below par. In large areas of Southern India, where milled rice is the staple article of diet, nearly all the pregnant females are in a state of a vitaminosis B. As a result the incidenceof premature births is three times as great as it is in the north of India (where wheat is the staple diet), and in consequence the infant mortality rate also is many times greater. The shortage of Ca and P is often as serious a factor as Vitamin D deficiency in the causation of rickets and osteomalacia in India. Tuberculosis is estimated to be twice as prevalent in South India as in the Punjab.

Ulcer of the stomach, rickets and anaemia are much more common in South India and Bengal than in Northern and North-west India. Aykroyd has found symptoms of Vitamin A deficiency quite commonamong children in Southern India, and suggests that Vitamin A deficiency may be a causative factor in the production of stone, which is widely prevalent both in Bengal and Madras. He observes: "While pellagra is uncommon in India a large percentage of children in South India show apellagra-like stomatitis, which is curable by foods rich in P-P factor. Xerophthalmia of varying degrees of severity is commonly met with, and kerato-malacia is one of the most blinding diseases in South India. Follicular keratosis of the skin, due to diet deficiency, is of extremely common occurrence." The high incidence of dysentery in the jails of Bengal as compared with the low incidence in those of the Punjab is also full of significance.

Infantile mortality is now being recognised as largely due to deficiency of vitamins, with its resulting gastro-intestinal and pulmonary disorders; and it is greater in Madras and Bengal than in the Punjab. The much higher incidence of leprosy in the south, west and east of India has also probably a nutritional basis. The increase of leprosy in the rice tracts of Northern Orissa, South-western Bengal, Deccan and Madras is perhaps connected with exhaustion of soil and deficiency of food values of rice grains.

Another significant instance of inappropriate food preparation is afforded by the use of boiled ghee. Vitamin A has been found fairly stable at temperatures up to 125°C., but is rapidly destroyed at higher temperatures. Throughout India ghee is subjected to high temperatures and thus Vitamin A is completely lost. The loss of the yellow colour of ghee runs parallel with the loss of Vitamin A and it takes a longer time for the buffalo ghee to lose its yellow colour.

The experiments of Papanicolaou and Stockard, the observation of Frederick von Mueller in the period of under-nutrition in Germany, and there searches of Professor H. Stieve indicate very strongly that underfeeding alters fertility and has profound effects upon the organs of generation; and also that it causes a retardation of development, especially of young animals and children, as well as symptoms of disease in fully developed adults. The everyday clinical experiments in rickets, scurvy, etc., show how important vitamins are to the growing child and even to the adult. Fertility, resistance to disease, height, weight, general endurance, learning capacity, and many of the qualities of personality are strongly influenced by diet in the sense that proper environment in relationship to the matters of diet and hygiene promotes the development of superior individuals, if we regard greater height, greater weight, resistance to infection, and better learning ability as evidence of superiority.

Deficiencies of Bengal and South Indian Diets

The distribution of protein, fat and carbohydrate in dietaries in different parts in India, indicates that the least satisfactory of all the Indian diets is that consisting of rice, dal, vegetables and condiments; this diet is used by millions of people in Bengal, Orissa, Madras and elsewhere. Such diet is associated with the lowest grade of physical efficiency and health in India, and McCarrison notes its following defects:" Poverty of protein, excess of starch, deficiency of certain mineral elements, deficiency in Vitamin A, deficiency in Vitamin B." Wright's investigations have shown that destruction of eyes as a result of Vitamin A deficiency is the commonest cause of blindness in the Madras Presidency. Systematic investigations will probably reveal eye and skin symptoms due to Vitamin A deficiency in almost any municipal or village school in Southern India. It is also probable, according to Aykroyd, that such diets also tend to be deficient in calcium, and deficiency in calcium affects adversely the functioning of every tissue in the body.

The foods richest in calcium are milk, cheese, green vegetables, and unmilled cereals. In striking contrast with the diet in Bengal and Madras, which predisposes the people to an unusual susceptibility to infection, a proneness to dysentery and diarrhoea and a marked tendency to deficiency diseases like epidemic dropsy and beriberi, we have the rich and nutritive diet of the Punjab and North-Western Frontier Province, with or without animal proteins but with its abundant supply of milk and milk products, fruits, and vegetables added to the basal whole meal bread, tubers and roots. We have already noted the abundant supply of calories (4,000) yielded by the menu consumed by the Jat cultivators in Lyallpur. In the United Provinces the diet of the western districts approximate to that of the Punjab. But in the eastern districts of the United Provinces and Bihar, which grow more rice than wheat, the diet becomes less nutritive and less balanced; yet in these areas wheat, flour, and ghee still retain their importance, and the protein element in the diet is greater than in Bengal.

The level of nitrogenous metabolism is at least 20 per cent higher in the North Indian peasant than in the peasant in Bengal; and his average weight also is greater, 120 Ibs. as compared with 110 Ibs. of the cultivators in Bengal and Madras.

The improvement of means of communications and transport and facilities of marketing have now overcome the natural handicaps of different parts of India in growing more nutritive cereals and pulses which form the staple foods of regions under more favourable conditions of soil and climate. Thus ignorance and conservatism have to be over- come in order that the average Bengalee and Madrassi, for instance, may consume wheat, ragi, and dal which have built up the larger, stronger and hardier body of the Punjabi. Rice-eating peoples preferring a mixed diet of wheat, barley and millets, which may be obtained at reasonable prices from other Provinces in combination with rice, will enormously improve their standards of nutrition and efficiency. Unpolished rice may be used in the form of roti of the flour and a mixture be formed with other grains or pulses. At present wheat and ragi are cheaper than rice both in Bengal and Madras. Further evidence of the health-giving properties of the Sikh diet is afforded by complete absence of any evidence of disease of the stock rats fed on this diet except an occasional cyst (tapeworm) in the liver.

Both McCay and McCarrison seem, however, to exaggerate the importance of the dietetic factor. Everywhere there is a reciprocal adaptation of climate, diet and stock. The lower metabolism of a Bengalee or South Indian accounts for the lower protein content of their diet, humidity being a highly important governing factor of basal metabolism. Nor can we say that the Punjabi's diet is adequate in quantity and quality. The Punjab enjoys during about half the year a remarkably stimulating climate. "It is possible," shrewdly observes Lt.-Col. C. A. Gill, "that the Punjabi is what he is not because of, but in spite of, his diet." An examination of the dietary of casual labourers employed in industrial enterprises in the Punjab yields a value of 2-347 calories only.

As one passes from the north to the west, east and south, rice begins gradually to replace wheat and so long as milk and milk-products are consumed insufficient amounts, or adequate animal proteins and fats from other sources are ingested together with fresh vegetable foods, there is no dietetic reason for physical deterioration. McCollum, one of the greatest authorities on nutrition, points out that in the warmest regions of the world, which are also characterised by excess of wetness, one of the most successful human dietaries have evolved. Such dietary consists of rice as the principal cereal, with additions of beans, pulses, various tubers and root vegetables and large amounts of leafy vegetables of all kinds. The leaf of the plant is superior to the seed, tuber, root or fruit in its dietetic property.

In fact the edible leaf, which is in itself complete from the standpoint of its dietetic principles, is widely used, especially in Bengal and Southern India. In these areas such leaves as Methi, Bathu, Palong and Pooin and those of gram and turnip are used in the mariner of spinach, and turnips, carrots and onions are generally eaten raw. A number of fruits such as mangoes, jack-fruits, guavas, plantains and lemons, eaten raw in the moist regions of India, contain vitamins in not inconsiderable quantities. Tamarind pulp and amchur or mango and lemon pickles are most important sources of vitamins consumed everywhere.

The juice of Tulsi leaves, green chillies, cabbage, bitter gourd, cauliflower and small radishes, containing a fairly large amount of Vitamin C, form common items of diet. In the wetter regions of India the masses consume habitually a variety of fruits, vegetables and leaves from season to season. The smaller weight, stature and physical capacity of the Bengalee or Madrassi, as compared with the Northerner, are governed by the ensemble of racial and environmental factors (especially temperature and humidity) of which a low protein dietary is only one. It is, however, going too far to condemn the Bengalee and the Madrassi for their in adequate and unbalanced diet and attribute only to this their inferior physique and lower efficiency. The physical characteristics of peoples and the nature of their diets are matters of environmental adjustment and neither the Bengalee nor the Madrassi, with his lower nitrogenous exchange, has proved a less successful farmer or less virile in the damp, moist climate. As between the Bengalees and South Indians it has been found on the basis of comparison of physical characteristics of children that the former are about 7 per cent superior in both height and weight, and that the Calcutta school-boys, even of the poor class, show a more regular gain in stature each year than the Coonoor, Calicut, Mettupalayamand Trivandrum boys studied. Whether this is due to climate, race or diet is not ascertained.

Index

A

Accounting 47, 48, 49, 213

Act 17, 136, 161, 165, 170, 180, 181, 182, 189, 191, 192, 193, 195, 258

Advantages 120, 157, 170, 238, 243, 256

Advertising 3, 48, 50, 54, 184, 181, 185

Agreement 57

Alcohol 21, 65, 73, 145, 178, 182

Alcoholic Beverages 64, 154, 157

Assistant Managers 2, 46, 47

Association 88, 105, 122, 211, 259, 265

Attacks 87, 165, 167, 185

B

Banquets 48

Bathrooms 43

Battle, legal 195

Benefits 9, 15, 22, 26, 99, 102, 104, 163, 166, 170, 188, 193, 194, 195, 210, 214, 215, 217, 219

Beverage 20, 47, 48, 55, 177, 211

Budget 219

C

California 64, 178, 200, 225

Catering 48, 52

Catering Managers 48

Committee 47, 218, 240

Communication 6

Company 4, 21, 24, 27, 37, 38, 54, 55, 65, 80, 102, 126, 182, 190, 193, 195, 197, 208

Compensation 4

Computers 4, 49

Convention 48

D

Dangerous 112, 123, 124, 125, 167, 170, 174, 176, 185, 220

Department 5, 7, 47, 103, 131, 180, 182, 200, 202, 206, 215, 221

Development 6, 9, 12, 14, 22, 26, 27, 48, 50, 53, 93, 103, 105, 108, 112, 115, 116, 152, 164, 178, 179, 187, 188, 196, 212, 215, 234, 235, 236, 239, 249, 255, 256, 257, 259, 267

Developments, key 116

Director 99

Diversity 12

E

Economics 11

Employee 2, 4, 5, 6, 48, 209, 210, 211

Equipment 1, 3, 4, 5, 11, 46, 52, 115, 118, 172, 176, 207

Executive 2, 3, 47, 48, 180

Executive Housekeepers 47

External 110, 120, 121, 150

F

Factors, Key 12, 199

Falls 137

Financing 212

Forest 245

Franchise 155

Front Office 8, 47

Functional 14, 105, 106, 144, 147

Furniture 3

G

General Manager 2, 46, 47

Guarantee 7, 10, 61

Guest 6, 8, 42, 44, 46, 47

H

Health 4, 12, 14, 28, 30, 35, 46, 99, 101, 103, 117, 119, 121, 123, 125, 137, 138, 152, 158, 163, 164, 166, 170, 171, 181, 184, 185, 191, 194, 195, 206, 222, 226, 233, 234, 249, 260, 267, 269

Hill 138

Holiday 48, 59

Hospitality 3, 5, 6, 42

Housekeepers 47

I

Importance 6, 7, 44, 107, 111, 210, 217, 220, 228, 232, 241, 242, 254, 256, 268, 269

Inadequate Rainfall 249

Incentives 218

Inflation 213, 219

Inspections 30, 185, 200

Inventory 1, 4, 78, 204, 205, 210

J

Job 6, 46, 210

Job Functions 210

Joint Ventures 157

K

Key 4, 6, 12, 45, 116, 154, 165, 190, 199, 213

Kitchen 1, 2, 3, 4, 27, 35, 48, 61, 84, 207

L

Labour 2, 23, 51, 53, 54, 55, 56, 58, 61, 62, 219, 228, 234, 242

Largo, Key 45

Laws 4, 23, 28, 48, 65, 71, 74, 151, 157, 158, 215, 216, 224, 228

Legal 71, 189, 195

Liability 206, 211

License 200

Limitations 114, 176

Location 5, 28, 42, 53, 116, 125, 209

M

Mail 46

Maintenance 1, 3, 40, 47, 48, 207, 243, 245, 246, 252, 255

Management 1, 2, 6, 23, 42, 47, 51, 80, 112, 171, 198, 208, 209, 210, 211, 212, 214, 215, 217, 255

Manufacturers 53, 115, 116, 159, 160, 162, 183, 188, 189, 190, 193, 194, 195, 201, 202, 203, 204, 205

Meetings 7, 42, 47, 48, 49

Motel 46

O

Occupancy 49

Operations 1, 2, 6, 25, 33, 46, 47, 48, 115, 199, 205, 218, 252, 230

Opportunities 69, 109, 115, 198, 205, 210, 218

P

Pastry 22, 62, 68

Payment 66, 90, 199, 201

Pennsylvania 59

Performance 2, 7, 107, 108, 111, 114, 115, 120, 173, 216, 249

Pool 19, 42, 47, 171, 193

Population 14, 50, 51, 54, 66, 113, 119, 127, 128, 129, 130, 154, 155, 161, 212, 228, 229, 230, 231, 232, 233, 234, 235, 236, 237, 239, 242, 243, 244, 245, 246, 247, 248, 249, 252, 256, 257, 258, 259, 260, 261, 263

Prevention 69, 70, 86, 99, 133, 164, 199, 221, 240

Processing 8, 9, 10, 11, 12, 13, 14, 20, 22, 23, 24, 25, 28, 29, 30, 31, 32, 38, 39, 50, 53, 54, 76, 92, 93, 95, 96, 103, 104, 107, 108, 110, 115, 116, 117, 118, 119, 120, 121, 132, 143, 146, 147, 148, 154, 155, 157, 158, 159, 168, 176, 177, 198, 199, 200, 201, 214, 217, 219, 220

Production 1, 7, 8, 15, 21, 22, 26, 37, 39, 50, 51, 52, 53, 54, 75, 76, 92, 103, 116, 134,

154, 155, 156, 157, 158, 159, 163, 178, 179, 185, 196, 198, 202, 203, 204, 212, 214, 216, 219, 229, 230, 231, 233, 234, 236, 237, 239, 240, 241, 242, 248, 255, 256, 257, 258, 259, 266

Profitability 7, 188

Promotions 5

Property 5, 47, 48, 110, 173, 215, 216, 220, 270

Property Protection 215, 216

Public Relations 47, 48, 50

Q

Quality 1, 2, 3, 10, 12, 14, 29, 34, 43, 46, 50, 72, 76, 77, 78, 80, 81, 82, 83, 84, 91, 95, 96, 97, 115, 116, 117, 118, 121, 123, 143, 154, 157, 160, 162, 186, 191, 199, 206, 209, 217, 233, 236, 241, 246, 250, 253, 255, 259, 262, 269

Quality Control 34

Quality of Life 10

Quality of the Food Supply 12

R

Rating Systems 43

Recognition 13, 15, 105

Reports 49, 119, 121, 158

Requirement, Legal 71

Reservation 5

Restaurant Industry 7

Restaurants 1, 2, 4, 5, 35, 42, 48, 198, 211

Revenue 49, 188

S

Safety 4, 9, 10, 11, 24, 29, 42, 50, 66, 76, 80, 85, 86, 95, 96, 98, 100, 101, 102, 103, 107, 108, 109, 115, 116, 123, 144, 152, 158, 162, 163, 166, 180, 183, 185, 186, 189, 190, 191, 194, 195, 196, 197, 214, 217, 219, 220

Senior Managers 47

Specialization 178

Staffing 48

T

Tax 4, 187, 258

Technology 4, 5, 9, 10, 11, 15, 50, 51, 53, 93, 94, 95, 96, 98, 102, 103, 104, 106, 154, 156, 177, 178, 179, 195, 214

Turnover 153

U

U.S. 23, 27, 52, 55, 75, 93, 100, 101, 107, 162, 163, 170, 179, 183, 188, 189, 190, 193, 200, 206, 215, 224

UAE 45

Unemployment 4

USA 26, 27, 28, 40, 74, 76, 126

USDA 52, 80, 85, 88, 94, 98,

101, 114, 154, 160, 161, 162, 164, 200, 202, 221, 225
Utter Inn 45

V

Vapour 110, 144, 176
Variation 1, 25
Vegetable 14, 16, 36, 40, 64, 96, 102, 135, 136, 137, 140, 145, 149, 160, 171, 200, 203, 204, 206, 227, 229, 231, 232, 234, 236, 238, 239, 242, 243, 244, 256, 260, 263, 269
Venizelos 50
Virginia 56
Vitamin 13, 81, 99, 120, 135, 137, 161, 166, 228, 232, 250, 264, 265, 266, 267, 270

W

Washington 59
Wildlife 44
Worker 222
World War 21, 26, 49, 93, 213
Worldwide 43, 52, 213

X

Xanthan Gum 147
Xerophthalmia 266

Y

Yeast 18, 21, 63, 64, 157, 160
Yield 7, 30, 115, 148, 169, 170, 213, 229, 230, 232, 233, 234, 235, 236, 237, 241, 243, 245, 247, 248, 257, 258
Young 37, 55, 83, 141, 142, 267
Yugoslavia 49

Z

Zone 78, 157, 229, 231
Zylphia Smith 206